Henry Allyn Frink, Austin Phelps

Rhetoric

Its theory and practice.

Henry Allyn Frink, Austin Phelps

Rhetoric
Its theory and practice.

ISBN/EAN: 9783337818500

Printed in Europe, USA, Canada, Australia, Japan

Cover: Foto ©ninafisch / pixelio.de

More available books at **www.hansebooks.com**

RHETORIC

ITS THEORY AND PRACTICE

"English Style in Public Discourse"

BY

AUSTIN PHELPS, D.D.
LATE BARTLET PROFESSOR OF SACRED RHETORIC IN ANDOVER
THEOLOGICAL SEMINARY

AND

HENRY ALLYN FRINK, Ph.D.
PROFESSOR OF LOGIC, RHETORIC, AND PUBLIC SPEAKING IN AMHERST COLLEGE
AND FORMERLY PROFESSOR OF ENGLISH LITERATURE AND ENGLISH
IN HAMILTON COLLEGE

NEW YORK
CHARLES SCRIBNER'S SONS
1895

PREFACE

ONE of the most valuable works that we have on the subject which it treats is " English Style in Public Discourse." When these lectures, which were originally delivered by the late lamented Professor Phelps to the students of Andover Theological Seminary, were given to the public, twelve years ago, their rare merit was at once recognized. Nor is " English Style in Public Discourse " to lose its place in the first rank of standard works on the characteristics and use of our language. The philosophical basis on which it rests ; the clear, interesting, and inspiring presentation of the subject ; the wealth of illustrations from the choicest fields of literature ; the fine, discriminating taste of its criticisms and suggestions ; the broad culture and good sense which mark its treatment of disputed points, make the book of permanent worth for reference and general reading. For such purposes the book may be still obtained in the form in which it first appeared. The publishers and the writer have thought, however, that these lectures, with alterations and additions, might have a larger usefulness where their influence seems especially to be needed, as a means of rhetorical instruction in our schools and colleges. An examination of " English Style in Public Discourse " in its present form will, therefore, show that it is a text-book which has peculiar claims to the consideration of teachers of rhetoric.

I. It aims with constant directness at the main purpose in the study of rhetoric, which is to give power to present effectively the thought of the writer or speaker to the reader or hearer. These lectures were prepared to teach young men how to write and to speak, who were almost immediately to put to the test every direction and suggestion made by their teacher, as they spoke on matters the most important that can command human attention. For this reason, the book does not resemble in its interest and stimulus the conventional text-book. Its instructions, thorough and complete as they are, have not the spirit of the drill sergeant, but of the officer who would prepare his soldiers to move into instant action. Hence, the book will not seem to the student a treatise on rhetorical terms and processes with which to be acquainted theoretically is enough. It is a book that, as he will soon learn, has for its one purpose to make him the immediate master of these terms and processes, and all other rhetorical resources for a practical end. Recognizing, as the student must, this purpose, and feeling, as he will, its inspiration, he will not share the indifference, and possibly aversion, which so many have to the study of rhetoric; for he will see the end of its instruction to be too real and vital for him to find in the means no interest.

II. The point of view from which the student considers the subject is also attractive and invigorating. When style seems to be only a dexterous manipulation of words, and composition mere verbal mechanism, the student is kept from the sources of his power and skill as a writer and speaker, and so from any progressive enjoyment in his work. But at every step this book shows that it is thought which is the basis of style and the source of its power and charm; and, that only in the conscientious observance of these essential relations between thought and style are to be gained clearness, force, and beauty of expression.

III. This book keeps constantly before the student not only the dependence of style on thought, but also, what is of great practical importance, the true relation of the writer to his reader or the speaker to his hearer. Of two large classes of writers and speakers, one class evidently understands the subject, but not the subject in relation to the reader or hearer; the other class has not simply a full knowledge of the subject, but also of the means by which it is to be made effective with those to whom it is especially addressed. It is unnecessary to say who are the writers and speakers of power. The lectures which form the foundation of this book were prepared originally, as has been intimated, to teach young men the art of oral address. This means that a guiding influence in its instruction are the relations between those who write and speak and those who read and hear.

It is to be remembered, however, that there is a large range of composition not intended to be spoken, yet which, to be effective in its purpose, must have the directness, force, and pointedness of oral address. In fact, nearly all successful composition—except, perhaps, the higher forms of literature, which are not a means, but in themselves an end—is marked by these characteristics of the spoken word. One of the most common mistakes in rhetorical training, is the failure to make the necessary distinction between this kind of composition and that of the purely literary type. Said a well-known professor of sacred rhetoric in one of our most prominent theological seminaries: "It is not often that I find a college graduate who is able, in his writing, to distinguish between composition addressed to the reader and to the hearer. I am, therefore, compelled to undo largely the rhetorical work of the college course before the student can put his sermon into a form which he can deliver, and to which a congregation will listen."

Literature proper which appeals to the thought, the imagination, the sensibilities, simply through the eye, is but slightly subject to the rules of rhetoric. The essential elements of literary power and beauty are indefinable, illusive, and are not to be communicated by direct instruction. The formal study of rhetoric will, therefore, be at the most no more than a preliminary step in helping to produce the successful sketch, story, or literary and critical essay.

If, however, "the oral," as Professor Earle says in his "English Prose," "is the source and parent of all that is developed in the literary," rhetorical training has a province largely and immediately fruitful in that broad range of practical composition, which, because it is so closely allied to oral address, permits instruction to be definite, positive, and helpful. But while this book perhaps stands alone as a text-book for schools and colleges in its peculiar adaptation to teach oral address, its range of instruction will be found to include all the rhetorical processes that can be directly taught with any degree of clearness and definiteness, and, hence with any measure of profit.

IV. A fourth claim that this book has to consideration is that indirectly it prepares for the study of English literature. This is not because it attempts to teach how to write a poem, to plan a story, or to portray a character. It is because the book in its original form is the product of a rare culture, and will give unconsciously that invaluable preparation for the study of literature which comes from intimate association with the highest type of literary taste and training. Nor have these lectures simply the literary spirit. They abound also in delightful references to the lives and works of representative writers, as well as draw largely their illustrations from the best that is to be found in literature. If such means fail to help awaken an early interest in literary studies and to serve in forming a good literary taste, it may be asked whence is to come the influence?

V. Another peculiar advantage which this book offers is the use that may be made of it in recitation and examination. A large practical acquaintance with students in writing and speaking shows me that young men now in college have not the ease and power of expression, oral or written, which students of the same age had several years ago. This, I believe, is to be accounted for mainly by the prevailing methods of instruction. The student, in the classroom, has not the daily drill in standing before his class and making an extended recitation, which formerly was an unconscious means of developing and training his powers of speech. Written examinations as most often conducted are not to be accepted as a substitute for this exercise. Whatever their benefits in other directions, they are, as a rule, not an aid but a hindrance to a command of language. Even increased attention, in secondary schools, to studies in English literature—if we are to judge from the examination papers, recently published by Harvard University, that are presented by students for entrance to college—does not seem as yet to give practical power in the use of English.

But if "the oral," to repeat Professor Earle's statement, "is the source and parent of all that is developed in the literary," then surely some opportunity ought to be given the student, in a course in rhetoric at least, to develop and train this power of oral expression. What is the value of such training I know from an extended observation. For eight or nine years I made it a feature of an early course in rhetoric with college classes, to have, for a part of each hour, a topical recitation of several minutes from certain members of the class. The student was required to give the substance of the lecture in his words, with the understanding, that, in this particular exercise, the merit of his work depended as much on the good form of his expression as on the evidence of his knowledge of the especial theme of the day. As the same student, in the later years of his course, stood before me in the extemporaneous work of debates, or as he prepared in written form his oration, discussion, or essay, he gave unmistakable proof of the value of that early discipline. Students coming from other institutions who had not been so trained, always acknowledged their disadvantage in competition with men who, in recitation, for a year, had been subjected to such rigorous exercise in this most practical form of composition.

We say to the student "speak as you talk! write as you talk!" But what opportunities do we give him to talk on subjects similar to those on which we expect him to write or to speak? For the purpose of giving such opportunities, and, therefore, such training, the method of presentation in this book is especially adapted. The orderly plan in the treatment of each division of the subject, and the full amplification and illustration of every principle and process, with the analysis which I have provided for each chapter, afford opportunity for the best kind of exercise, in reproducing the thought of the author in the expression of the student.

The chapters of the book are also equally well adapted for reproduction in written work. No better exercise in early composition can be required than for the student to reproduce in the class-room, without the book, one, two, or more chapters, according to the general plan and its various divisions, with the examples and illustrations under each division of the subject of the chapter.

VI. To make this work complete as a text-book for schools and colleges I have added Part II., which consists mainly of practical examples and exercises that illustrate fully every principle and process of the most important chapters. These examples and exercises in number go into the hundreds, and are of such wide range and variety as to give the student not only adequate practice in each element of style, but also an intimate acquaintance with the prominent characteristics of the English language.

Exercises of a large number have been so arranged that in their preparation the student must consult dictionaries and other works of reference, and by independent investigation and study reach his conclusion, and prepare himself to defend it before the teacher and the class. Some of the work in this direction will be found to be of the highest value; and none of it, I am sure, will fail to reward well the time and thought which the student and the teacher may give to the exercise. While it is hoped that the method indicated by these exercises will be closely followed, yet there are examples and exercises in great number which can be prepared by using only the text-book.

It will be observed, however, that in regard to examples about which critics and general good usage are at variance, I have, as a rule, referred the student to the works where these points are fully discussed. This has been done that the student may early see what is the relative authority of usage and of the laws of language. Moreover, in no other way, at this period of his studies, can he so well learn the characteristics of English speech as by following, with the guidance of his teacher, some of the discussions to which I have referred him. When opinions have been indicated in the exercises on these disputed matters, the decision has not been so much from the arbitrary point of view of the purist, as it has been in accordance with the needs of the language and the usage of good writers and speakers. The student should be kept from license in the use of English; but he should be permitted also to know the full liberty of our noble speech.

The reason why examples and exercises have not been provided for the chapters on Elegance and Naturalness, is because I think that these elements of style are not to be taught directly by formal application of rule and process. If taught at all beyond the general instruction of the chapters, they will be taught by finer methods, which the defects or aptitudes of the individual student must largely determine.

In adapting to the requirements of a text-book for schools and colleges the lectures of Professor Phelps, I have reduced them by omissions, condensation, and alterations nearly one third. Great care has been taken, however, that the continuity of thought should not be broken, nor the force of its presentation weakened. Not to deprive the book of its original life and interest, a number of illustrations has been retained that in an ordinary text-book would probably be rejected. If the book is used in recitation and examination, as has been suggested, the illustrations will not seem too many. Should circumstances not favor this method of work, the book may be successfully used with various other methods. While it may be said that the book is unique in its adaptation to certain kinds of rhetorical work, it is a flexible text-book. In connection with the examples and exercises which go with the first eighteen chapters, it is possible not simply to vary the instruction from class to class, but to give each student work fitted to his especial needs or gifts at almost every step in the course.

HENRY ALLYN FRINK.

AMHERST COLLEGE, September 27, 1894.

CONTENTS

PART I
ENGLISH STYLE

CHAPTER I
STYLE
PAGE

Style defined by Wordsworth, Swift, and Buffon—Style defined by the Author—Popular Conception of Style as Sophistry or Ornament—Qualities of Style as Qualities of Thought—Classification of the Fundamental Qualities of Style—Purity and Precision—Individuality — Perspicuity, Energy, Elegance — Naturalness—Reasons why Individuality should not be Studied as a Quality of Style, ... 1

CHAPTER II
PURITY OF STYLE

Its Definition—Its Standards—The Laws of Language and Usage—Restrictions on Usage—Present Usage—National Usage—Reputable Usage, ... 10

CHAPTER III
VIOLATIONS OF PURITY OF STYLE

Obsolete and Obsolescent Words—James Russell Lowell's Test—The Obsolete in Poetry, in Prayer, in Ordinary Discourse — New Words—Absolute Creations — Contractions — Expansions—New Words Formed Facetiously—New Words by Union of Greek Terminations and Old Substantives, by Compounding Old Words, ... 19

CHAPTER IV

Violations of Purity of Style (Continued)

New Words a Necessity—Six Principles by which to test New Words —Importation of Foreign Words; often caused by Pedantry, by Undue Regard for Etymology, by the Composite Character of English—Provincialisms—Vulgarisms, ... 27

CHAPTER V

Reasons for the Cultivation of Purity of Style

Value of Purity of Style—Purity the Foundation of the Most Effective Style—An Aid to Perspicuity, to Energy, to the Best Results of Public Oral Discourse—Testimony of Literary Authority— Rapid Spread of English—English the Language of Colonization and of Commerce, ... 37

CHAPTER VI

Purity of Style (Concluded)

Reasons for its Cultivation (Continued)—Danger that the English Language will be Corrupted in this Country; by Republican Influence, by Extent of Territory; by Variety of the Immigrants—Means of Acquiring Purity of Style—Classic Conversation—Classic Authorship—Use of Treatises on Language—Habits of Composing, 45

CHAPTER VII

Precision of Style

Its Definition—Its Violations by the Omission of Single Words; by the Wrong Use or the Omission of "It;" by Wrong Use of Moods and Tenses of Verbs; by Wrong Use of Connectives, . . 54

CHAPTER VIII

Precision of Style (Continued)

Its Violation by a Confused Use of Literal and Figurative Words; by Confounding Synonyms and Words Similar in Orthography; by Defect in the Number of Words; by Excessive Conciseness; by Excessive Redundancy; by Looseness of Construction, ... 60

CHAPTER IX

Precision of Style (Continued)

Causes of the Formation of a Loose Style—Indiscriminate Thinking—Excessive Care for Expression—Want of Command of Language—Means of Acquiring a Command of Language; by Power to Select and Reject Words; by Critical Study and Use of Language; by Knowledge of the Synonyms of Words, of the Figurative Uses of Words; by Retentive Control of a Good Vocabulary—Command of Language an Acquisition not a Gift—The Vocabulary of Effective Speech not Voluminous, ... 68

CHAPTER X

Precision of Style (Concluded)

Popular Idea of a Precise Style—Inducements to the Cultivation of a Precise Style—It is not Pedantic; it promotes Perspicuity, Energy, Elegance, and Genuineness of Style; it is approved for Its Own Sake; it is a Popular Style, ... 79

CHAPTER XI

Perspicuity of Style

Its Foundation in Clearness of Thought—Obscurity from Absence of Thought; from Vagueness of Thought; from the Affectation of Profound Thought; from Real Profoundness of Thought; from Rapidity in the Succession of Thought, ... 87

CHAPTER XII

Perspicuity of Style (Continued)

Perspicuity as Affected by the Use of Imagery; by Incongruous Imagery; by Mixed Imagery; by Learned Imagery; by Excess of Imagery; by Entire Absence of Imagery—Perspicuity as Affected by the Words of Discourse; by Absence of a Saxon Style; by Use of Ambiguous Words, of General for Specific Words, of Abstract for Concrete Words; by Excessive Diffuseness; by Excessive Conciseness, ... 96

CHAPTER XIII
Perspicuity of Style (Continued)

Perspicuity of Construction—Defective Arrangement of Pronouns and Antecedents—Repetition of Pronouns with Different Antecedents—Defective Arrangement of Adjectives and Adverbs—Defective Arrangement of Qualifying Clauses, ... 107

CHAPTER XIV
Perspicuity of Style (Concluded)

Wrong Order of Thought in the Whole Structure—Excessive or Careless Use of Ellipsis—Abuse of the Parenthesis—Use of the Anacoluthon—The Introduction of Irrelevant Matter, ... 116

CHAPTER XV
Energy of Style

Its Definition—Improper Subjects of Energetic Expressions—Unimportant Thought—Indefinite Thought—Conditions of Forcible Composition—Enthusiasm—An Immediate Object in View—Self-Possession, ... 124

CHAPTER XVI
Energy and Language

Energy as Promoted by the Use of Pure Words, of Specific Words, of Short Words, of Words whose Sound is Significant of their Sense—Conciseness as an Element of Energy—Tautology—Verboseness—Circumlocution of Thought, ... 134

CHAPTER XVII
Energy and Language (Continued)

Exception in which Conciseness is not Favorable to Energy ; in Affectation of Conciseness ; in Composition requiring Diffuseness ; in Descriptive Writing ; in Expressing Intense Emotion—Construction of the Sentence an Element of Energy—The Placing of Emphatic Words—The Use and the Omission of Conjunctive Beginnings—The Use of the Periodic Structure—Advantages of the Period, ... 145

CHAPTER XVIII

ENERGY AND LANGUAGE (CONCLUDED)

PAGE

Energy as Promoted by Rhetorical Figure—Climax—Anthesis—Interrogation—Colloquy—Hyperbole—Irony — Exclamation — Vision—Apostrophe, ... 156

CHAPTER XIX

ELEGANCE OF STYLE

Its Definition—Elegance of Style Dependent on Delicacy of Thought—Smallness of Object Essential to Beauty—Feminine Qualities of Truth—Prejudice Against an Elegant Style—Intensified by our Temperament—Aggravated by Literary Affectations—Answers to this Prejudice—Means of Acquiring Delicacy of Thought ; by Cultivating Refinement of Perception ; by Believing it a Possible Attainment for Everyone, ... 164

CHAPTER XX

ELEGANCE OF STYLE (CONTINUED)

Offences Against Elegance of Style in Choice and Arrangement of Words ; in Construction ; in Imagery, Inelegant Imagery, Commonplace Imagery, Unfinished Imagery, Mongrel Imagery—Elegance as an Aid to other Qualities of Style—Elegance and Energy—Chief Peril of a Studied Beauty, ... 171

CHAPTER XXI

ELEGANCE OF STYLE (CONCLUDED)

Vividness as an Element of Elegance of Style—Demands of Vividness—Distinctness of Thought—Sensitiveness of Feeling—Simplicity of Language—An Easy Command of Imagery—Variety as an Element of Elegance of Style—Means of Acquiring Variety—Versatility of Thought—Varied Means of Presenting a Subject—Varied Vocabulary and Constructions—Varied Illustrations—Varied Delivery, ... 180

CHAPTER XXII

NATURALNESS OF STYLE

Its Definition—Relation to all other Qualities of Style—Characteristics of Naturalness—Fitness of Style to Subject—Fitness of Style to the Relations of Hearers—Fitness of Style to the Relations of the Speaker—Characteristics of Unnaturalness—An Apologetic Style—An Apathetic Style—Naturalness Adapted to Oral Discourse—Means of Acquiring Naturalness of Style—Mastery of Subject—Self-forgetfulness in Composing—Absorbing Interest in the Aim of Discourse—Practice of Composition, ... 192

PART II

PRACTICAL EXERCISES IN THE FUNDAMENTAL QUALITIES OF ENGLISH STYLE

EXERCISES IN PURITY OF STYLE

(CHAPTERS II., III., IV., V., AND VI. OF PART I)

Obsolete and Obsolescent Words—Contractions and Abbreviations—Expansion of Old Words—New Words—Americanisms—American and English Usage of Words—Words Condemned by Verbal Critics—Colloquial Words, Cant, and Slang—Errors in the Use of Prepositions—Miscellaneous Errors, ... 209

EXERCISES WITHOUT REFERENCE TO DICTIONARIES AND OTHER BOOKS

Notes by Professor Phelps on Violations of Purity—Exercise in Applying the Criticisms of Professor Phelps, ... 229

EXERCISES IN PRECISION OF STYLE

(CHAPTERS VII., VIII., IX. AND X. OF PART I)

Errors in the Use of "It"—Errors in Comparison—Errors in the Use of Tenses—Errors in the Use of Verbs from Ellipsis—Errors in the Use of the Subjunctive Mood—Errors in the Use of Connectives—Errors in the Use of Synonyms and of Words of Similar Orthography—Blunders in Construction—Synonyms to be prepared from Worcester's Unabridged Dictionary—From Webster's International Dictionary, ... 248

EXERCISES WITHOUT REFERENCE TO DICTIONARIES AND OTHER BOOKS

Notes by Professor Phelps on Violations of Precision, ... 265

EXERCISES IN PERSPICUITY OF STYLE

(CHAPTERS XI., XII., XIII., AND XIV. OF PART I)

Figurative Language—Saxon-English Words Substituted for Words of Latin or Greek Origin—Generic Words and Specific Words—Abstract Words and Concrete Words—Errors in the Arrangement of Pronouns and their Antecedents—Errors in the Use of the Same Pronoun with Different Antecedents—Errors in the Case of Pronouns—Errors in the Number of the Verb when a Pronoun is the Nominative—Errors in the Omission of Relative Pronouns—Errors in the Arrangement of Adjectives and Adverbs—Errors in the Arrangement of Qualifying Clauses—Errors in the Whole Structure of the Sentence—Errors in the Use of Ellipsis—Errors in the Introduction of Irrelevant Matter, ... 275

EXERCISES IN ENERGY OF STYLE

(CHAPTERS XV., XVI., XVII., AND XVIII. OF PART I.)

Short Words and Long Words—Words having Sounds Significant of their Sense—Examples for Correction in Tautology, in Verboseness; in Circumlocution—Examples of Conciseness for Approval or Criticism—Examples for Correction in Placing Important Words and Parts of the Sentence; in the Wrong Use, or the Omission of Connectives—The Loose Sentence and the Period—Climax—Antithesis—Interrogation, ... 292

PART I
ENGLISH STYLE

ENGLISH STYLE

CHAPTER I

STYLE

I.—Definition of Style.

What is style? One critic answers, "Style relates to the words and sentences of composition." True: but so does grammar; so does syntax; so does language. Are these the synonyms of style? Another declares, "Style is that part of rhetoric which treats of the expression of thought by language." But argument does the same; grammar also does the same. Are these synonymous with style? A third defines, "Style is the body of thought;" or, as Wordsworth puts it, "Style is the incarnation of thought." But this is description, not definition. A fourth says, after Dean Swift, "Style is proper words in proper places." But any good composition is that: "Paradise Lost" is that. Have we no conception of style, abstract from its illustrations? A fifth responds, "Style is character." Buffon has it, "Style is the man himself." But body and soul are that: are they style? This, again, is descriptive, not definitive. Sometimes it is not true. The chief thing which does *not* appear in some specimens of style is the person of the writer. Anonymous authorship might be well-nigh impossible if style always disclosed the writer's individuality. Of acknowledged authorship, are we not often obliged to confess, in reading a book, that we cannot become *acquainted* with the man who wrote it? He remains at the end as much a stranger to the reader as the reader is to him.

The chief difficulty in framing a definition of style is to distinguish it from the term "language." Let the following be tested as an experiment: "*Style is the expression of the qualities of thought in language.*" The pith of this formula is, that it builds style upon thought, not upon expression alone; yet not upon thought alone, but upon expression as well. This is probably all that De Quincey means when he calls style "the organ of thinking."

II.—Two Popular Conceptions of Style.

Two popular conceptions of style demand notice, however, between which it vibrates. One is that of sophistry, expression used to mislead: the other is that of ornament, expression used for display. Both of these assume that style is all outside. It is cunning in the use of words. It is the dress, the shell, the husk. A thought is a thought "for a' that." So the good sense of men will reason on any such theory as this. One writer expresses with amusing artlessness this degrading conception by soberly defining style to be "the art of arrangement applied to words." Observe it is an art, it is an art of arrangement only, it is an art applied from without, it is concerned with words only. Not a glimpse is visible here of thought, of organic growth, of words created and swayed by things. A comic song is a more respectable product than such a specimen of style. A "negro melody," in which rhythm supplants thought, would fill such a formula. A Cherokee war-song is vastly more worthy of scholarly study. If style be such, the study of it is contemptible.

[marginal note: Sophistry—Ornament.]

Test the correctness of the principle here advanced by a criticism of a few specimens of striking composition. What can you conceive the style to be, as distinct from the thought, in the first stanza of Wordsworth's "Ode on Immortality?" *"Ode on Immortality."*

> " Our birth is but a sleep and a forgetting:
> The soul that riseth with us, our life's star,
> Hath had elsewhere its setting,
> And cometh from afar.
> Not in entire forgetfulness,
> And not in utter nakedness,
> But trailing clouds of glory, do we come,
> From God who is our home."

This we call an imaginative, a figurative, a poetic style. True: but divest it of its imaginative forms, and yet express all the weight it carries, if you can. It is impossible. The very measure is an element in the expression of the ideas. The thought is shorn of somewhat if you change the measure. The style grows to the thought, as the sea-shell to its occupant. Poetic rhythm often is to thought what the down is on the cheek of a peach: without it the peach is something less. But admit that you can transform poetry to prose, then what is the thought as distinct from the prose style? Change the language; say something else than "trailing clouds of glory;" divest the style of figure—and have you not clipped the thought? The figure *is* the thought, in part: every curve, every indentation of it, every vibration of its winged utterance, is necessary to the full and rounded expression of the idea.

The Lord's Prayer is, perhaps, the simplest form of speech in any language. It is taught to children. It is used in the precative mood, which, of all moods, is the least friendly to artifice. *The Lord's Prayer.* Here, then, if anywhere, mere forms of speech might be supposed to be interchangeable, and therefore the choice of forms of no moment. But change the style of the Lord's Prayer, and yet express all the thought, with all its suggested and related ideas, if you can. You cannot do it. Even translation does affect this most perfect original of the precative style. It is not equal to itself in all languages.

III.—Qualities of Style are Qualities of Thought.

The principle, then, holds good everywhere; and, the more perfect the style, the more absolute is the principle. Style *is* thought. Qualities of style are qualities of thought. Forms of style are thought in form. In every specimen of perfect style this principle tolerates no question of its authority. Not only is thought primary, and expression secondary: thought is absolute, it is imperial. Expression as an independent entity is words without sense. This principle is the corner-stone of all manly criticism in literature. Every possible excellence in style grows out of it: every possible defect grows out of the neglect or denial of it. A writer of superior mental force, starting with this principle alone, might, in time, work his way, by the sheer force of original thinking, to supreme perfection in literary expression. Yet, starting without it, a lifetime of criticism and experiment could not create a style of tolerable quality.

margin: Style is thought.

IV.—Classification of the Fundamental Qualities of Style.

An important preliminary to our discussion is the *classification* of the fundamental qualities of style. Four distinct things lie at the basis of these qualities. These are THOUGHT, LANGUAGE, the SPEAKER, and the HEARER. Out of the relations of these four things the fundamental qualities of a good style grow.

margin: Four distinct things.

Out of the relations of thought to language grow Purity and Precision. PURITY comprises all those qualities which grow out of the laws of grammar. A good style is conformed to certain laws of language which are expressed in grammar. PRECISION includes all that is essential to the expression of no more, no less, and no other, than the meaning which the writer purposes to express.

One quality fundamental to a good style grows out of the relation of thought and language to the writer or speaker. We term it INDIVIDUALITY. It is that quality by which the speaker diffuses himself through his style; not merely that by which he impresses himself upon his style, but that by which he lives and breathes within and throughout its every variation and sinuosity of expression. It is that which Buffon had in mind when he said, "Style is the man himself," and which others have meant by saying that "style is character."

Out of the relations of thought and language, and the speaker to the hearer, grow three qualities of a good style. They are perspicuity, energy, and elegance. PERSPICUITY expresses the clearness of the thought to the *perceptions* of the hearer. ENERGY expresses the force of the thought to the *sensibilities* of the hearer. ELEGANCE expresses the beauty of the thought to the *taste* of the hearer. All these are relative to the culture of the hearer.

One quality remains. It results from a fit selection and a due proportioning of the qualities already named. It is NATURALNESS of style. It is that quality by which thought, as expressed in language, appeals to the sense of fitness in the hearer.

These seven qualities, and only these, are fundamental in the criticism of style. All other qualities naturally fall into the rank of tributaries to these. These will therefore constitute the themes in the ensuing chapters, but with one exception; viz., that of Individuality of style.

At the first view it may seem unreasonable to make this omission; but it is made deliberately, after vain attempts to *Why individuality is not to be considered.* discuss this quality in a manner fitted to the practical uses of a public speaker. As a subject of theoretic criticism only, it can be discussed, of course, *ad libitum;* but, as a subject of practical use, it is not a proper theme of critical research. The more sedulously a speaker studies and strives to gain it, the less will he have of it. He must be a man of rare genius if he does not fall into servitude to some counterfeit of it.

When a man sits for his portrait, the surest way of securing upon the canvas another man, not him, is that he *A man and his portrait.* should set himself to work profoundly thinking of himself—how he looks: are his eyes upon the right point of the compass? is his mouth closed with the proper degree of compression? are wrinkles visible in his forehead? is the head poised at the right angle? do the arms hang limp, or stiff? and so on. The more he thinks thus of himself, the less will he *be* himself on the canvas. He can defeat the genius of a prince of artists, solely by the conscious intentness of his own mind upon his body. Many of the most perfect likenesses are taken without the knowledge of the subjects of them. Portraits of artists painted by themselves are never their best work. The gallery of such portraits in Florence is justly criticised by Hawthorne as abounding with autobiographic peculi*Hawthorne.* arities which in perfect likenesses would be invisible. <u>To be himself in anything a man must</u> not think of being it. An English officer said of the Duke of Wellington that he did not write as well after *The Duke of Wellington.* the battle of Waterloo as before; because he knew that whatever he wrote would be printed and he wrote thinking how it would look in print.

The principle illustrated in these examples governs the art of acquiring individuality of style. A speaker cannot impress his own individuality upon his discourse consciously. He cannot, therefore, study this quality successfully for any practical uses. As a theme of rhetorical science, with frequent incursions into psychological science, it can be studied; but, as a theme of practical criticism for uses in public speech, the less a man knows of it the better. It is a quality which must come unbidden, as happiness does to the unconscious recipient: it cannot be produced by force of will, nor acquired by studious discipline.

When to be studied and when not to be studied.

ANALYSIS.

STYLE.

I. Definition of Style.
   1. Definition by Wordsworth, Swift, Buffon and others.
   2. Definition by the Author.

II. Two Popular Conceptions of Style.
   1. Sophistry.
   2. Ornament.
      (a) "Ode on Immortality."
      (b) The Lord's Prayer.

III. Qualities of Style are Qualities of Thought.

IV. Classification of the Fundamental Qualities of Style.
   1. Relations of Thought and Language—Purity and Precision.
   2. Relations of Thought and Language to the Writer or Speaker—Individuality.
   3. Relations of Thought and Language, and the Speaker to the Hearer—Perspicuity, Energy, Elegance.
   4. Due proportion of Purity, Precision, Individuality, Perspicuity, Energy and Elegance—Naturalness.
   5. Reasons why Individuality should not be studied as a quality of style.

CHAPTER II

PURITY OF ENGLISH STYLE

I.—Definition of Purity.

Purity may be more specifically defined by several memoranda, of which the first is, that it *relates to three things;* viz., the form of words, the construction of words in continuous discourse, and the meaning of words and phrases. The second, therefore, is that it *requires three things ;* viz., that the words used should belong to the English language, that the construction be accordant with English idiom, and that words and phrases be employed in the senses recognized by good English authority. The third is, that therefore the violations of English purity are *offences against the three departments of scientific grammar.* In the form of a word, a violation of purity is an offence against the laws of English etymology and their modifications by usage. In the construction of sentences, a violation of purity is an offence against English syntax. In the meaning of words or phrases, a violation of purity is an offence against the authority of lexicography. The fourth is, that the names given to the chief violations of purity are three. In the forms of words, a violation of purity is a *barbarism ;* in the constructions, a violation of purity is a *solecism ;* in the meanings of words and phrases, a violation of purity is an *impropriety.*

II.—Standard of English Purity of Style.

A further topic fundamental to the subject is the inquiry, What is the standard of English purity of style?

The history of this question in the rhetorical literature of the language discloses but two opinions which deserve debate. They may be represented by the formula, "Usage *versus* Laws of Language." One opinion gives the ascendency to usage, the other to the laws of the language, as the ultimate authority. One class of writers adopts an extreme utilitarianism, saying, "If a man makes himself understood by those who *use* the language, why should he care for a pure style beyond that?" This is the one extreme. At the opposite extreme are the "Purists." They hold in theory, that, be the usage of a people what it may, the laws of a language must be authoritative to scholars. *Two extremes.* Purists in the use of language have existed in every country which has had a literature. In the first half of the sixteenth century, Italian scholars would employ none but the purest Augustan Latin. Erasmus contended that the true rule for a scholarly author was to write as Cicero would have written if he had lived to modern times. He rejected *Erasmus.* as unscholarly all the languages of modern Europe. It was one of his chief objections to the Reformation, that it employed the language of the German people. The principles of Luther he approved, but he could not admit that Christianity could ever outgrow the Latin tongue. His life was a sacrifice of the Christian religion to the conservatism of literature. All the modern languages of Europe had a similar conflict with the ancient classic Latin. The action was, "The Aristocracy of Learning *versus* the Democracy of Usage." Usage triumphed, and forced new languages into being. The conclusion was foregone from the beginning.

Two principles, which practically qualify and limit each other, seem to indicate the true theory on the subject. One is, that the laws of a language are the proximate standard of purity. A language is the production of the national mind. In it the national mind has ex- *The true theory.*

pressed its unconscious will. Like every other national growth, it is a thing of law. If exposed to the inroad of alien or mongrel words, or barbarous idioms, the interests of culture require, that, if possible, it should be protected by appeal to its inherent laws. A violation of those laws is to scholarly taste an evil. It is an excrescence on the national tongue, to be excluded if possible; to be checked in its growth if it cannot be excluded; to be often only tolerated if it cannot be checked, till the national usage shall possibly right itself, and go back to the purer forms of speech.

<small>Language and its laws.</small>

But another principle qualifies and controls this: it is, that usage must be the ultimate standard of purity. Recognizing the conservative authority of scholarly taste as expressed in the laws of the language, we must submit to usage if that insists on change. This principle rests on several reasons. One is that of simple necessity. A language is a nation's property. The many make it, not the few. If the many choose to change it, enlarge it, bring importations into it, even load it with absolutely new creations, how shall the few who object on grounds of scholarly taste help themselves? The nation retains the most absolute of all rights—the rights of creatorship. It is sufficient to say, that scholarly taste must yield because it must. Usage may be tyrannical. It may create words by sheer whim. It may indulge a taste for vulgarisms. This makes no difference. If scholarly authority cannot make itself felt as a conservative influence, it has no power to act as a conservative force.

<small>Why usage is the ultimate standard.</small>

An amateur in philological studies once found, as he believed, a Norman origin for the word "quiz." But Smart, the author of an English dictionary, gives to the word a more simple and probable origin. He says, that the manager of a theatre in Dublin once

<small>Origin of quiz.</small>

passed an evening with certain amateurs in literature; and he staked a sum of money on the proposal that he would create a word which should belong to no language on the globe, and should be absolutely void of sense, yet it should become the subject of the common talk of the town in twenty-four hours. The wager was accepted. He then sent his servants through the most densely peopled streets of the city, with directions to chalk in large capitals the letters Q U I Z on each alternate door and shop-window. The next day was Sunday. Stores were closed, and the throng in the streets had leisure to read the enigmatical letters. Everyone who saw it repeated it to his neighbor; and his neighbor responded, "What does 'quiz' mean?" It had no meaning. No language owned it. Scholarly taste scouted it. Yet everybody laughed at it, and that gave it a meaning. From that day to this, scholarship has been compelled to recognize the word, and to use it as good sound English. In such a case usage declares its will, and says to scholarship, "What will you do about it?"

Further: the principle before us rests on its usefulness. *Languages need improvement.* The most finished languages admit of improvement. The Greek, the nearest perfect of any medium of human speech the world has known, never saw the time when it could not have been improved. Sixty years ago the Prussian Government published a dictionary, to be used in the public service, restricted to words of strictly national origin and then in use. It was an attempt, by authority of law, to prevent the introduction of new and foreign words. It was, by the nature of the case, doomed to failure. A national mind grows; it accumulates a history; new ideas are born; new institutions are created; new wants arise. Language, therefore, must grow, to express these novel facts. We must have new words, new idioms, new constructions, new combinations, and new senses of old words.

<small>A Prussian dictionary.</small>

Specially is this true of every new epoch in a nation's history. Such events as the rise of Greek art, the growth of the Roman Empire, the irruption of the northern tribes into Italy, the rise of the Papacy, the Reformation, the French Revolution, the downfall of American slavery, either create, or are created by, new ideas, which exceed the capacities of language as before organized and fixed. Moreover, one national mind originates ideas not original to another. One language also gives birth to words more felicitously expressive than their synonyms in another of ideas common to both. One, therefore, must borrow from another: there is no shame in that. Our English word "humbug," for instance, is an English original. Good authority states, that it cannot be reproduced in one word in any other living tongue. Yet it is too valuable a word to be excluded from any language.

<small>The demand of every new epoch.</small>

In the French language a dictionary is extant containing only the words born into the language since the Revolution of 1789. Among the old books in the British Museum is found a dictionary, of which this is the title, "A Dictionary of all words born since 1640, in speeches, prayers, and sermons: as well those that signify something as nothing." These dictionaries were published after periods of popular ferment. The passions of nations had been raging. They had forced national growth, and therefore the expansion of languages. Such epochs are sure to create words which "signify something."

<small>A French dictionary.</small>

<small>An English dictionary.</small>

The usefulness of a language, then, necessitates a scholarly obedience to usage as the authority of last resort. We not only must obey because we must, we must obey in order that our language may conform to the national wants, and be an honest expression of the national mind.

III.—Usage as Influenced by the Laws of a Language.

The foregoing views suggest the inquiry, To what restrictions is usage practically subjected by the conservative influence of the laws of a language?

In the first place, that which we recognize as our ultimate standard of purity should be the *present* usage; not the usage of a past age, not the possible usage of a future age. The laws of a language protect it, not as it was, not as it may or will or ought to be, but as it is. Conservative presumption always favors the thing that is. The great majority of things in human life prove their right to be by being.

<small>Present usage.</small>

Again: that which we accept as authority should be the *national* usage. The laws of a language protect it from the errors of foreign usage; that is, the usage of those to whom it is not vernacular. M. Guizot, for instance, wrote and spoke the English language with almost the accuracy of an English scholar, but he was not an authority on a question of English purity. *The authoritative use is the vernacular use.* The laws of a language also prescribe the national usage as distinct from any sectional use. The English-speaking world abounds in provincialisms. Scotticisms, Americanisms, Irish idioms, Australian *patois*, the Chinook dialect of Oregon, are no part of the English language, because they have not the stamp of universal use. The laws of a language further support the national usage as distinct from clannish use. Why is not the lingo of the forecastle pure English? Why not the jargon of the thieves of London? Why not the cant of religious enthusiasts? Why not the slang of American colleges? Because these are clannish. No national authority supports them.

<small>National usage.</small>

The third restriction which the laws of a language lay upon the usage to which we appeal for our authority is, that *Reputable usage.* it shall be *reputable* usage. This principle grows out of the obvious and necessary difference between the colloquial use of the language by all classes, and the use of it in continuous discourse by public speakers and writers. Every man who uses the language much in both these modes adopts inevitably different styles. Words and constructions which conversation tolerates, perhaps requires, are often unfit for discourse, either written or oral. Not only the book, but the speech, demands elements of diction for which conversation provides no range.

A critic in *Blackwood's Magazine* says, that " at the present day, in the English portions of the world—European, Asiatic, *Three different kinds of English.* Australian, African, and American—all educated people use three different kinds of English: *old Saxon English* when they go to church, or read good poetry ; *vernacular or colloquial English*, not altogether free from slang and vulgarity, when they talk to one another in the ordinary intercourse of life ; and *literary English* when they make speeches or sermons, and write or read articles in reviews or books. This threefold division of the language has always existed ; though the great bulk of the people, up to recent times, may have only been familiar with the first, with its limited range of nouns, verbs, and adjectives." A scholar of thoroughly good taste must demur to this analysis of existing usage in some respects , yet a foundation for some similar distinction exists in the necessities of the case. It is obvious, that one who writes or speaks much in public must have a standard of pure English other than the usage of numerical majorities. Majorities use the language only colloquially. We are driven to look above them for a standard of classic purity. We find it in the usage of reputable authors.

What do we mean by reputable authors? We mean those authors, who, by the common consent, have been successful in the use of their language. Reputation proves success; not notoriety, but good repute. Literary fame entitles an author to rank as a standard in literary style, on the same principle on which fame at the bar and on the bench renders a lawyer an authority to his profession. Pope, Dryden, Macaulay, Everett, Irving, are standards of pure English, as Blackstone, Brougham, Marshall, Story, are standards in jurisprudence. By unwritten common law, such names have the voice of the nations behind them, and speaking in them. Scholarly taste obliges writers and public speakers to acknowledge this standard. It is unscholarly not to do so. Even the common, uneducated mind has a dim sense of this claim of pure English on an educated speaker. The common people like to be addressed in sound old English which has the centuries behind it. They desire it to be plain, direct, strong, racy, but they never as a body desire it to be low. Marines do not like to be preached to in the dialect of the forecastle. When one preacher of distinction in our metropolis endeavored to preach thus on a man-of-war in Boston harbor, his hearers said, when his back was turned, that "there were two things which he did not understand—religion and navigation." A rabble in the street will often hoot if they are addressed in bad grammar.

Who are reputable authors?

Pure English and the common people.

Patrick Henry thought to win the favor of the backwoodsmen of Virginia by imitating their colloquial dialect, of which his biographer gives the following specimen from one of his speeches: "All the larnin upon the yairth are not to be compared with naiteral pairts." But his hearers, backwoodsmen though they were, knew better than that; and they knew that a statesman of the Old Dominion ought to speak good English. They

Patrick Henry.

were his severest critics. The common people know good English when they hear it; they understand it; men crave it who never use it. In their unconscious criticism of a speaker, his right to their hearing depends on his ability to say something worth their hearing; and one of the first evidences they look for of that ability is that he speaks better English than they do.

ANALYSIS.

PURITY OF STYLE.

I. Definition.
1. Purity relates to three things.
2. Purity requires three things.
3. Purity violated in three ways.
4. Barbarism, Solecism, Impropriety,

II. Standard of Purity.
1. Two extremes.
2. Two principles indicate the true theory.
   A. Language as a national growth is a thing of law.
   B. Language a nation's property, and thus usage is the ultimate standard.
      (a) "Quiz."
   C. Languages need improvement.
      (a) A Prussian dictionary.
      (b) A French dictionary.
      (c) An English dictionary.

III. Usage as Influenced by the Laws of a Language.
1. Present usage.
2. National usage.
3. Reputable usage.
   (a) Three different kinds of English.
   (b) Reputable authors.
   (c) Kind of English desired by the common people.

CHAPTER III

VIOLATIONS OF PURITY OF STYLE

THE consideration of the standards of English purity in the last chapter leads us to observe, as the fourth general topic of discussion, the most important violations of a pure style. What are they? We have observed their well-known names in defining this quality; viz., the barbarism, the solecism, and the impropriety.

I.—OBSOLETE WORDS.

We note them now more specifically by observing that purity is violated by the use of the *obsolete* in language; that is, by obsolete words, or constructions, or significations. Present usage being the standard, it is not sufficient, to authorize the use of a word, a construction, or a signification, that it has once been pure English. Old words are often like old ploughs. They must give way if the national civilization has outlived them. Why may we not now employ the words "peradventure," "forsooth," "yclept," "whilom"? In Latimer's day it was no violation of good taste to use the word *alonely*. These words are all barbarisms now, because they are obsolete. Dr. Barrow says, "It is our duty to testify an affectionate *resentment* to God." "Resentment" once signified the act of acknowledging a favor, Jeremy Taylor says, "Humility is a duty in great ones no less than in *idiots*." "Idiot," in his day, meant a private man only, retaining the etymological sense of the original Greek. A writer of the same period speaks of

Alonely.

Resentment.

Idiot.

Lord Bacon as a man of "very wise *prejudices.*" "Prejudice" then meant only a prejudgment. "Humility" and "pusillanimity" were once synonyms. The history of these words illustrates the conflict of Christianity with Paganism to make the lowly virtues respectable. The word "painful" has a similar history. It once signified, not "producing pain," but "taking pains.' Richard Baxter was called by his contemporaries "a most painful preacher." Wren, once Bishop of Ely, was charged by the Puritans with "having banished fifty godly, learned, and painful preachers" from the kingdom.

Humility.

Painful.

Several inquiries deserve answer respecting the obsolete in style. When does a word become obsolete? "Whereof the memory of man runneth not to the contrary" is the hint given by Dr. Campbell and others; that is, if a word has not been in current use within the memory of any man living, it must be considered as lost to the living tongue. This appears reasonable: scholarly taste has suggested no better principle.

Time when words become obsolete.

Should obsolescent words be retained? Critics agree, as a general thing, in the negative. Words usually die, as men do, because of some infirmity. They are ill formed, or difficult of enunciation, or redundant, or inferior to their synonyms; or that which called them into being has ceased to be. For one reason, or more, the words are not needed; and the national mind parts with them unconsciously. None but a decadent people will commonly permit a valuable word to die.

Why obsolescent words should not be retained.

But exceptions to the general rule exist, in which scholarly effort is needed to keep a good word alive. When the loss of a word would cause an obvious deterioration of a language, then culture should exert its influence to conserve the word. James Russell Lowell says that "*an archaism is permissible*

Test given by James Russell Lowell.

when a word has been supplanted by one less apt, and yet has not become unintelligible. An obsolescent word may be necessary to the precision of a language. The word "concept" is an old English word, signifying, not the act of conceiving, but the idea conceived. It passed out of use for a time; and "conception" took its place, and is now used to signify both the act and the thing. But Sir William Hamilton revived the more ancient word, because it adds to the philosophical precision of the language to have two words to express the two ideas.

The obsolescence of a word may indicate a moral decay in the language, and may for that reason be wisely arrested. The Italians have permitted the word *virtuoso* to lose its old element of moral virtue, and to decline to the expression of a "connoisseur of art." The French have suffered the word *honnêteté* to lose its original sense of "honesty," and to descend to the idea of "civility." In both these cases the languages would have been the richer if the old significations had been retained. Milton saved some words to our language, which in his day were obsolescent, but which he thought ought not to die. Missionaries in heathen lands are sometimes able to secure a new medium of appeal to the heathen mind by resuscitating obsolescent words which the nations are losing through the decay of their moral sensibilities, and therefore of moral ideas. Verbal obsolescence and moral decay.

What principle should govern the use of obsolete words in poetry? The general taste of scholars makes an exception to the rule in behalf of obsolete words in poetic style. The necessities of rhythm often require this. A reason for it exists also in the nature of poetry. The distance of an object quickens the play of the imagination toward it. An obsolete phraseology, therefore, is in keeping with the design of poetic expression. The style of Spenser in "The Faerie Queene" is designedly Obsolete words in poetry.

archaic. He multiplied obsolete and obsolescent words purposely, in order to throw back the style into a bygone age. Guizot thinks that Shakespeare, in "King Lear," intentionally violated grammatical construction in order to locate the drama in a period in which the language was in its infancy. Dramatic congruity admits of this license.

What principle should guide us in the use of obsolete words in prayer? Prayer in this respect partakes of the nature of poetry. German critics have suggested, that, rhetorically considered, prayer *is* poetry. A reverent diction, like the poetic, invites a certain infusion of the antique element. Therefore we retain the obsolete termination of verbs in "th." We say "maketh," "believeth," "saith." This is not pure English in oratorical style, but it is such in the precative style.

<small>Obsolete words in prayer.</small>

It is, however, different when a writer in ordinary discourse seeks for an obsolete style for effect. Even when this is prompted by a struggle to clothe a thought with power, it is objectionable. More power is lost than gained by the expedient. Hearers feel it to be an expedient, and the effect is to attract attention to the style by distracting attention from the thought. One often feels this defect in reading certain productions of De Quincey. It is true that force is sometimes gained by it, but it is an artificial force. Good taste approves only the force gained by the purest and simplest English.

<small>Obsolete words in ordinary discourse.</small>

II.—New Words.

Passing, now, from the consideration of an obsolete style, we observe another class of violations of purity, in the *coining* of *novelties*. Present usage being our standard, novel words, novel constructions, novel significations, do not belong to the language. The objection is as valid against a possibly future use as against one which time has ejected. A scholarly regard for English purity will act conservatively against new coinage.

Professor Park of Andover has observed that barbarisms from new coinage occur chiefly in three ways—by the creation of new words, by the enlargement or contraction of old words, and by the compounding of old words. In an early edition of one of our two standard dictionaries, the following words are found: "unwappered," "intersomnious," "circumbendibus," "jiggumbob," "solumnigate," "grammatication," "somniative," "scrimption," "solivagous," "slubberdegullion," "transmogrification."

1. These are *absolute creations* by somebody. They are not English: they never have been. By what authority do they find a place in a dictionary of a civilized tongue? Their only becoming place is in that ancient lexicon in the British Museum to which allusion has been made, as compiled, in part, of "words which signify nothing." Absolute creations.

2. *Contractions of old words* appear chiefly in the form of vulgarisms. Contraction in speech is a most singular development of the natural *inertia* of the human mind. Even the tongue, the most nimble of human organs, will utter only that which it must utter. A syllable, a letter, an accent, which it can slur, it will slur. The contraction "ain't" for "isn't" is a vulgarism which ought not to need criticism. The safe rule respecting contractions is never to use them in public speech. This is the instinct of a perfect taste. It is said that Edward Everett never employed them, even in epistolary style. Some critics do not consider it fastidious to avoid them in colloquial usage. Contractions of old words.

3. *Expansions of old words* are more frequent than con-

tractions. "Preventative" and "intensitive" are examples; the pure forms are "preventive" and "intensive."

<small>Expansions of old words.</small> Unauthorized prefixes and suffixes create a multitude of barbarisms. In a standard dictionary are found the following: "untriumph," "untrussed," "unuplifted," "unwormwooded," "unruinable," "unvulgarized," "unquarrelable," "unquaker," "unrenavigable," all coined, chiefly, by the unauthorized prefix "un" to words, which, either in part or in whole, are in good use. Here are found also, "cockneyfy," "dandyize," "dandyling," "incoherentific," "imperiwigged," "fiddlefaddler," "sapientize," "wegotism," "weism," "perfectionation," "maximize," "pishpash," "fiddle-de-dee," most of which are coined by unwarrantable additions to the end of good words. Such dictionaries are emphatically "dictionaries unabridged."

4. *New words are sometimes created facetiously.* De Quincey speaks of Suetonius, the story-teller of antiquity, as a <small>New words created facetiously.</small> "curious collector of anecdotage." Words originating in a facetious mood of authorship or oratory sometimes have a vitality to which no real worth in such words should seem to entitle them. It is one of the collateral evidences that man was made to be happy, that the risible faculty has so much power as it has in public speech. Very little is required to make an audience laugh. The same principle it is, probably, which gives ready rootage to words which are coined by the risible emotions. A multitude of such words die; but, if they express any genuine humor, they have peculiar chances of life.

5. It deserves remark, that writers coin many words, in the haste of composition, *by adding the Greek termination* <small>New words from adding "ize" to substantives.</small> *"ize" to substantives.* A new verb is thus created, which in not one case in a hundred becomes permanent in the language. "Jeopardize," "municipalize," "chartize," "deputize," are found almost at random in one volume.

6. *Good words compounded by means of a hyphen*, are another form of barbarisms from new coinage. The pulpit, from time immemorial, has been in this respect, if not a "den of thieves," a nest of counterfeiters. "Heaven-descended," "soul-destroying," "God-forgetting," "God-defying," are among the counterfeit words of this construction for which the pulpit is responsible. Very few of these long-winded, long-waisted, long-tongued, long-tailed, and long-*eared* compounds, are authorized English.

<small>New words from compounding old words.</small>

A young writer has no protection against the barbarisms of this class, unless he finds it in his scholarly tastes and his scholarly reading. When once fixed in a writer's style, they form one of the most debilitating features, especially in the style of a public speaker. The taste for them destroys the taste for monosyllabic words, on which the force of a spoken style so greatly depends. A subtle sympathy exists between these compounds and long, involuted sentences. Be not deceived, if occasionally they appear to strengthen style. In the general effect they dilute and flatten it. They invite a drawl in delivery. They *are* a drawl in expression. Few forms of mannerism run to such extremes as this, when once the scruples of good taste are broken down. Mrs. Henry Wood, in "Roland Yorke," speaks of the "not-attempted-to-be-concealed care." Another author remarks upon "the-sudden-at-the-moment-though-from-lingering-illness-often-previously-expected death" of the heroine. It does not require scholarly erudition to decide that such a tape-worm as this has no proper place above ground. The taste which could tolerate it is hopeless barbarism. The next phase of such culture is cannibalism.

<small>Effect of compounded words on style.</small>

ANALYSIS.

VIOLATIONS OF PURITY.

I. Obsolete Words.
   1. James Russell Lowell's Test.
   2. Use in Poetry.
   3. Use in Prayer.
   4. Use in Ordinary Discourse.

II. New Words.
   1. Absolute Creations.
   2. Contractions of Old Words.
   3. Expansions of Old Words.
   4. New Words formed Facetiously.
   5. Union of Greek Terminations and Old Substantives.
   6. New Words by Compounding Old Words.

CHAPTER IV

VIOLATIONS OF PURITY OF STYLE (CONTINUED)

We have observed that the growth of a national civilization necessitates the growth of its language. No other one thing expresses a nation's mind so exactly as its language does. The growth of the language must be, in part, by new coinage. How, then, shall we judge when to reject, and when to employ, new words? By the common consent of scholars the following principles are recognized.

I.—Six Principles Which are to Determine the Acceptance or the Rejection of New Words.

1. One is, that an acknowledged master of a science or of literary acquisitions may coin such new words as, in his judgment, the necessities of the language require. Modern physical science has received immense expansion. Its nomenclature is almost wholly new, created by experts in the sciences. Even mental science claims this prerogative. Coleridge claimed the right, as an expert in psychology, to introduce into our language the German distinction between the understanding and the reason. That use of these words is thus far technical to the science which has created it. If philosophers generally accept it, by the laws of good taste it becomes authoritative in our dictionaries. Criticism must not condemn it as a novelty or an importation. Mr. Grote, in his "History of Greece," coins the word "dicast." It means nearly, yet not exactly, the same as our word "juryman." Mr.

Men of science.

Coleridge.

Mr. Grote.

Grote therefore exercises his literary right as an historian to import the word from the Greek, which is its original. He cannot otherwise express the idea without a cumbrous circumlocution.

2. Another principle which criticism admits is, that an acknowledged master of the English tongue may coin such words as, in his judgment, it requires for its precision or its affluence of expression. Scholarly taste allows this as one of the prerogatives of scholarly authorship. The prerogative is unquestioned in proportion to the critical care of the author who claims it. A new word used by Addison, Swift, Macaulay, Irving, Everett, would have a claim to recognition which a word coined by Carlyle would not have. The writers first named are known to have been scrupulous in their use of good English, and no other. Carlyle is notorious for his recklessness of scholarly taste, neither cherishing it himself, nor respecting it in others. De Quincey advances, as one test of an author's sway over the national mind, how many original words, phrases, idioms, significations, does he succeed in ingrafting upon the national tongue?

Masters of English

Carlyle and other writers.

3. Another principle which critics admit with restrictions is, that some novelties in language may be created by authors of only provincial or local fame. "With restrictions," it is to be remembered: criticism here only conforms to facts. The number of words thus originated is incalculable: the number that live is very small. It is the authors of inferior power and repute who are most free in such coinage: their authority is in inverse proportion to their presumption. Yet a small fraction of the language owes its origin to them. Robert Southey coined the word "deicide." He gave three reasons for it; that it is in strict analogy with other words in good use— " suicide," " fratricide," " parricide," " regicide ; " that its

Writers of only local fame.

meaning is obvious; and that no other word in the language expresses the same idea. Very good reasons these: it would be hard to answer them. Yet the word has not yet found its way into the usage of the first class of authors.

4. A fourth principle is, that it is a doubtful experiment with any man to add a word to his native tongue. The creation of a word is a great assumption over human thought. It is a challenge to a nation's mind. It may be an assault on a nation's prejudices. It may be resisted by the whole momentum of a nation's history. It may be ejected by the force of a nation's whims. The chances are as a thousand to one against its success. Such a word may have every scholarly quality in its favor, and yet it may die of sheer neglect. It dies without so much as a burial. The nation often does not resist it, does not argue about it, but simply says, "We do not want it." Cicero had no superior as an authority in Roman literature, yet he failed more frequently than he succeeded in his attempts to improve the vernacular of his countrymen. The same is true of Milton and of Coleridge, both of whom were students of the forces of language, masters of racy English, and experimenters in the creation of novel words.

The creation of a word a doubtful experiment.

Cicero.

5. A fifth principle bearing upon the subject grows out of a peculiarity of modern literature: it is, that new coinage by journalists should be accepted with great caution. Journalists are a class of writers of recent origin. They include in their guild very many rudely educated men. They write much in haste; they write by shorthand; they write often in a somnolent state, in the small hours of the morning. The consequence is, that they coin words recklessly. Theirs is not often leisurely and scholarly authorship. Very few of them attain to the first rank in literature. Where can be found

Words coined by journalists.

among them the peer of Bryant? Their suggestions of new words are often crude. One of them, for example, proposes the word "thalagram," to express a message through the Atlantic cable. He coins it from Greek originals. But, so far as is known, no second writer has approved it, and for the very good reason, that nobody needs it. Why do we need any other than the word "telegram?" We say, "A telegram from Chicago," as we say, "A telegram from London." Why do we need a word to remind us that the one came from under the sea, more than a word to remind us that the other came through a line of cedar posts and insulated wires? Good taste forbids overloading the language with rubbish. A language should be like a library, well selected, not conglomerated. This new coin, "thalagram," has fallen flat on the national taste, as it is to be hoped will be the fate of the still more wretched medley, "cablegram." Two languages are searched for the rubbish which is patched to make this barbarism. The decisive test of new coinage in a language is the question of necessity. Does the language need it? If not, no other reason for it can commend it to good taste.

"Thalagram."

"Cablegram."

6. A sixth principle that the usage of good writers practically applies to the subject to be noted is, that authors of the first class, acknowledged by all others as literary authorities, may *occasionally* coin a word which they would not recommend as good English, and would not introduce into a standard dictionary if they could. They may do it as an exception to their general rule. Thus Coleridge writes: "If the reader will pardon an uncouth and new-coined word, there is, I should say, not seldom, a *matter-of-fact-ness* in certain poems." Coleridge here coins a word, which, though he was very unequal in his choice of English, he evidently would not recommend. He apolo-

New words not good English may be sometimes coined.

Coleridge.

gizes for it. He employs it exceptionally. The liberty to do this is a perilous one : a young writer may more wisely refrain from assuming it. The tendency to corruption is so strong, that while one's style is in the process of formation, as it is in the early years of one's practice, the safe course is, not to use any word which writers of the first order would not recommend, as well as indulge exceptionally. Yet the indulgence in question must be named because it exists, and it is sometimes indulged by the best writers. We cannot hope to enforce a style which is better than the best.

James Russell Lowell, for example, is one of the most scholarly critics and authors in our language. A word coined by him with expressed approval would carry all the authority which any one man's name can give to a word. *James Russell Lowell.* But when he coins, as he does, such words as "cloudbergs" and "otherworldliness" and "Dr. Wattsiness," he descends from style to slang. He coins them as an exceptional and rare indulgence. He does not expect to see them in the next edition of Worcester's Dictionary. He would be ashamed to see them there with his name as their authority. He would be the last man to authorize such words by scholarly criticism. He knows, and the world of scholars knows, that his own scholarly reputation will bear such occasional departures from good English, somewhat as a very saintly man can bear to be seen carrying a flask of brandy in the street. That which is a literary peccadillo from James Russell Lowell's pen may be unscholarly slovenliness from the pen of one unknown to fame. It is due to fact to recognize this exceptional license in authors of good repute, because it is a fact; yet we do not thereby commend it as a rule, nor even as an exception. It exists : that is all that we can say of it.

II.—Importation of Foreign Words.

Similar to the effect of unnecessary novelties upon a pure style is that of needless importation of foreign contributions to the language. The vernacular tongue is the tongue of a man who means to be understood. We commit a barbarism if we import a foreign word when an English word will express our thought as well.

1. It deserves mention, first, that this error is often caused by a pedantic attachment to foreign languages.

Greek and Latin. Professors of the Greek language often think in Greek. They use a Greek word, therefore, when no poverty of the English tongue creates the necessity. In the seventeenth century the taste of English scholars was infected with a morbid preference for the Latin language to their own. This led to the introduction of extremely ungainly words, which good use has never adopted.

Milton. Milton's style is defaced by such words as "ludibundness," "subsammation," "septemfluous." Even Milton's authority has not forced these words into the language: the national good sense has been too strong for that. Dr. Samuel Johnson's Latinized style is one of the fruits of a similar freak in

Dr. Johnson. the taste of a later age. In him it manifested itself, not only in the use of words not English, but in distorting the proportion of words of Latin to those of Saxon derivation, and in an imitation of Latin construction also, which renders his style one of the most foreign to the genius of our language to be found in our literature. Yet his was a mind compact with sturdy and solid English elements, which gave to his literary opinions, as Carlyle says, "a gigantic calmness." They made his conversation the antipodes of his written style. In conversation he was racy, laconic, fleet; in writing he was ponderous, lumbering, logy. In conversation he was an antelope: in his books he was a whale.

2. Again: an undue regard for the etymology of words often leads to improprieties from foreign importation. A word often has in its Greek or Latin root a meaning which its English form has entirely lost. *Etymology.* You find a familiar illustration of this in the word "prevent," which King James's translators of the Bible, following the usage of their age, have retained in its etymological meaning—a meaning which later usage has abandoned. Many contested passages in Shakespeare depend on the question, whether he adopted the pure English, or the etymological English, of his times. *Shakespeare.* Meaningless words become rich in sense, and obscure words become clear often, in his plays, by reading them, not as modern English, but with their etymology in mind. An affectation of etymological science is apt to infect the style of a writer who reads more in foreign languages than in his own. De Quincey is often guilty of this. It is the more inexcusable defect in a modern author; because he has what Shakespeare and Milton had not—a matured language at his command.

3. Further: the composite character of our English tongue has a twofold bearing upon the question of admitting importations. Our language is largely made up of accretions from abroad. It is, in this respect, very unlike the ancient Greek and Latin languages and the modern German. *Composite character of English.* Those were, to a great extent, evolved from internal resources. Our own language grows very slowly by such evolution. Its history is a history of innovations. As our national stock is a composite one, made up from many tributary migrations, so our language is a composite product, made up from almost all the civilized languages on the globe. If we want a new word, we instinctively go for it to some foreign source. Thus the English

nomenclature of the natural sciences is almost wholly Greek and Latin. One critic contends that ours is a decadent tongue, because it shows so little power of growth from within. This composite character of our language, to repeat, has a twofold bearing on the question of foreign imports.

It should render our taste tolerant of such imports, when they are necessary to the affluence of the language. This being the composite structure of it, an importation from abroad is a less evil than it was to the Greek language of the Augustan age. It does less violence to the genius of the English than it did to that of the Augustan Greek. Some importations every language must have. Every finished language has words for ideas which no other language expresses as well. We are already borrowing some philosophical words from Germany. We are obliged to do so, because we borrow the ideas there. Some French words express ideas which no corresponding English terms express as well. De Quincey asks, How can the idea of a "post-office" be expressed in Greek? or that of a "coquette," in Hebrew? If a language needs the foreign word to give utterance to the foreign thought, it must import the foreign word. Words are made for thought, not thought for words.

Why we should be tolerant of such imports.

But, on the other hand, the composite structure of our language should make us intolerant of importations when they are needless. This dependence on foreign sources for linguistic growth is an evil. Any language will be the more symmetrical, and free from anomalies, if developed from its native stock. A graft makes a gnarl in a tree: so does an importation make a protuberance in a language. Let the natural resources, therefore, be developed if they can be: let us take the alien tribute only when we must. There was great significance in Cæsar's rule of composition: "Always shun, if possible, the *insolens verbum*."

Why we should be intolerant of such imports.

III.—PROVINCIALISMS.

Purity of style is further impaired by the needless use of provincialisms. National usage being our standard, that is not pure English which has only sectional authority, unless sectional necessities compel its use.

It should be remarked, however, that words of provincial origin often become good English. Such words may force their way into universal use. All words begin to be somewhere. They may have at first a small constituency. Many of the most impressive words in the language had a provincial origin. The word "caucus" is of American birth: it was first used by old Samuel Adams. Now no English dictionary would be complete without it. *Words of provincial origin.*

Further: words remaining provincial may be good English. They may be necessitated by provincial peculiarities—peculiarities of climate, of soil, of productions, of institutions, of history. Americanisms, especially, are very numerous, which must still be accepted on the score of provincial necessity. "Senatorial," "gubernatorial," "mileage," "prairie," "backwoods," "clearings," "pine-barrens," "savannas," "federalist," "nullifiers," "anti-renters," "free-soilers," "pro-slavery," and many others, have been created by peculiarities in our provincial soil, or climate, or institutions, or history. *Words remaining provincial.*

IV.—VULGARISMS.

The most unscholarly violations of purity consist of vulgarisms. Reputable usage being our standard only that is pure style which has the authority of authors and speakers of national fame. Several things here deserve attention. One is, that the adoption in dignified writings of the usage of the illiterate is the *Pure style.*

chief source of corruption to any language. The language of common life is full of slang : nothing controls it but the taste of scholars. It is intelligible, often forcible : its very vulgarity gives it a rude strength. A large class of middlemen between the scholars and the vulgar do not know enough, or do not care enough, about the principles of taste, to refrain from slang in their own practice. Newspapers constantly seek notoriety by the use of it. A vast amount of the facetiousness of journalists is made up of it. It is, therefore, an ever open doorway for the inroad of corrupt taste into scholarly usage.

Prevalence of slang.

ANALYSIS.

VIOLATIONS OF PURITY OF STYLE (CONTINUED).

I. **Six Principles Determining the Acceptance or Rejection of New Words.**
   1. As offered by Men of Science.
   2. As offered by Masters of the English Tongue.
   3. As offered by Writers of only Local Fame.
   4. As offered by any man a Doubtful Experiment.
   5. As offered by Journalists.
   6. As offered by Authors when the words are not recommended as Good English.
      (a) Coleridge.
      (b) James Russell Lowell.

II. **Importation of Foreign Words.**
   1. From the Study of Greek and Latin.
   2. From the Study of Etymology.
   3. From the Composite Character of English.
      (a) Why we should be Tolerant of such Imports.
      (b) Why we should be Intolerant of such Imports.

III. **Provincialisms.**
   1. What Provincialisms may be Good English.

IV. **Vulgarisms.**

CHAPTER V

REASONS FOR THE CULTIVATION OF PURITY OF STYLE

I.—Value of Purity of Style.

The question is not an unnatural one—probably every public speaker asks it when his attention is first called to the subject—Is the use of scholarly English of sufficient practical value to repay one for the time and labor it will cost to acquire it and to make it habitual? If I make myself understood as a public speaker, do I not accomplish the great object of speaking? Is not a scrupulous regard for a scholarly selection of words the fruit of a squeamish taste? At the most, is it not an accomplishment of literary leisure rather than a necessity to literary labor?

1. Let it be observed, then, that literary authority is uniform in support of purity as the foundation of the *most effective style*. Cicero declares this in unqualified terms; and in so doing he speaks the judgment of the ablest authors, speakers, critics, of all time. No writer of distinction depreciates it theoretically. Carlyle represents a class of authors who ignore it practically, but I do not know that he has ever written a line decrying it in theory. Literary opinion claims for it the rank of a practical necessity. It is not primarily an accomplishment, but a power. Speakers should cultivate it, because they need it. It is the most direct and effective instrument for their purpose. The best style for all the ends of public discourse is a pure style. This is the ground taken by liter-

Marginal notes: Foundation of the most effective style. Carlyle.

ary opinion on the subject. It ought to be authoritative to any public speaker of sufficient education to enable him to understand the argument. The scholarly judgment of the world would not be thus uniform if it were not true.

2. But, more specifically, a pure style is tributary to the *most perfect perspicuity of expression.* When an objector says, "If I make myself understood, let that suffice," he begs the question. The surest way to be understood is to speak your pure mother-tongue. Perspicuity is relative to the intelligence of hearers, but pure English all hearers understand. The provincial dialects of Great Britain are such, that the people of different shires can with difficulty understand each other; but pure English they all understand. A speaker who employs classic English can go from one end of the kingdom to the other, and be perfectly understood by people who can scarcely make themselves intelligible to one another. Yet an eminent English critic, speaking of the English peasantry, says that "a rustic language, purified from all provincialism and grossness, and so far reconstructed as to be consistent with the rules of grammar, will not differ from the language of any other man of common sense." That is to say, the popular dialects of Great Britain comprise, for their staple in colloquial use, good English. It requires but a sprinkling of provincial words to make a *patois.* Pure English in place of these makes a perfect instrument of popular speech.

An aid to perspicuity.

Classic English.

The chief reason why the English Bible is so clear, except where the argument is abstruse, is, that its vocabulary is such pure and simple English. It is this which gives to the English Scriptures their clearness, prolonged to successive generations. They were published in the same age with Spenser's "Faerie Queene." Now the "Faerie Queene" needs a glossary, while the Bible is as intelligible as ever. Two

The English Bible and "Faerie Queene."

hundred and fifty years is a long while for the lifetime of a book. No book can live so long which is not written in the purest vernacular of the people. One of the reasons of the sway of the Bible over the other literature of the English tongue is that its style is so pure. An accomplished expert in English literature says that " our poetry could not have been, as it is, the noblest body of poetry in the world, if the divines and scholars of King James's era had taken it upon themselves to translate the Bible into the polite language of the court, or into any other than that used by the common people." The secret of the sway of the Scriptures over English literature is, that, by using in a scholarly way the language of the people, our translators fell back upon the purest vocabulary of their times ; and that vocabulary continues to be perspicuous to all classes of mind to this day. The purest style is not only the most perspicuous for the time being, but it has the longest heritage of perspicuity to subsequent generations. The purest style has the longest life.

2. Purity is tributary, also, to the *most forcible style*. A vernacular tongue carries weight because it is vernacular. Indefinable magnetic threads connect the pure vernacular with the sensibilities of the people who use it. Love of language is more potent than love of country. The native country, men call the *father*-land : the native language, they call the *mother*-tongue. The ballads of a nation which move its sensibili- Love of language and love of country. ties most profoundly are written in the purest dialect. That which Milton said of books is more profoundly true of a great nation's language in its untainted purity : " Books are not dead things, but they do carry a potency of life in them." So that style which " carries a potency of life " in it to the hearts of hearers is the style in which they recognize their purest vernacular vocabulary. They feel it as their own. It has roots running under their whole in-

tellectual life, and going back to their infancy. Swiss soldiers in the Austrian service used to be forbidden to sing their country's songs in their native tongue because it tempted so many to desertion.

This force of a vernacular style is the more powerful in the English language because of the intrinsic vigor of its chief fundamental element, the Saxon. "Saxon" has be- *The Saxon element.* come a synonym of "strong." This is the element most active in the vitality of the English Bible, to which I have referred. How long could the Lord's Prayer in English form live if it had been translated into Latinized English like that of Sir Thomas Browne? Suppose the style of it to have been as technical to religious thought as the following is to the science of medicine. A lady has died suddenly, and the reporter thus describes the event: "An autopsy was held, which revealed extensive cardiac disease, consisting of hypertrophy, with aneurism of the aorta just below its bifurcation, the rupture of which was the proximate cause of dissolution." It requires a classical scholar to understand from this that the person died of heart disease. How long would the readers of that rural newspaper continue their use of the Lord's Prayer if it had been taught to them by our translators in such a style as this?

4. Moreover, the genius of the English mind has given to the language the resources which specially adapt it to pub- *Demanded for the best results in public oral discourse.* lic oral discourse, as distinct from that of scholastic research. The English mind is pre-eminently the practical mind of modern times. As the German is the philosophic, and the French the scientific, so the English is the national mind most heartily given to the practical civilization of the age. The English are also a nation of public speakers. The same is true of the American people. In no other countries in the world is language so much used in public oral discourse as

in these. In the eloquence of the pulpit, of the bar, of the senate, of the platform, our language is the best fitted for use, in part because it is most abundantly used in all these varieties of public speech. Such a language as this, with such a history behind it, and the force of such a history in its structure, deserves to be employed with scholarly care.

5. Lest the estimate here given of the intrinsic value of our language should seem extravagant, let us observe the testimony of European scholars. The first is that of Jacob Grimm, the German lexicographer. *Testimony of Jacob Grimm.* From the midst of the most learned etymological studies of the age he once sent forth this tribute to a language not his own. "The English language," he wrote, "has a veritable power of expression such as, perhaps, never stood at the command of any other language of men. Its spiritual genius, its wonderfully happy development, have been the result of a surprisingly intimate union of the two noblest languages of modern Europe—the Teutonic and the Romanza. In truth, the English tongue, which by no mere accident has produced and upborne the greatest poet of modern times, may with all right be called a world-language. Like the English people, it appears destined to prevail, with a sway more extensive even than its present, over all portions of the globe. For in wealth, good sense, and closeness of structure, no other languages at this day spoken, not even our German, deserve to be compared to it." This is the judgment of a German, who would not needlessly exalt a foreign tongue at the expense of his own. It is the judgment of a philologist, who would not indulge in declamation on such a theme. It is the judgment of one of the most learned men of the age, who knew whereof he affirmed.

The late Baron Humboldt expressed, not long before his decease, substantially the same opinion of the capacities of the English as compared with the classic languages of antiquity. The Academy of Berlin once gave a prize for the best essay on a comparison of fourteen of the ancient and modern tongues. The prize was awarded to Jenisch, and the essay assigned the palm of excellence over all the rest to the English. Guizot claims the superiority, in some respects, for the French tongue; yet he concedes the pre-eminence of Shakespeare over all other modern poets, and affirms that Shakespeare could not have written his unequalled dramas in any other than the English language. No English, no Shakespeare, is the gist of his criticism. The point to which such testimony is to be bent is this, that such a language deserves protection from decadence and corruption. Its purity is its glory. Scholarly taste ought to stand sentinel over such a national treasure in the persons of the authors and public speakers who use the language in dignified discourse.

Guizot.

II.—Purity Ought to Characterize the Ruling Language of the World.

1. Another reason for the scholarly conservation of our language in its purity is the fact that the knowledge and the use of it are rapidly extending over the nations of the world. It is now the mother-tongue of the masters of one-fourth of the civilized globe. De Quincey expresses the opinion that the English and the Spanish are destined to contest the control of the civilization of the future. Why the Spanish should be thought able to engage in such a competition is probably because Spain has been what England is—the great colonizing power of the globe. Its language, therefore, has a lodgment at many commanding points on both continents. A short time ago seventeen different governments corresponded with the Department of

Rapid spread of English.

De Quincey.

State at Washington in Spanish—a larger number, probably, than that of correspondents in any other tongue. Alison the historian gives it as the result of his studies of the institutions of Europe, that the language of half the world, for ages, will be our own. Other ethnologists and philologians express the same or a similar opinion.

Alison.

2. The fact also deserves more particular notice, that English is the language of colonization and of commerce the world over. Those agencies which are most effective in extending commerce, and colonizing new lands, are rooted in the nations to which English speech is vernacular. In these lines of expansion, the French, the Spanish, and the German—the only tongues which in other respects can compete with ours—have no future comparable with that of ours. The absorption of them, wherever they come into rivalship with English on a large scale and on a new soil, is only a question of time. If new and uninhabited lands are to be discovered on the globe, the chances are that the first foot planted on their soil will be that of an Englishman or an American, and that the first word of human speech heard there will be from our mother-tongue. Even in Central Europe, English is gaining ground as the language of culture. The ability to speak it is recognized both as an accomplishment of culture and a necessity of commerce. The old idea of making Latin the dialect of learning is now shut up to the universities. The later fashion, of making French the dialect of courts, is also yielding ground. In many German cities English is spoken in every other store one enters. Ask for a hat in broken German, and the chance is, that you will be asked in return, in a dialect as pure as yours, "Can you speak English?"

The language of colonization and commerce.

English in Central Europe.

Commerce and colonization have effected such an extension of the use of this language, that an English traveller, not long ago, starting from Liverpool, and following the sun, travelled on a belt around the globe, and never was for twenty-four hours on land out of hearing of his native tongue, spoken by natives of the countries he visited. Dilke's "Greater Britain" is well worth reading, for the conception it gives one of the steadiness and the grandeur with which English speech is marching over the habitable world. It is more sublime than the tramp of an army. Mr. Webster gave expression to a profound fact, prophetic of this world's destiny, when he represented the globe as surrounded with one "continuous and unbroken strain of the martial airs of England."

Experience of an English traveller.

ANALYSIS.

REASONS FOR THE CULTIVATION OF PURITY OF STYLE.

I. **Value of Purity of Style.**
  1. Purity the Foundation of the Most Effective Style.
  2. Purity an aid to Clearness or Perspicuity.
  3. Purity an aid to Force or Energy.
  4. Purity demanded for the Best Results of Public Oral Discourse.
  5. Testimony as to the Value of English by European Scholars.

II. **Purity ought to Characterize the Ruling Language of the World.**
  1. Rapid spread of English.
  2. English the Language of Colonization and of Commerce.

CHAPTER VI

PURITY OF STYLE (CONCLUDED)

I.—Why American Writers and Speakers Should use Pure English.

AMERICAN speakers and writers should cultivate the use of pure English because the language is in special danger of corruption in this country. The danger arises from several causes, which can be but briefly noticed here.

One is, that republican institutions favor the influence of the illiterate upon the language. Our people are intelligent, yet in the main illiterate. Republicanism creates a multitude of illiterate speakers. *Influence of the illiterate.*
It tends, also, to promote the use of the language in address to the illiterate. As a nation we have no such knowledge as that which extensive reading gives, and no such delicacy of ear for the sounds of the language as the people of Athens had in their better days. Popular influence on the use of the language, therefore, is powerful, and at the same time not subject to good taste. Public speakers of all classes are tempted to speak for sensational effect. Members of the American Senate illustrate the force of this temptation in the prejudice which some of them have expressed in words quite equal to the dignity of the sentiment, against "literary fellers" among their associates. The late Hon. Stephen A. Douglas once declared it to be a disqualification for the duties of senator, that a man had a classical education. *Stephen A. Douglas.*

2. Again: the extent of our territory favors the formation of provincial dialects. The dialects in the different shires of England have been mentioned. In France the same thing abounds. The peasantry of different departments find it difficult to understand each other. Yet France has a territory not so large as Texas. Herodotus tells us, that the dialects of ancient Greece often could not be intelligibly interchanged by those who used them. Yet Greece comprised a landed area less than that of one-half of the State of Pennsylvania. What shall prevent the growth of provincial tongues in a territory measured by thousands of miles from sea to sea, divided by such lines of demarcation as the Rocky Mountains, and embracing every variety of climate and production within the temperate zone?

The extent of our territory.

What is actually going on on the Pacific coast, the "Chinook dialect" in Oregon illustrates. A few years ago that dialect was in full play as an infant language by itself. It was originally compounded by members and employees of the Hudson's Bay Company to facilitate trade with the Indians. A dictionary of it has been printed, containing about twelve hundred words made up of English, French, and German, with a sprinkling of Indian words. Of forty tribes of Indians, no two use the same language; but they all understand "Chinook."

"Chinook dialect."

3. Further: the multitude of nations represented in the emigration to this country also fosters the growth of dialects. The Dutch settlers in Eastern New York were from the first hemmed in by strong English populations; yet they have left an impression on the colloquial language of that region which lives to this day, and this after the lapse of two hundred years. In some inland villages not far from the Hudson the mixture of Dutch and English words is obvious. It is not long since persons were found

The variety of immigrants.

New York State.

there who spoke Dutch alone, yet were natives of the Empire State. In Oneida County, a few years ago, you might have travelled for miles, and heard only the Welsh language.

If a few Dutch and Welsh immigrants could give to their languages such vitality in the midst of a thickly settled English State, what must be the effect produced by the thousands of Germans, Swedes, and Norwegians, in the Northwestern States? These have newspapers in their native tongues, and schools in which those tongues are used. Sometimes even the laws of the State have to be printed in a foreign language. In the city of Chicago the gospel is preached in eight different dialects to-day.

The Northwest.

In California the more familiar Spanish terms have become ingrafted on our English, so that they never can be detached again. Words from every language on the earth are working in, from Chinese to Kanaka. A shoemaker in San Francisco was asked by a customer, "Can you speak English?" and he replied, unhesitatingly, "Si Signor, certainement! you bet!" There were three languages in one sentence; and the good man straightened himself up with a look of proud satisfaction at the thought that he could speak English like a native. He was an Italian.

California.

The effect of this condition of things must subject our language to a very severe process of transition, in which dialects will be almost inevitable. The danger is, that the language will be seriously weakened for the high purposes it has served hitherto, and which have resulted in the noblest body of literature in the world.

Good taste, however, does not favor any quixotic enterprise. Changes cannot be wholly prevented. It is not desirable that they should be. But it is desirable and practicable to guard the old English of scholars and public speakers from reckless change, from ignorant change, from change fostered by the <u>indolence of</u> authors and the coarse-ness of readers. Keep the old English literature within the homely language of the people, as it is now, by keeping the language substantially what it is now. Do not allow such a magnificent literature to become obsolete through the obsolescence of the tongue in which it is now treasured. Think of it! Shall an American a hundred years hence be unable to read "The Pilgrim's Progress" in the *original?* Shall an American child then need a glossary to decipher the present form of "The Lord's Prayer," as we do to read the translation of it by Wickliffe? It would be a catastrophe to all high culture and to Christianity itself. Yet any language will die out thus, if authors and speakers leave it unguarded to drift with illiterate and vulgar usage. They are its natural conservators.

The way to guard our language.

II.—Why Educated People Should Use Pure English.

Indispensable to thorough and refined scholarship is a taste for a pure style. Observe critically the character of educated men, and you will find that their genuine culture in other things is proportioned to their taste for good English in their public speech. The accuracy of a man's learning, the soundness of his philosophy, the trustworthiness of his literary judgments, the value of his opinions of books, of educational enterprises and expedients, and the general symmetry of his culture, may be graded by his taste for pure English in his own use of language. The study of this quality of speech lies deeper in the ground-work of culture than at the first view it appears to do. Its roots run into and under the foundation of scholarship. This is the chief reason why so large a space is given here to its discussion.

An essential condition of genuine culture.

It is not because purity of style is immediately and intrinsically more important than other qualities, but that it lies at the basis of them all.

III.—Means of Acquiring a Pure Style.

The only remaining topic in the discussion of the theme before us is the inquiry, What are the most effective means of acquiring a pure style? These relate to several things.

1. One of these is our habitual conversation. We should distinguish between colloquial usage and that of continuous discourse. Conversation tolerates a freedom which is not authorized in discourse, written or oral. Colloquial usage admits provincialisms, contractions, even imports from other tongues, more freely than the usage of public speech or of authorship. For instance, a scholarly spirit does not recoil at hearing, in the freedom of conversation, such contractions as "don't," "can't," "won't." But, when Daniel Webster used them in the United States Senate, he violated the canons of cultivated taste. He did not do it in the earlier and more vigorous years of his life. His style in this, and in some other respects, deteriorated. We often say of a man's written style, that it needs more of the colloquial elements. That criticism commonly refers, not to vocabulary, but to construction, and specially to the ease and flexibility of structure which conversation creates more readily than written discourse. *[margin: Habitual conversation. Daniel Webster.]*

But it is not fastidious criticism to subject even conversation to substantially the same rules respecting a pure vocabulary by which we form the diction of discourse. Use pure English in common talk. This is not "talking like a book." It is using in speech the best elements of the language—the best for clearness, for force, for elegance. Observe for yourself the *[margin: Pure English in common talk.]*

conversation of the best class of educated men: you will detect an indefinable charm in it, which is due almost wholly to its selection of pure words, the predominance of Saxon words, the avoidance of slang, of contractions, of vulgarisms, of pedantic importations. The colloquial style of Edward Everett by the hour together might have been transferred to print without an omission or a correction. So might that of Washington Irving. One reason why they wrote as they did, in pure classic English, was that they talked in pure classic English. The habit of the tongue became the habit of the pen.

An educated man should never translate educated speech into slang facetiously. A man's jests may be a cause, as well as a sign, of literary decline. The majority of men of culture would be surprised to discover how much of such facetiousness exists among them, and how insidious its influence is on refinement both of thought and speech. Some conversationalists seem to know no other way of giving mother-wit to their talk than that of translating pure English into the dialect of low life. The apology for it is, that it is so expressive. But so is profaneness expressive. Vulgarity in all forms is expressive. You can command entranced attention in the pulpit by the utterance of an oath. But neither is a necessity to the bold and manly purposes of conversation. The princes in colloquial expression employ a vocabulary of which the most fastidious scholar need not be ashamed. The most forcible elements of common talk are its purest elements.

<small>Use of slang.</small>

The habit of ignoring those elements in favor of their vulgar equivalents is degrading to a man's habits of thinking. It fills his mind with coarse expressions of energy; and, in the haste of dignified speech, these will crowd their way in, to the displacement of those refined forms which a scholar's taste prefers, and

<small>Effect of the use of slang.</small>

the superiority of which every man feels. Such forms of vulgar force, once rooted in a speaker's vocabulary, may not die out of it in a lifetime. De Quincey, for instance, must first have allowed his colloquial dialect to be corrupted, before he could, with his princely command of language, have indulged himself in writing, as he does, of Greece as having been very proud of having "licked" her enemy "into almighty smash;" and again, of Apollodorus as being "cock of the walk." An author's pen does not commit such crimes against the mother-tongue if his own tongue has not first been guilty of degrading colloquial liberty into colloquial vulgarity.

2. A pure style may be fostered by the reading of classic English authors. The most lasting influence which forms a speaker's style is commonly that of the authors of whom he is most fond. The influence is a silent one, and its growth imperceptible; but it is creative. That which an educated man reads with most profound reverence and enjoyment he will most nearly resemble in the end. Delight in pure English, and you will compose in pure English. Let your tastes be formed upon the models of Addison, David Hume, Wordsworth, Macaulay, Whately, Washington Irving, Edward Everett, Motley, and Prescott, and you can scarcely fail to write and speak with a pure vocabulary. *Reading of classic English authors.*

On the other hand, read with scholarly caution authors who by reputation are indifferent to the purity of their language. Do not accept as authorities Coleridge, Carlyle, Emerson. Read with critical care against abuses of languages those authors whose culture has been chiefly derived from German literature. We may be unable to assign a reason for it; but it is a fact, that German writers, when they become the favorites of an American speaker, are more efficient in corrupting his English style than those of any other foreign *Authors who are to be read with critical care.*

tongue. This, probably, was the chief source of the degeneracy of Carlyle's English. It is reported that when he began his literary career, before German studies had become ascendant in his reading, he wrote a diction not at all noticeable for unscholarly features. The degradation of his style to the most monstrous contortions that have defaced any modern literature of equal rank seems to have been consciously and voluntarily invited on his part, by the sacrifice of his English to his German masters.

3. Purity of style may be assisted in its growth by a discreet use of dictionaries, grammars, and other treatises upon language. Robert Hall never wrote for the press without keeping Johnson's Dictionary open before him for reference. Yet he might have been pardoned, if any man might, for writing recklessly; for he probably never had a painless waking hour in his life after reaching the age of manhood. He lived and died in extreme neuralgic suffering. If Carlyle had been such a sufferer as Hall was, one might pardon his style for howling and growling in outlandish English.

Discreet use of dictionaries.

4. Purity of style may obviously be cultivated by a scholarly care in one's own habits of composing. Never use a doubtful word without investigation. Generally give the preference to Saxon words. A Saxon style is almost certain to be a pure style. Criticise your own composition after the excitement of the work is over. By directing your own attention consciously to the barbarisms already familiar to your pen, you most easily expel them from your use. Write also with the assistance of a manuscript catalogue of words which you detect as impure or doubtful English in your reading. For convenience' sake, such a list of words should include also those which are violations of precision, to avoid the necessity of constructing two. Words obsolete, words obsolescent, words doubtful, words whose structure or sense

Scholarly care in composition.

should not invite their introduction to the language, words not precise as commonly employed, unauthorized compounds, words improperly imported—these and similar violations of good style may be accumulated as a ready guide to one's own critical taste. Knowing what to shun is the chief thing in learning what to use. The very writing of such a catalogue will of itself improve one's critical taste. It is also the most effective method of keeping one's self informed of the progress of the language.

ANALYSIS.

PURITY OF STYLE (CONCLUDED).

1. Why American Writers and Speakers should use Pure English.
1. Influence of the Illiterate in this Country.
2. The Extent of Our Country.
3. The Variety of the Immigrants.
    (a) Foreigners in New York State.
    (b) Foreigners in the Northwest.
    (c) Foreigners in California.

II. Why Educated People should use Pure English.

III. Means of Acquiring Pure English.
1. Habitual Conversation.
    (a) What it is to Use pure English in Common Talk.
    (b) Use of Slang.
    (c) Effect of the Use of Slang.
2. Reading of Classic English Authors.
3. A Discreet Use of Dictionaries, Grammars, and Other Treatises on Language.
4. Scholarly Care in Composition.

CHAPTER VII.

PRECISION OF STYLE

I.—Definition of Precision of Style.

PRECISION of style—what is its characteristic idea? This is figuratively suggested by its etymology—*præcido.* To eliminate redundancies, to supply deficiencies, and to remove inaccuracies, is its aim. Precision, then, is the synonym of exactness. More fully, *it is that quality by which a writer's style expresses no more, no less, and no other, than the thought which he means to express.*

II.—Precision Distinguished from Other Qualities of Style.

Precision needs to be distinguished from certain other qualities which it resembles. It is distinct from *propriety* of style. Propriety, as we have seen, relates to the signification of language as fixed by usage: precision relates to the signification of language as demanded by the thought to be expressed. Propriety is satisfied if we write good English; precision demands such a choice of good English as shall express our meaning.

<small>Distinguished from propriety.</small>

Precision is distinct, also, from *perspicuity* of style. Precision, as above remarked, is satisfied if we express in good English our thought, no more, no less, no other. Perspicuity requires such a selection of good English as shall make our thought clear to the hearer. The thought may be precisely expressed, yet not

<small>Distinguished from perspicuity.</small>

be understood by the hearer. It may be clothed in unfamiliar English, yet with no want of precision. You may soliloquize your thought exactly: you do not thereby communicate it clearly. Perspicuity demands an adjustment of style to the capacity and culture of an audience; precision, only an adjustment of it to the thought of the speaker. Profound thinkers are not necessarily expert communicators. Style, then, may be precise, and not perspicuous: it may be perspicuous, and not precise. Connection may neutralize the want of precision. It may be clear that a speaker means what he does not say. One may not always easily determine at what point the want of precision passes over into a want of perspicuity. That depends on the quality of the hearing.

To recapitulate these distinctions: *propriety* requires only good English; *precision* requires such a choice of good English as shall express the speaker's mind; *perspicuity* requires such a choice of good English as shall make the speaker's mind clear to the hearer.

III.—Violations of Precision.

1. One class of offences against precision concerns *the use or omission of single words*. The wrong use or omission of a word sometimes affects grammatical construction to the injury of this quality. Omission of single words. "Certainly I nor any man has a right," etc., thus writes De Quincey. Ungrammatical structure here is occasioned by the omission of the word "neither." "No writer was ever guilty of so much false and absurd criticism," thus writes Macaulay of Sir Horace Walpole. The omission of the word "other" impairs precision. If no writer was ever thus guilty, then Walpole was not guilty. But Macaulay means to say the opposite. Scores of instances of this offence against precision are found in Macaulay's writ-

ings. A model of precision as he is in other respects, he seems never to have observed the nice requirement of our syntax in this.

2. The word "*it*" is often so used or omitted as to injure exactness of expression. William Cobbett says, "Never put an 'it' on paper without thinking what you are about." Often the thing needs to be expressed to which the impersonal pronoun refers. Sometimes the demonstratives "this" or "that" need to be substituted for "it." Your reading, if your attention is directed to the fact, will disclose to you the enormous amount of material which this word is made to carry in the usage of authors. The freedom of its use exposes it to abuse. The possessive case of "it" is of recent origin in the language. Our English translators of the Bible did not recognize it. They employed "his" for "its." The impersonal form of the possessive does not occur except by interpolation. It was not common in King James's day.

<small>Wrong use or omission of "it."</small>

3. A wrong choice of single words leads often to the loss of precision *in the moods and tenses of verbs*. "I intended to go," "I had intended to go," "I intended to have gone"—these forms express different shades of thought; yet some writers use them interchangeably. De Quincey writes: "With the exception of Wordsworth, no celebrated writer of this day has written a hundred pages consecutively without some flagrant impropriety of grammar, such as the eternal confusion of the preterite with the past participle, confusion of verbs transitive with verbs intransitive, or some violation more or less of the vernacular idiom." This is an extravagant criticism, but it indicates the general impression left by a voluminous range of reading upon one of the keenest of modern critics.

<small>Wrong use of moods and tenses of verbs.</small>

<small>De Quincey.</small>

One of the permanent questions of literary criticism is when to use the subjunctive mood. A very difficult question it is, except to a writer whose habit of critical observation has been disciplined by extensive reading of the best authors. Hallam says that the use of misplaced inflections was one of the chief things in which the decadence of both the Greek and the Latin languages first showed itself. Teachers of the freedmen of our own country find the similar defect one of the most difficult things to correct in the negro dialect. In that dialect it often extends to the connection of different verbs utterly without sense, as in the phrase "done gone." A singular power is observable, in such corruptions, to migrate from one language to another, apparently through the national blood. Livingstone found, in some of the African dialects, phrases corresponding to this "done gone" in the *patois* of the Southern plantation.

<small>Hallam.</small>

The instinct of literary taste is seldom, if ever, sufficient to guide a writer in the use of the verbal moods and tenses. We need elaborate study of them with grammar in hand, and also a large range of good reading behind to determine points which grammars do not specifically treat. Think on these topics with the pen; write down errors and their corrections, and fix thus in mind the underlying philosophy of grammar. There is no less elaborate method by which one can become an accomplished scholar in English idioms. The majority of the graduates of American colleges understand the Latin and Greek languages more philosophically than they do the English. The study of our own tongue as the subject of philosophical analysis is a modern addition to our collegiate curriculum. One expedient which facilitates the study of it is to study the English verb in comparison with the Greek verb.

<small>Means to a right use of verbal moods and tenses.</small>

4. This suggests, further, that the wrong use or omission of *connective* words is often the occasion of looseness of style. The superior precision of the Greek tongue is said,

by those who are experts in teaching it, to be in part due to the abundance of connectives in its vocabulary.

Wrong use or omission of connective words. For some of its connective particles our language has no equivalents; yet such as we have serve often to knit one's style together in exact and forcible collocations. Coleridge says that a master of our language may be known by his skilful use of connectives. This is one secret of the vigor of Coleridge's own style. His prolonged and involuted sentences derive from this source often a wonderful continuity, without which his profound conceptions could not find adequate expression. In order to represent some thoughts, style needs a certain sweep of sustained expression, like the sailing of an eagle on wings of scarcely visible vibration. Such, often, is Coleridge's style; and his command of it is often due to his precise use of connective words. It is still more abundantly and grandly illustrated in the prose style of Milton. Hence

Milton. arises the independence of both of fragmentary expression such as the majority of writers would think to be all that some thoughts admit of in human speech. Hence their freedom from that which Southey calls the "Anglo-Gallican style, whose cementless periods are understood beforehand, they are so free from all the connections of logic." Dr. Arnold, speaking of this feature in the thinking of Coleridge, says that he would have been more perfectly understood if he had written in classic Greek.

This which I have termed the "involuted style" is essential to the loftiest flights of eloquence in oral address. No

The "involuted style." man can be supremely eloquent in laconics. You cannot express the rising and the expanding and the sweep, and the circling of eloquent thought borne up on eloquent feeling, in a style resembling that which seamen call "a chopping sea." For such thinking, you must have at command a style of which an oceanic ground-swell, or the Gothic interweaving of forest-trees, is the more becoming symbol. You must have long sentences, euphonious sentences, sentences which invite a rotund and lofty delivery. This diction is often censured by critics as "fine writing." But you must have such a style for the most exact utterance of certain elevated and impassioned thoughts. Yet, in the construction of such a style, you must use connective words—links elaborately forged, inserted in the right joints of style, to make them flexible without loss of compactness. One word of such exact connective force in the right place, with the right surroundings before and after, may make all the difference between a disjointed and a linked style.

ANALYSIS.

PRECISION OF STYLE.

I. **Definition.**

II. **Precision Distinguished from other Qualities of Style.**
    (a) From Propriety.
    (b) From Perspicuity.

III. **Violations of Precision.**
1. Omission of Single Words.
2. Wrong Use or Omission of It.
3. Wrong Use of Moods and Tenses of Verbs.
    (a) Statement of De Quincey.
    (b) The Subjunctive Mood.
    (c) Means to a Right Use of Verbal Moods and Tenses.
4. Wrong Use of Connective Words.
    (a) Remark of Coleridge.
    (b) The Prose Style of Milton.
    (c) The "Involuted Style."

CHAPTER VIII

PRECISION OF STYLE (CONTINUED)

I.—Violations of Precision in the Use of Single Words.

Another class of offences against precision concerns the literal and the figurative uses of the same words. The style of oral address naturally multiplies the figurative uses of words. There is something in the correspondence of *eyes* between a speaker and his hearers, which prompts the use of pictorial language with a freedom not so natural to the style of books. The magnetism of vision invites a speaker to paint his thought to the waiting and eager eyes before him. Good hearers are always good spectators. No man hears perfectly with his eyes shut.

<small>The literal and the figurative use of the same word.</small>

The connection, whether in oral or written address, does not always determine which of the two uses of a word, the literal and the figurative, an author means. What, for instance, does Aristotle mean when he speaks of a " perfect thief " ?—a sinless thief, on the principle of Spartan ethics, which made the wrong of theft consist in its detection ? or a thief perfectly trained in the arts of his trade ? What does a celebrated English physician mean, when he describes a " beautiful ulcer " ?

2. Excessive figure in style obviously exposes it to a loss of precision. The style of some writers is a winged chariot; it bears up everything into the air, soaring on a figurative vocabulary. A reader often doubts how much is figurative, and how much

<small>Excessive use of figure in style.</small>

literal. Something must be literal in any sensible style. Good sense must have literal expression; it must often be pedestrian. What is the literal conception is often the vexed question. The style of Ruskin abounds with illustrations of this. Turn to one of his pages, and you will find a description of the flowing of a brook in summer: "Cressed brook, lifted, even in flood, scarcely over its stepping-stones, but through all sweet summer keeping tremulous music with harp-strings of dark water among the silver fingering of the pebbles." A precise reader, accustomed to look for exact ideas, will read this a second time, and perhaps not even then discern its meaning.

Ruskin.

II.—VIOLATIONS OF PRECISION IN CONFOUNDING SYNONYMS.

1. Another class of offenses against precision of style consists of synonyms confounded. The composite structure of our language has multiplied synonyms immensely. The two great branches of the language, the Saxon and the Norman, have specially wrought this result. To illustrate the extent to which these heterogeneous elements have accumulated synonyms, let a single example be given, which I take, in part, from Trench. We have the words "trick," "device," "finesse," "artifice," "ruse," "stratagem," "maneuver," "wile," "intrigue," "fraud"— at least ten words to express a group of ideas all having a common centre. These words are contributions from five different stocks of language. "Trick" and "wile" are Saxon; "device" and "intrigue" are Italian; "finesse," "maneuver," "ruse," and "intrigue" also are French; "artifice" and "fraud" are Latin; and "stratagem" is Greek. We have more than thirty words to express different varieties of the single passion of anger. It is obvious at a

The Saxon and the Norman.

Trench.

glance, that, in this multitude of synonyms, our language presents great facilities for looseness of diction.

2. Some writers are deceived by the similarity in the orthography of certain words. Such words as "ingenuous" and "ingenious," "guile" and "guilt," "fictitious" and "factitious," "genius" and "genus," "human" and "humane," "depreciate" and "deprecate," "extenuate" and "attenuate," "subtle" and "subtile," "imperative" and "imperious," "healthy" and "healthful," "impassable" and "impassible," "conjúre" and "cónjure," are often confounded. A store-keeper gives notice in his window, "Umbrellas recovered here." What does he mean?—"recovered" or "re-covered"? The two words "healthy" and "healthful" are so frequently interchanged, that our dictionaries define them, in part, as if they were exact synonyms; which they are not. The best usage of authors expresses by one of them the state of health, and by the other the act of producing health. "Health" is "not diseased:" "healthful" is "tending to promote health." The physician implied precise English, when, to the inquiry whether oysters were "healthy" at certain seasons, he replied, "I have never heard one complain of an ache or an ail." The distinction between these two words is parallel to that of a large group of words in our vocabulary, by which we distinguish between a condition, and a tendency to produce it. A man advertises the patent for a proprietary medicine for sale and observes, "It can be made very profitable to the *undertaker.*" Here the confounding of the general with the technical meanings of the last word, through sameness of orthography, gives a very dubious commendation to the drug.

Words confounded by similarity of orthography.

Healthy and healthful.

The "Undertaker."

3. The use and the neglect of the etymology of words are often the occasion of a loss of precision. "Sympathy" and

"pity" are confounded by neglect of etymology. Συν-παθος, the root of the word "sympathy," indicates a much finer feeling than that of pity. On the other hand, more often still, adherence to the etymological sense of a word when that sense has become obsolete, impairs precision.

Words confounded by neglect of etymology.

Command of the etymological senses of words is a rare gift, often as valuable as it is rare. Sometimes the etymological idea in a word is so remote from its real meaning, that the use of it amounts to an original figure, as when Mr. Choate in speaking of a disappointed candidate for office, said, "The convention *ejaculated* him out of the window." This latent force, which always lies in the etymology of words, tempts writers of classic training to resort to it, to the loss of precision. Thus Bishop Lowth writes, "The Emperor Julian very *judiciously* planned the overthrow of Christianity." Paley speaks of the "judiciousness of God." Guizot writes of the "duplicity" of certain of Shakespeare's plays, meaning only their dual structure. Bancroft writes of the "versatility" of the English government, meaning its fickleness. De Quincey speaks of "chastity," meaning "chasteness," "of taste." He speaks also of a "licentious" style when he means a style rhetorically loose.

Choate.

Paley, Guizot, Bancroft, De Quincey.

In all these cases the obsolete etymological significations are recalled, and allowed to displace the later usage. If a writer so keen of eye as De Quincey can commit this error, more feeble or less practised writers must be in constant peril of saying what they do not mean. No other quality of a good style demands such incessant care as this of precision. One's mind must be wide-awake, and always awake, in its choice of vocabulary.

III.—Violations of Precision by Defect in the Number of Words.

Not single words only may impair precision, but it is often sacrificed by defect respecting the number of words employed. Two forms of error in this respect lie opposite to each other.

1. One is the sacrifice of precision through excess of conciseness. In the manufacture of bullets, one part of the process is that of compressing the bulk of the metal without lessening its weight. By this means is gained increase of momentum in the discharge. This is a pertinent emblem of genuine conciseness in style. Only that is true conciseness which compacts thought without loss to the exactness of its expression. Precision is impaired if words are not numerous enough to express the whole thought.

An excessive conciseness.

Writers who affect conciseness inevitably commit this error. Ralph Waldo Emerson is often guilty of it, through the affectation of laconic style. Dr. South is not always free from it. The different degrees of comparison are often expressed with deficiency of words. "As many and even more hearers were assembled than before." What is the defect here? The writer should have said, by some reconstruction, "As many as, and even more than," etc. The inflections of verbs, also, are often put into excessively concise forms. "Men always have and always will reject the doctrine of fatalism." What is the error? The form should have been, "Men always have rejected, and always will reject," etc. The late Rev. Dr. Sears, writing of a certain rule in German grammar, says, "If this rule were established in all languages, this subject would be attended with fewer difficulties than it actually is." He should have said, "than it actually is attended with."

2. Some errors of this class arise from hopeless blundering. Says an editor, who still survives the achievement, "Chaffee's majority was thirteen hundred and ninety-two—just one hundred less than Christopher Columbus discovered America." A bridge in Denver, a few years ago, contained this record of municipal law: "No vehicle drawn by more than one horse is allowed to cross this bridge in opposite directions at the same time." The civil code of California once contained this statute: "All marriages of white persons and negroes and mulattoes are illegal and void." Who were, then, the legally married people of California? None but the Indians and Chinese. Such errors, or their equals in blundering expression, will occur in every writer's first thoughts of construction in composing, and will be paralleled in his written style if he trusts implicitly to first thoughts. They suggest a good general rule, that we should not shrink from repetition of words if that is necessary to precision. The elegance of a precise style is often disclosed where the precision is gained by repetition. Macaulay's writings abound with illustrations.

Hopeless blundering.

3. Precision may be sacrificed, not only by excessive conciseness, but by its opposite—a redundance in the number of words. Writers—and, still more, speakers—are exposed to this error, who have at command a diffuse vocabulary. A voluminous vocabulary by no means insures a full expression. One to whom thought comes in a volume of words may express more, he may express less, he may express other, than his real meaning. He to whom words occur with difficulty is the more apt to have a studied expression, and therefore an exact expression.

An excessive redundancy.

Looseness from redundance is specially apt to occur in speaking on difficult themes to the popular mind. Under such conditions, one is apt to explain, to qualify, to repeat, to speak in circumlocutory phrase, to experiment with variations. These easily overwhelm the thought with words.

<small>Redundancy in popular address.</small> One then loses precision in the effort to be perspicuous. Style moves aslant and askew in the struggle to move at all. Sometimes the very struggle to be precise—the mind, in the very act of composing, being intent on precision—may defeat itself. Here, again, thought is overborne by the machinery employed to give it utterance. Writers who pride themselves on philosophical accuracy are apt to multiply qualifications, and cir- <small>Philosophical accuracy.</small> cumstantial incidents, and secondary clauses, and parenthetical inclosures, so that no possible error shall be affirmed ; but that very strain after accuracy defeats its aim through the mere expansion of bulk and involution of connections. When a dozen words might have been understood, a dozen dozen may fall dead on the ear.

Edmund Burke sometimes illustrates this. In one of his elaborated sentences you will sometimes find words and <small>Edmund Burke.</small> clauses selected and multiplied and arranged and compacted and qualified and defined and repeated, for the very purpose of extending and limiting the truth to its exact and undoubted measure. He obviously labors to say just what he means, no more, no less, no other. Still, on the whole, he fails, because he is so elaborately precise in details. The thought is suffocated by the multitude of words employed to give it life. It is buried alive. To change the figure, you can divide and subdivide a field into so many, so small, so regular, and so exact patches, that the chief impression it shall leave on your eye is that of the fences. Similar is the impression of an excessively precise style.

Such a style is peculiarly inapt to oral delivery. That <small>Excessive precision in oral delivery.</small> which gives a dim idea to the reader may give none to the hearer. A style which must be critically analyzed to discover its contents has no chance in the rapidity of oral speech. Beginning, it may be, with a defect in precision, it ends with a defect in perspicuity.

4. Precision may be sacrificed further by looseness of *construction*. This class of errors runs parallel to a similar class, which we shall have occasion to consider in the study of perspicuity of style. *Looseness of construction.* The difference between the two is only a difference of degree. The same peculiarity of construction which in one degree of it is an example of looseness, in a greater degree becomes an example of obscurity. To avoid repetition, therefore, illustrations of these offences are deferred till we are led to recall this construction in our discussion of the corresponding class, on the subject of perspicuity.

ANALYSIS.

PRECISION OF STYLE (CONTINUED).

I. Violations of Precision in the Use of Single Words.
   1. Literal and Figurative Use of the Same Word.
   2. Excessive Use of Figure in Style.

II. Violations of Precision in Confounding Synonyms.
   1. The Saxon and the Norman in our Language.
      (a) Example from Trench.
   2. Certain Words Confounded by Similarity of Orthography.
   3. Certain Words Confounded by Neglect of Etymology.
      (a) Use of Words by Choate, Paley, Guizot, Bancroft and De Quincey.

III. Violations of Precision by Defect in the Number of Words.
   1. An Excessive Conciseness.
   2. Hopeless Blundering.
   3. An Excessive Redundancy.
      (a) Redundancy in Popular Address.
      (b) Writers of Philosophical Accuracy.
      (c) Some of Burke's Sentences.
   4. Looseness of Construction.

CHAPTER IX

PRECISION OF STYLE (CONTINUED)

The violations of precision in style which we have considered, we may assume to be of such significance as to give importance to a third general inquiry, to which we now proceed; viz., what are the chief causes of a loose style?

I.—Chief Causes of a Loose Style.

1. Of these, the first and chief is the habit of indiscriminate thinking. Other causes will give way to time if this one be entirely removed. Let a speaker habitually think with exactness, and a precise style will be at last inevitable. The power will grow to meet the demand of the thinking mind. Such is the subjective relation of language to thought, that the mental force which originates exact thinking will at length command exact expression.

Indiscriminate thinking.

Coleridge lets us into the secret of much which is called study, and is not such, when, in a letter to Wordsworth, he complains that he loses so much of his time in "leaning back in his chair, and looking up to the ceiling, in the bodily act of contracting the muscles of the brows and the forehead, and unconsciously attending to the sensation."

Coleridge.

Be it remembered, then, that the foundation of precision, as of all other qualities of masterly discourse, lies in one's habits of thinking; not in one's thoughts on a given subject alone, but in one's mental habits. Style, like character, is the mirror of habits. The

The foundation of precision.

thing needed is that, which, in painting, Ruskin calls the "power of mental grasp." This, he says, "implies strange and sublime qualities of mind." It is a power which must be elaborately gained—gained by thinking on difficult themes, by cultivating mastery of such themes, till they become the easy and natural subjects of one's daily meditations, and the joy of one's mental life.

2. A second cause of the formation of a loose style is the indulgence of excessive care for expression as distinct from thought. A writer is often anxious, not so much to say somewhat as to say it somehow. *Excessive care for expression.* Most of the faults of a juvenile style result from this cause. Diffuseness, repetition, bombast, result inevitably from the study of expression as distinct from thought. The temptation is constant to abandon the precise word, known to be the precise word, felt to be the only precise word, and to go roving for a substitute which may have every quality but the necessary one of saying what is meant. Watch the growth of an emphatic sentence in your own mind. Do you never find your tentative efforts to frame it following the *The growth of an emphatic sentence.* lead of a favorite turn of expression, which is not the lead of your thought? Have you never chosen a word which you were conscious did not, so well as another, express your meaning, yet chosen it because it was a novel word, or an odd word, or a strong word, or a euphonious word, or an archaic word? Yet that is mannerism in style. It is not honest work.

The most offensive variety of the error in question arises from a morbid fancy for some one quality of style. Often this form of the defect becomes a servile imitation. An illustrious author who has a *Servile imitation.* marked individuality in his style is very apt to have a crowd of imitators. That which is original to him is copy to them. Their own individuality is sacrificed to his.

In this way, at one period arose a "Chalmerian" style, and again a "Johnsonian" style, and another, which one critic has labelled as "Carlylese." Even so manly a man as Robert Hall confesses to having fallen in early life into subjection to the Johnsonian dialect. His criticism of himself illustrates with what scorn a robust mind will fling off such a mask as soon as it discovers that there is a mask. He says of himself, "I aped Johnson, I preached Johnson. It was a youthful folly, a very great folly. I might as well have attempted to dance a hornpipe in the dress of Gog and Magog. My puny thoughts could not sustain the load of words in which I tried to clothe them."

<small>Robert Hall.</small>

The first lesson to be learned by a young writer, yet often the last that is learned, is, that expression is to thought what countenance is to character. The one cannot exist without the other. Thought is the fixture; expression should be fluid in its capacity to adapt itself to the configuration of the thought. Hugh Miller gives a hint of the truth in his criticism of the poet Cowper. He says, "Cowper possessed, above all other modern poets, the power of bending the most stubborn and intractable words in the language around his thinking, so as to fit its every indentation and irregularity of outline, as a ship-carpenter adjusts the planking, grown flexible in his hand, to the exact mould of his vessel."

<small>Hugh Miller and Cowper.</small>

3. Precision often suffers from another cause, which is not peculiar to this quality, but affects others as well. It is the want of a command of language. This may result either from natural defect, or from the want of studious practice in the use of the language. A speaker cannot express his thought if he cannot command the requisite vocabulary.

<small>Want of a command of language.</small>

II.—Means of Acquiring a Command of Language.

How can the want of a command of language be remedied? The inquiry is pertinent to all the qualities of a good style, though especially so to the one before us.

1. In the first place, be it observed with emphasis, that command of language is not attainable by the mere accumulation of words in a ready memory. Vocabulary alone may stifle thought. A true command of language consists in a command of the forces of expression which the language carries. With emphasis, it is a *command* of language. It consists in the power of selection and rejection, rather than in that of accumulation. It is the power to use and to lay the spirits, as well as to summon them. Command of words, and command of the linguistic forces, are by no means one thing. Words come in troops at the bidding of one man: they fall into rank at the bidding of another.

<small>Power to select and to reject words.</small>

These two varieties of power are illustrated in the styles of Daniel Webster and Rufus Choate. Both were powerful speakers; but Webster was the superior, because of his superior power of selection. Much as one is dazzled by Choate's marvellous command of vocabulary, still one cannot avoid thinking of his style in the reading. That always indicates a defect. An absolutely perfect style attracts no attention to itself. Criticism of it is an after-thought. Members of the Boston bar all alike yielded to the spell of Choate's rhetoric; yet, in the very act of admiring, they found leisure to note that he "drove the substantive and six," alluding to the multitude of adjectives which he harnessed to a noun. Men with tears coursing down their cheeks, in listening to his sonorous periods in his eulogy upon Webster yet slily made a memorandum that they would count the words in some

<small>Daniel Webster and Rufus Choate.</small>

of those periods when they should be printed, and afterward remarked, that one of them was the longest but one in the English language. Who ever heard of any such arithmetical criticism of Webster's reply to Hayne of South Carolina? When Choate spoke, men said, "What a marvellous style! How beautiful! how grand! how immense his vocabulary! how intricate his combinations! how adroit his sway over the mother-tongue!" When Webster spoke, men said, "He will gain his case." Webster's vocabulary was much more limited than that of Choate, but he had a much sterner power of selection and rejection. His command of language was like Darwin's law of species in the struggle for existence—only that lived which deserved to live.

2. The most effective, indeed, the only effective means of obtaining command of the forces of expression which the language contains, is the persistent union of a critical study of the language with its critical use. Language needs to be searched. Words need to be weighed. Then use must make them familiar and ready to the pen or tongue. In oral delivery, words vary in their momentum. We need to graduate their movement by unconscious thought which shall guide selection to the purpose. A speaker makes a great acquisition when he adds to his practicable vocabulary one new word of which he has entire mastery. Mastery of a word means more than is commonly understood by it: it includes knowledge of all the shades of thought which good use attaches to the definition of a word. Look at Noah Webster's definitions of standard words. Are you never surprised, as by a discovery, at the secondary senses of a word which you thought you knew by heart? Do we not all know something of the experience of which Maurice speaks, when he says that "a light flashes out of a word sometimes which frightens one. If it is a common word . . . one wonders how one has dared to

Critical study and use of language.

Maurice.

use it so frequently and so carelessly, when there were such meanings hidden in it."

3. Command of a word implies also knowledge of its synonyms. Words have a science corresponding to that of comparative anatomy. No man knows a word all around, till he knows in what and why it is superior, or not so, to its synonyms. *Knowledge of the synonyms of a word.* Such knowledge includes, further, perception of the forces of a word in varieties of connection. The life of a word, like that of a tree, is seldom in one tap-root, so that it always signifies the same thing, and carries the same weight, and gives to thought the same momentum in oral speech. It commonly has fibres, by which connection modifies force. Look at the idiomatic phrases in our language, of which the word "come" is the centre—"come at," "come to," "come short," "come off," "come by." See Webster's Dictionary.

4. Mastery of a word involves, also, knowledge of its possible figurative uses; not only of those which dictionaries define, but of other forces which a writer may originate by a figurative combination. The heavy preponderance of the weights of language is in the scale of its figurative senses. *Knowledge of the possible figurative uses of a word.* Analogies connect all words with all words. By means of figurative speech, all departments of thought illumine each other. Originality in style appears chiefly in the discovery of analogies, and fitting them to use. Who but DeQuincey, for instance, would ever have discovered the analogies of thought which enabled him to describe in a breath the style of Dr. Johnson, by calling it the "plethoric tympany of style"? Yet all language is veined by such analogies, in which every writer may range at will.

5. Once more : mastery of language includes a retentive control of a vocabulary and of varieties of English construction, by which they shall always be at hand for uncon-

scious use. Do we not often fret for the right word, which is just outside of the closed door of memory? We know that there is such a word; we know that it is precisely the word we want; no other can fill its place; we saw it mentally a short half-hour ago: but we beat the air for it now. The power we crave is the power to store words within reach, and hold them in mental reserve till they are wanted, and then to summon them by the unconscious vibration of a thought. Nothing can give it to us but study and use of the language in long-continued and critical practice. It is the slow fruitage of a growing mind.

Retentive control of a good vocabulary.

Walter Scott, for instance, saunters through the streets of Edinburgh, and overhears a word, which, in its colloquial connections, expresses a shade of thought which is novel to him. He pauses, and makes a note of it, and walks on, pondering it, till it has made a nest for itself in his brain; and at length that word reappears in one of the most graphic scenes in the "Fortunes of Nigel."

Walter Scott.

Washington Irving relates, that he was once riding with Thomas Moore in Paris, when the hackney-coach went suddenly into a rut, out of which it came with such a jolt as to send their heads bumping against the roof. "By Jove, I've got it!" cried Moore, clapping his hands with great glee. "Got what?" said Irving. "Why," said the poet, "that *word* which I've been hunting for for six weeks to complete my last song. That rascally driver has jolted it out of me."

Thomas Moore.

The late Hon. Caleb Cushing, of Massachusetts, spent the larger part of his mature life as a member of legislative bodies. For years he was the Mentor of the Massachusetts Legislature at a time when his politics put him always in a minority on any political measure. Yet he saved the State from much unconstitu-

Caleb Cushing.

tional legislation by his power of command over the English language. It has been said that no suit at law is known to have been brought into court by any lawyer, in which the success of the suit depended on proving to be unconstitutional or defective any statute of which Caleb Cushing had the control in the committee which framed it. He was able to say, and to assist legislators to say, so exactly what was meant, that no clear-headed advocate could misunderstand the statute, or find a flaw in it by which to sustain a lawsuit. The explanation of that rare power of his, of precise utterance, as given by those who knew him best, is, that he read and conversed in half a dozen languages, and made language the study of his life. In the convention for the settlement of the "Alabama Claims" he was the only man who could converse intelligibly with all the members of the convention in their several vernaculars.

Reading which covers as broad a range of literature as critical reading can cover, is a necessary adjunct to a speaker's studies. Rufus Choate writes in his diary, "I have long been in the habit of reading daily some first-class English author, chiefly for the *copia verborum*, to avoid sinking into cheap and bald fluency, to give elevation, dignity, sonorousness, and refinement to my vocabulary." This hint discloses to us one of the sources of his magnificent and superabundant diction.

Choate.

Great importance is, therefore, clearly to be attached to the early favorites of a young man when his style is forming. If he does not form a taste for scholarly precision then, he is not likely ever to form it. A certain peculiarity of shadow, it is said by critics of art, is perceptible in all the paintings of Rembrandt. Experts have attributed it to the fact that his father's mill, in which his early studies of his art were practised, received its light through an aperture in the roof. So it is in the kindred art of literary composition. A very insignificant fascination by a very inferior author may give to a young man's style a monotone which shall last through a lifetime. Precision especially is one of those products of scholarly taste which is not apt to attract a man for the first time in middle life or old age. Youth must plant it, or it will not flourish in mature age.

III.—Two Facts to Encourage Young Writers and Speakers.

Before closing these remarks on command of language, let two facts be named for the encouragement of young writers and speakers.

1. One is, that a genuine command of language is an acquisition, never a gift. There is a certain leakage of words, which popular slang defines as "the gift of the gab," which may be a gift, but is no sign of control over one's mother-tongue, but the reverse rather. That control is an acquisition by the ablest as by the most feeble writers. We read the writings of De Quincey with a discouraging admiration of his marvellous uses of English. Whatever other excellence he has not, he certainly has this, of the power to summon and put to use a large and forcible vocabulary. The exuberance of his style is excessive. The growth is rank. Yet he tells us that in early life he labored under a "peculiar penury of words." He regarded the infirmity of his mind in that respect as extreme. It gave him, he says, "a distinguished talent for silence." What young writer or speaker does not know the experience of that "distinguished talent for silence?" De Quincey's acquired power of utterance is finely illustrated in his subsequent description of his early reticence. He says, "I labored like a Sibyl instinct with prophetic woe, as often as I found myself dealing with any topic in which the understanding combined with deep feelings to

[margin: Command of language an acquisition.]

[margin: De Quincey.]

suggest mixed and tangled thoughts." He adds, that Wordsworth also suffered in early manhood from the same cause. In both cases, doubtless, the ultimate affluence of style was an acquisition. It was a laborious acquisition. It grew hardily and thriftily, as an oak does, out of the very toughness of the native soil.

2. The other fact to be remembered for our encouragement is, that the vocabulary which is necessary to effective speech is much less voluminous than is often supposed. Our language, it is estimated, contains about one hundred and twenty-five thousand words; yet, of this immense number, it is surprising how few are in common use. *The vocabulary of effective speech not voluminous.* The majority even of educated men, it is believed by careful critics, not only do not use more than one-tenth of them, but would not recognize more than that as having been met with in their reading. The obsolete and obsolescent words, the vulgarisms, the provincialisms, the terms technical to the arts and the professions, the imports from other languages, the words of recent coinage which have not acquired naturalization in the language, and the words which a public speaker would not employ twice in a lifetime, probably comprise by far the larger part of Webster's Dictionary. *Webster's Dictionary.*

It is stated on scholarly authority, that a child does not commonly use more than a hundred words; and, unless he belongs to a cultivated family, he will never habitually employ more than three or four hundred. *Words used by a child.* An eminent American scholar estimates that few practised writers or speakers use as many as ten thousand words in threescore years of public life. Speakers employ not so many, by a large count, as writers employ. *Words used by practised speakers.* Max Müller says, that "a well-educated person who has been at a public school in England and at an English university, who reads his Bible and Shakespeare, and all the books in

Mudie's Library, that is, nineteen-twentieths of all the books published in England, seldom uses more than three or four thousand words in actual conversation." Eloquent speakers, he thinks, may rise to a command of ten thousand. "Even Milton," writes another critic—"Milton, whose wealth of words seems amazing, and whom Dr. Johnson charges with using a Babylonish dialect, uses only about eight thousand; and Shakespeare 'the myriad-minded,' only fifteen thousand." The Old Testament contains less by some hundreds than six thousand words. These facts go to show that a scholarly mastery of an English vocabulary, large and varied enough for forcible public speech, ought not to be looked upon with awe, as an impossible or very difficult achievement.

ANALYSIS.

PRECISION OF STYLE (CONTINUED).

I. **Chief Causes of a Loose Style.**
 1. Indiscriminate Thinking.
   (a) The Foundation of Precision.
 2. Excessive Care for Expression.
   (a) Servile Imitation.
   (b) Robert Hall's Confession.
 3. Want of a Command of Language.

II. **Means of Acquiring a Command of Language.**
 1. By Power to select and to reject Words.
 2. By Union of Critical Study and Use of Language.
 3. By Knowledge of the Synonyms of Words.
 4. By Knowledge of the Figurative Uses of Words.
 5. By Retentive Control of a Good Vocabulary.
   (a) Walter Scott, Thomas Moore, and Caleb Cushing as Examples.
   (b) The Reading of Good Literature.

III. **Two Facts to encourage Young Writers and Speakers.**
 1. Command of Language an Acquisition not a Gift.
 2. The Vocabulary of Effective Speech not Voluminous.

CHAPTER X

PRECISION OF STYLE (CONCLUDED)

The Inducements to the Cultivation of Precision of Style by a Public Speaker.

The only branch of the subject before us which remains to be considered is the inquiry, Why should a speaker to a promiscuous assembly be scrupulous to cultivate a precise style? Scarcely any other quality of speech has been made the object of so much impatient and sarcastic criticism as this of precision.

I.—Popular Idea of a Precise Style.

Quintilian said of a certain author, and it has been repeated of scores of others, for it is the keenest remark that Quintilian ever made, "that his greatest excellence was, that he had no faults; and his greatest fault, that he had no excellences." This is often nearly the popular idea of a precise style. Preciseness in manners is ranked as its twin-brother. Robust men are not charmed with prigs in oral speech any more than in morals. It is instructive to observe the complacency with which some educated men will express contempt for the class of studies which that of precision represents. When a celebrated preacher was once asked what principles he followed in regulating his own style, he answered, "I have but two. One is, have something to say; and the other, say it." A truth was contained in the aphorism, but by no means all the truth, or

Quintilian.

A popular preacher's rules.

the best of it. It would be as apt a reply if an architect, when asked on what rules of architecture he constructed a cathedral, had said, "I have had but two: one was to get the job, and the other, to execute it."

Robert Southey says, with scarcely more discernment of the merits of the question, "I have but three rules of com-

Robert Southey. position—to write as clearly as I can, to write as concisely as I can, and to write as impressively as I can." "As clearly as I can"—was the study of precision useless to that? "As concisely as I can"—had precision no concern with that? "As impressively as I can"—could precision give no aid to that? Southey's neglect of critical study of language had its natural effect on his own style. He is distinguished as a voluminous rather than a powerful author. He would have doubled the duration of his influence on English literature if he had published less, and elaborated more. Ralph Waldo Emerson dismisses his name with a sneer—"Who is Southey?"

II.—INDUCEMENTS TO THE CULTIVATION OF A PRECISE STYLE.

1. In opposition to such unscholarly neglect of the study of those elements in style which precision represents, let it

It does not imply anything pedantic. be remarked, first, that this study does not necessitate in the result the acquisition of any thing pedantic or unpractical. You do not become a mere word-hunter by hunting words. The fact remains unanswered, that the most powerful masters of English speech are those who have studied the resources of the language most critically. The ablest thinkers are they who can put thought into its most exact expression. Those who are most successful in making style the servitor of thought are they who have most thoroughly weighed words. Such authors and speakers command the words they need, and use no more and no other. They are free from the entire class of literary defects which arise from the tyranny of expression over thought.

2. Precision and the study of it are essential to certain other qualities of a good style; for instance, they assist clearness of style. A speaker, especially, who must deal with difficult themes, and in oral address, and to the popular mind, will often find, that if he would be understood, if he would not be misunderstood, he must say exactly what he means. He must put into language intelligible to the common mind his ultimate thoughts on the subject in hand. Not a word too many, not a word too few, not an ill-chosen word, not a misplaced word, not a word untruthful in its connections, not a figurative word which can be mistaken in a literal sense, not a word exaggerating the shade of his thought—such must his style be if he would express himself at all, on a certain theme, to a promiscuous audience. *It promotes clearness.*

3. Precision and the study of it also promote energy of style. The most intense energy often depends on precision. There is an energy which is created by a voluminous vocabulary, but the supreme energy in speech is from a well-chosen vocabulary. Force of style is specially intensified by the compression which precision tends to secure. Take an example, almost at random, from John Foster: "The rude faculty which is not expanded into intelligence may be sharpened into cunning." How otherwise could so forcible an expression be given to his thought in a literal form? He adds a figurative form of the same idea: "The spirit which cannot grow into an eagle may take the form and action of a snake." *It promotes energy. John Foster.*

How could you define lightning to a man who never saw it? Witness the struggles of blind men to conceive of colors. When one said, "The color of scarlet is *like* the sound of a trumpet," he illustrated the struggle of the mind to conceive and express an impossible thought by the aid of a simile. Like that is the aid of figure to the precision of all difficult thought. Hyperbole may assist precision, even when it falsifies fact. Said John Randolph, when seeking to provoke a duel with Henry Clay, "A hyperbole for meanness is an ellipsis for Clay." Though false to fact, it was not so to the real meaning of the speaker. He meant all that he said; and the reason for his unconscious choice of figurative style was, that in no other way could he approximate the whole of his meaning. We miss the breadth of significance in the term "precision," when we restrict it to the exactness of a philosophical definition and a mathematical demonstration.

<small>John Randolph and Henry Clay.</small>

4. Again: precision promotes elegance of style. This it does by promoting the fitness of style to sentiment. Our sense of beauty depends largely on our sense of fitness. This we feel, not in words only, but in construction as well. What is the defect in the following specimen? A church which was burnt in Saco, Me., was thus discoursed upon by a rural editor: "The church was erected during the ministry of the Rev. Elihu Whitcomb; and the dedication sermon was preached February 12, 1806. *It* was ninety feet in length and fifty-four in breadth." We detect in this no want of purity, the words are good English; no want of energy, the style is as forcible as the thought is, and no style should be more; no want of perspicuity, for it is clear that the writer meant what he did not say; no reader can mistake the sense. The defect is a want of precision of construction. No writer would be guilty of it who was accustomed to study precision as a tribute to elegance.

<small>It promotes elegance.</small>

5. Further: precision is the most effective test of af-

fected style as distinct from genuine style. In affected style, expression is estranged from thought. Apply the test of precision, and the mask drops. In a certain treatise on political economy may be found this declaration : " As much food as a man can buy for as much wages as a man can get for as much work as a man can do, ought to satisfy every citizen of the state." A profound principle of political science appears here to be expressed in pithy, condensed, forcible diction. A world of axiomatic wisdom seems to be packed into this monosyllabic sentence. Probably the writer himself believed, certainly meant that his readers should believe, that this was a marvel of laconic force.

It promotes genuineness of style.

An example from political economy.

Now analyze it by the inquiry, What exactly does it mean ? Reverse the order of the thoughts, for the sake of clearing it of its deceptive axiomatic forms, and it reads thus : " A good citizen will first do as much work as he can do ; for his work he will ask as much wages as he can get ; and then he will spend it all on food, and be content." He may not possess a hat, or a shoe, or a coat, or a book. Yet he has done his whole duty to the state ; and the state, its duty to him. Even with largest allowance for latent and understood ideas, it amounts only to this : that a man should be content with the best he can do and the best he can get. What concern has this with the elements of political economy ? It reminds one of another notable example of economic wisdom, in which the author advanced as an elementary principle of population which Malthus had never discovered, " that a large town densely peopled must commonly support a greater number of inhabitants than a small place sparsely settled, especially if it be in the rural districts." Apply to any form of affectation in style the query, " What precisely does the writer mean ? " and the glamour of affected excellence disappears.

6. Precision is not only auxiliary to other qualities of a good style, but it has an independent virtue of its own. This is not easily defined, yet we all feel it. We respond approvingly to a precise style, not merely because it is a perspicuous style, not merely because it is a vigorous style, not merely because it is a becoming style. We approve of it for its own sake. That is a keen mind which *can* say what it means, and all that it means; and we respect a keen mind. That is an honest mind which *does* say all that it means; and we trust an honest mind. That is often a bold mind which does not *fear* to say all that it means; and men are attracted always by the bold virtues. "He says what he means" is often the highest encomium which the popular verdict gives to a public speaker.

It is a style approved for its own sake.

7. We often think of precision as one of the peculiarly scholarly virtues. It is that; but the popular mind is passionately fond of it as well. A common audience often makes a blunt demand for it in an extreme. They silently crowd upon a speaker the mandate: "Say what you think; out with it!" Nothing wearies them more quickly than a style which beats about the bush. They never read diplomatic papers. One reason for the popular simile, "As dull as a sermon," is, that sermons are so often written in a style indicative of self-restraint—a style which a certain critic has described as one in which "words spend their time in dodging things."

It is a popular style.

Men crave a coarse precision, a savage form of truth. Yet it is the truth after all. The common mind will not long retain a label of a distinguished contemporary if it is not true. Popular slang, in such cases, though etymologically loose, is commonly definite to the popular ear, and substantially exact. No language is more so. Thus, when a prince has proved himself bold, quick, decisive, ponderous in character, the popular

Popular slang.

voice has summed up its verdict in one figurative but exact title, "Charles the Hammer." When a military chief has proved himself sanguinary, cruel, ferocious, relentless, the people have told the whole story of his life in the single phrase, "Alva the Butcher."

The watchwords of political parties again illustrate the same thing. These are often intensely figurative; yet, if they have great force with the people, they are as intensely true. No style can express the truth with more of that vividness which is often necessary to precise ideas in the popular mind. General Harrison owed his elevation to the presidency of our republic, in large measure, to his supposed sympathy with the simple and rude usages of backwoodsmen; and this was expressed in the old war-cry of the Whigs of 1840: "Log Cabin and Hard Cider." General Taylor owed his election to the same office, largely to the sobriquet which his soldiers gave him in the Mexican war, "Old Rough and Ready." General Scott was believed to have lost his election because of the nickname by which his enemies ridiculed his well-known fondness for military etiquette, "Old Fuss and Feathers." Thousands of voters who cared nothing, and knew nothing, about the policies of the contending parties, knew as definitely as you do what those watchwords meant; and they voted for and against the things which those words painted to their mental vision. A style in which men said what they meant, and meant what they believed, carried the day, although it was made up of popular slang.

[sidenote: Watchwords of political parties.]

ANALYSIS.

PRECISION OF STYLE (CONTINUED).

I. **Popular Idea of a Precise Style.**
   1. A Popular Preacher's Rules.
   2. Robert Southey's Rules.

II. Inducements to the Cultivation of a Precise Style.
1. It does not imply anything Pedantic.
2. It promotes Perspicuity of Style.
3. It promotes Energy of Style.
4. It promotes Elegance of Style.
5. It promotes Genuineness of Style.
6. It is a Style approved for Its Own Sake.
7. It is a Popular Style.

CHAPTER XI

PERSPICUITY OF STYLE

I.—General Divisions of the Subject.

For the object of the present discussions, perspicuity of style needs to be considered in reference to four things—*thoughts, imagery, words, construction.*

II.—Perspicuity as Affected by Thought.

Perspicuity must, like every other quality of a good style, find its foundation in the thought to be expressed. An important class of the causes of obscurity, therefore, concerns the thoughts of a discourse.

1. Obscurity may arise from the absence of thought. Dr. Campbell writes: "It hath been said, that in madmen there is as great a variety of character as in those who enjoy the use of reason; and in like manner it may be said of nonsense, that in writing it, there is as great scope for variety of style as there is in writing sense." Men may write nonsense unconsciously. What conception of truth have preachers had in discoursing of "the eternal Now"? Certain it is, that if the pulpit has meant by this phrase anything more or other than the omniscience of the Divine Mind, they have experimented with an inconceivable idea. Language is at a deadlock at the outset. If the phrase means the absence, from the consciousness of the Divine Mind, of all knowledge of succession in time, it is nonsense, in the sense of being an impossible notion of the Deity.

[margin note: Obscurity arising from absence of thought.]

A preacher is mentioned also by Dr. Campbell, who once remarked, as evidence of the goodness of God, that to our minds the moments of time come in succession, and not simultaneously; "for," said he sagely, "if they had been so ordered as to come simultaneously, the result would have been infinite confusion." It reminds one of Southey's crit-

Southey.

icism on a literary production which he deemed a monument of folly. He said that "such pure, involuntary, unconscious nonsense is inimitable by any effort of sense."

This is, sometimes, the real and only cause of obscure passages in public discourses otherwise intelligible—that the speaker talks on when he has nothing to say. He plays on the keys of the organ, with no wind in the pipes. His mind is vacant of thought; and to fill up time, or to round out the rhythm of a sentence, he speaks words—words—words! For the moment he belongs to the class

Whately.

of authors of whom Whately says, "They aim at nothing, and hit it." Patches of such vacuity may be found in compositions which as a whole are thoughtful.

2. A much more frequent cause of obscure expression is vagueness of thought. Vague thinking necessitates indefinite utterance. Utterance can be no wiser than the

Obscurity arising from vagueness of thought.

thought is. A man cannot say what is not in him to say. The style of vague thinking cannot be specific. It has no point. The thinking is not forceful enough to compel clear expression.

It used to be said of Napoleon that he did not understand diplomacy, and that he never practised the diplomatic

Napoleon and diplomacy.

style. The statesmen of Europe were perplexed, because they could always understand him; that is, his style was that obvious style which cannot be misunderstood, if the author has written what he meant.

When he left Paris for Waterloo, he declared his purpose to deliver a pitched battle at or near that locality, in language so plain, that his opponents could not believe that he was not deceiving them. They well-nigh lost the battle by not taking him at his word. A certain critic of Napoleon's style attributes this clearness of it, so uncommon in the despatches of statesmen, to the uniform intensity of his thinking. His mental working in all things was so intense that his style was illuminated. He could not help saying what he meant, though Europe was in a maze because they could always understand him. This is the kind of mental working which the effective writer or speaker needs—intense working, which sets style on fire by the friction of thought and language.

Fontenelle's rule in composition was this: "I always try first to understand myself." No man will write obscurely who thoroughly understands himself. No speaker will speak obscurely in oral address who will first faithfully practise his speech on himself as an imaginary hearer. "Should I understand this discourse if it came first upon me with no preparatory thinking, and in oral form, in the style which I have given to it?" Apply this test, and the probabilities are that it will never delude you into composition of the nebulous order. *Fontenelle.*

The remedy, therefore, for obscurity of style arising from vagueness of thought, is either a more thorough discipline or a more thorough furnishing of the mind. In such an exigency one must have a more vigorous thinking power, or certain materials of thought which are absent. Sometimes both are needed. The vital point to be observed is, that no mere study of diction as such can remedy such an evil as this. Study of one's style may disclose the evil, but cannot remedy it. The remedy lies back of rhetorical criticism. More power or more knowledge, or both, must fit a man to *The remedy for vagueness of thought.*

discuss subjects on which his style exhibits such incompetence.

3. Obscurity of style related to the thoughts of discourse may spring also from the affectation of profound thought.

<small>Obscurity arising from affectation of profound thought.</small> It is one of the subtle laws of nature, that nothing which is affected is so clear as that which is genuine. In judging men, we call a genuine character a transparent character. So, in style, nature is more intelligible than art.

Let it be observed, that clear thinking may be made obscure in the expression by the attempt to clothe it in the philosophical forms of profound thinking.

<small>George Brimley.</small> The real thought, the kernel when the husk is off, may be so simple that it is the last thing a hearer would suspect of being so magnificently hidden. Let this be illustrated by an extract from the essays of the late George Brimley, librarian of Trinity College at Cambridge. He is discoursing upon the nature of poetry, and he soliloquizes thus: "A poetical view of the universe is an exhaustive presentation of all phenomena, as individual phenomenal wholes, of ascending orders of complexity, whose earliest stage is the organization of single coexisting phenomena into concrete individuals, and its apotheosis the marvellous picture of the infinite life, no longer conceived as the oceanic pulsation which the understanding called cause and effect." Indeed! Yet the writer was no fool. His essays show that he had some thoughts. Probably one is struggling, like Milton's half-created lion, to see the light in this fathomless and boundless revery. The kernel of it was probably a very simple thought, which Dugald Stewart would have expressed in three lines which an educated man need not have read a second time. Read this of George Brimley's the twenty-second time, and are you the wiser?

The fact deserves notice, that, in the study of modern

philosophy, a professional man needs to be on his guard lest his style of public speech should become infected with the disease of artificial depth. In much of the philosophical style of our age there is a needless multiplication of novel words, odd words, imported words, archaic words, general words for specific thoughts, and a haziness of general effect, which wearies a reader as a blurred picture wearies the eye. When the writers are charged with obscurity of diction, and they excuse it on the ground of its necessity to that which they call "the higher thinking," we may well be incredulous. Many thoughts which are wrapped up in this style of "the higher thinking" do not look, when one comes at them, to be so inexpressibly lofty. They lie on a plane a long way this side of the third heaven. Often they are very simple thoughts, not novelties in philosophy, but susceptible of expression in very homely English.

Effect of the study of modern philosophy.

That was a perilous principle which Coleridge advanced respecting the capacity of human language, that it cannot express certain metaphysical ideas, and therefore that clearness of style in a metaphysical treatise is, *prima facie*, evidence of superficialness. As Coleridge was accustomed to illustrate it, the pool in which you can count the pebbles at the bottom is shallow water : the fathomless depth is that in which you can see only the reflection of your own face. This would be true if thinking were water. But the principle opens the way to the most stupendous impositions upon speculative science. It tempts authors to the grossest affectations in style. In the study of modern psychology, therefore, a writer needs to be on his guard. We may safely treat as a fiction in philosophy anything which claims to be a discovery, yet cannot make itself understood without huge and unmanageable contortions of the English tongue.

Coleridge.

4. Thought may give occasion for obscurity of style by

its real profoundness. Subjects may be too abstruse for oral discussion. Speculation may be too refined for popular comprehension. Argument may be too long-protracted for the power of attention in a promiscuous assembly.

Obscurity arising from real profoundness of thought.

One form of this defect is that of pursuing simple themes into complicated relations. No theme is so simple that it cannot be handled abstrusely. The most simple truths are elemental truths. They are principles. They are foundations and pillars on which systems of truth are constructed. Language cannot render all the relations of such truths clear to all minds in oral speech.

Robert Southey says of Edmund Burke, " Few converts were made by him, because, instead of making difficult things easy, he made things easy in themselves difficult to be comprehended, by the manner in which he presented them ; evolving their causes, and involving their consequences, till the reader whose mind was not habituated to metaphysical discussion knew neither in what his argument began, nor in what it ended."

Method of Edmund Burke.

A caution, however, needs to be observed on this danger ; it is, that we should not underrate the power of language to make difficult things clear to the popular comprehension.

The most successful speakers to the popular mind on secular themes are, after all, the men of thought. There is a certain tact often witnessed in secular speech which plants itself never below the level of the popular thought, always above that level, yet so near it as to secure popular sympathy, and always to make itself understood. It is doubtful whether this tact is ever consciously chosen as an expedient : it is a gift. But the men who possess it never fail to gain a hearing ; and as a rule they succeed, when demagogues who despise the people, yet truckle to their tastes, fail.

When President Lincoln was once inquired of what was the secret of his success as a popular debater, he replied, "I always assume that my audience are in many things wiser than I am, and I say the most sensible thing I can to them. I never found that they did not understand me." *Method of President Lincoln.* Two things here were all that Mr. Lincoln was conscious of, respect for the intellect of his audience, and the effort to say the most *sensible* thing. He could not know how those two things affected the respect of his audience for *him*, their trust in him as their superior, and their inclination to obey him on the instant when they felt the magnetism of his voice. But he saw, that, say what he might in that mood, he got a hearing, he was understood, he was obeyed.

Good sense can make anything intelligible which good sense will wish to utter to the popular mind, or which good sense will care to hear. We are in more danger of suppressing truth which hearers can understand than of attempting to express truth which is above them. "Overshooting" is not so frequent as shooting into the ground. *Wordsworth.* Wordsworth says, "There is no excuse for obscurity in writing; because, if we would give our whole souls to anything, as a bee does to a flower, there would be little difficulty in any intellectual employment." John Foster was a marvel and a model of patience and of energy in forcing profound thought into expression. *Method of John Foster.* He often spent hours, as he tells us, in the labor which he calls "pumping;" that is, forcing his thoughts up to the surface of a familiar diction. Read his essays; see what his thoughts were; then observe the transparency of his style. With such an example in view, one need never despair of discussing intelligibly in public speech any subject which ought ever to be generally discussed.

5. Thought may lead to obscure expression through ra-

pidity in the succession of thoughts. The majority of minds require time to take in a difficult thought, and make acquaintance with it. They need to dwell upon the point of an argument. They require illustration, varied statement, repetition. A diffuse style, therefore, the sign of a slow succession of thought, is a necessary style for some subjects and some audiences.

Obscurity arising from rapidity of thought.

Rapid succession of disorderly thought is the general infirmity of excited minds. Extemporaneous speakers are often thus embarrassed. The wheel takes fire from the friction of its own revolutions. This is the cause of the majority of the blunders of extemporaneous speaking. Irish "bulls" have their counterparts in some of the phenomena of extemporaneous oratory. They are not expressive of a vacant mind, but of the reverse. They indicate a freshet of thought. The speaker in the English Parliament, who, in the tumult of patriotic enthusiasm, said, " Sir, I would give up half, yes, the whole, of the constitution, to save the other half," had a thought to express, and a valuable one ; but it overslaughed his tongue. The speaker, who, in a paroxysm of tempestuous loyalty, said, " Sir, I stand prostrate at the feet of my sovereign," was not affecting any feat of gymnastic agility. His thought formed itself first in the standing posture : the prostration was an after-thought.

A speaker in the English Parliament.

Sir Roche Boyle, whose speeches have so long been a thesaurus to rhetorical writers of illustrations of rhetorical blunders, was not void of thought, even in the well-known instance of his inquiry, " What has posterity done for us ? " He had a thought which was entirely logical to his purpose. It was that of the reasonableness of reciprocity of service. Probably he was driven into a vacuum of thought by the burst of laughter which followed, and which he met by explaining, " By

Sir Roche Boyle.

posterity, sir, I do not mean our ancestors, but those who are to come immediately after." One of the aims of conquest in the mastery of extemporaneous speech is that of beating back the rush and trampling of thoughts which huddle themselves into these bovine forms of style.

ANALYSIS.

PERSPICUITY OF STYLE.

I. **General Divisions of Subject.**

II. **Perspicuity as Affected by Thought.**
  1. Obscurity arising from Absence of Thought.
  2. Obscurity arising from Vagueness of Thought.
      (a) Napoleon's Diplomacy.
      (b) Fontenelle's Rule.
      (c) The Remedy for Vagueness of Thought.
  3. Obscurity arising from Affectation of Profound Thought.
      (a) Effect of the Study of Modern Philosophy.
      (b) Statement of Coleridge.
  4. Obscurity arising from Real Profoundness of Thought.
      (a) Method of Edmund Burke.
      (b) Method of President Lincoln.
  5. Obscurity arising from Rapidity of Thought.
      (a) A Speaker in the House of Parliament.
      (b) Sir Roche Boyle's Inquiry.

CHAPTER XII

PERSPICUITY OF STYLE (CONTINUED)

I.—Perspicuity as Affected by the Use of Imagery.

PERSPICUITY of style, having its foundation in the thoughts to be expressed, is further affected by *the use of imagery*.

1. Obscurity may arise from incongruous imagery. Imagery is painting. The expressiveness of it is measured by its congruity. More frequently than otherwise, the incongruity of imagery consists in its irrelevance. It may not be contradictory to the truth, but may have no natural concern with it. Lord Shaftesbury speaks of a "wilderness of mind." What clear idea does one receive from that? He also writes of an "obscure climate" of the human intellect. What is an obscure climate, what is any "climate" of the intellect? *Make pictures mentally of these attempts at imagery, and what is the look of them?* Such images blur thought by taxing the attention to discover resemblances which do not exist. *Congruity is the first requisite and test of a genuine imaginative diction.*

<small>Incongruous imagery.</small>

2. Similar is the obscurity caused by the use of mixed imagery. The Hon. Henry A. Wise, of Virginia, will be immortalized for having executed John Brown, rather than for perpetrating the following before the House of Burgesses: "Virginia has an *iron chain* of mountains running through her centre, which God has placed there to *milk* the clouds and to be the source of her *silver rivers*." What, in detail, is the fact corresponding to a chain of iron drawing milk from the clouds, which flows in rivers of silver?

<small>Mixed imagery.</small>

<small>Governor Wise.</small>

The juxtaposition, also, of the milk and the river, is quite too suggestive of a less dignified occurrence. Surely the mind of man, when it seriously expresses itself in such inconceivable compounds, seems fearfully and wonderfully made.

3. Obscurity, again, may be occasioned by the employment of learned imagery. *Learned Imagery.*

The style of Jeremy Taylor, for the practical uses of preaching, was well-nigh ruined by his excessive use of his classical library. Imagine a man rehearsing the following passage in a sermon anywhere outside of a Latin school : " They thought there was . . . in the shades below no numbering of healths by the numeral letters of Philenium's name, no fat mullets, no oysters of Lucrinus, no Lesbian or Chian wines. Therefore now enjoy the descending wines distilled through the limbec of thy tongue and larynx ; suck the juices of fishes, and the lard of Apulian swine, and the condited bellies of the scarus : but lose no time, for the sun drives hard, and the shadow is long, and the days of mourning are at hand." *Jeremy Taylor.* Jeremy Taylor preached this gospel to an audience of less than fifty, of whom possibly five remembered dimly something of their studies of Horace at Oxford, and the rest knew no more of what the preacher meant than of the sources of the Nile.

It has been elsewhere noticed that Charles Sumner obscured his oratory by excessive indulgence in classical allusions, which, even in the United States Senate, belong to the dying reminiscences of collegiate life. *Charles Sumner.* He used to roll forth from a too faithful memory a string of classical recollections, which his hearers felt to be untimely when the liberty of the nation was trembling in the scale. His opponents could charge upon him sentiments which he disowned, because the clearness of his meaning was obscured through the loss of force occasioned by illustrative materials which were not in keeping with a national emergency.

4. Another cause of obscurity in the use of imagery is an excess of imagery. This may obscure the meaning by exaggeration. It may produce the same effect by overloading a thought. Imagery not needed to illustrate a thought must tend to cover it from the hearer's sight. A hearer's power of perception may be impaired by it through mental weariness. Few things are so wearisome to the brain as a rapid review of a gallery of paintings. Aside from weariness of eye, there is an expenditure of thought in that which the spectator must supply by his own imagination. An excessively pictorial style makes a similar demand, and produces a similar effect. Mental weariness thus induced diminishes the clearness of a hearer's perception. Such a discourse, therefore, lives in his memory, only as a jumble of pictures.

An excess of imagery.

A gallery of paintings.

The same result may be produced, if weariness is not, by attracting attention to the style for its own sake. Attraction to the style is distraction from the thought. Edmund Burke often obscured an argument by excess of imagery. Byron said of Curran, that he had heard Curran speak more poetry than he had ever seen written. It was no compliment to an orator.

5. Yet a truth lies over against that which has just been named. If excess of imagery may obscure one's meaning, on the other hand, it may be obscured by the entire absence of imagery as well. Abstract thought often needs to be made palpable: the senses must be called in to the aid of the intellect. When the meaning is not positively vague, it is not impressively clear without a picture. A certain degree of dulness for the want of imagery amounts to obscurity. A very simple book may be unintelligible to a child for the want of pictures.

Entire absence of imagery.

Military commanders say, that in battle it is the eye which is first vanquished. Similar is the experience of the popular mind under the sway of oral discourse. The first sign that an audience has fairly taken in a speaker's thought, and the whole of it, may often be seen in a hearer's eye. It is often produced by an illustration which has flashed the meaning upon his vision. *The eye in battle.*

The most successful pleaders before juries are of two classes. The one class achieves success mainly by solid logic; the other class by pictorial vividness. To the latter class belong nearly all the great criminal lawyers in modern practice.

Why did Judge Pierrepont, in the trial of Surratt for the assassination of President Lincoln, parade before the jury the maps showing Surratt's line of travel, the guns hidden at Lloyd's tavern, the diary of Booth, his eye-glass, and the registers of the hotels at which Surratt lodged? Not one of these was necessary to a literal statement of the facts, and all could have been proved by testimony. But testimony could not paint the facts to the eye of the jury as this was done by the table on which these mementos were spread out before them. The aim of the prosecution was a purely rhetorical, not a logical one. It was to make the facts more clear by visible symbols. True, it was, in part, to make the facts vivid as well as clear; but it is impossible to separate the two things. Where the aim at perspicuity ends, and the aim at vividness begins, criticism cannot determine. Perspicuity is insured if vividness is gained. *Judge Pierrepont.*

Vividness and clearness differ only in degree. Do we not all obtain clearness of conception from the pictorial newspapers? Why are pictorial illustrations deemed necessary to a modern dictionary of the first class as an aid to definition?

II.—Perspicuity as Affected by the Words of Discourse.

The course of these discussions leads us now to observe the relation of perspicuity of style to *the words of a discourse*.

1. Obscurity may be induced by the preponderance in style of other than the Saxon elements of our language. *Absence of a Saxon style.* With no conscious cultivation of a Saxon style, a writer who is eminently clear will possess a style in which the Saxon words outnumber all others. In the English version of the Lord's Prayer not more than one word in eleven are of other than Saxon origin. This is probably a fair index to the proportions of the language as actually used by the masses of an English-speaking people. It does not follow that the same proportions are necessary to render discourse intelligible to them from the lips of others; but it does follow that a style which is pre-eminent for perspicuity will be, in the main, from Saxon roots. Transparent discourse to a popular audience will be largely Saxon in its vocabulary. Discourse not positively obscure may be difficult of comprehension if other than a Saxon vocabulary preponderates. Such a style as the prose style of Milton, even though every word be authorized English, may require in oral address a closeness of attention by the hearer which few audiences will give.

Specially should the emphatic words of a sentence, if possible, be Saxon. What is the defect of Edmund Burke's *Edmund Burke.* celebrated diatribe against metaphysicians? "Their hearts," he says, "are like that of the principle of evil himself—incorporeal, pure, unmixed, dephlegmated, defecated evil." The use of two unusual and Latinized words obscures the climax of the invective. Few hearers understand them. Journalists especially are often affected in their use of the Latin and Greek elements of the language. One writes of "lethal weapons:" he could not say "deadly weapons," for he would have been too easily understood. Another says, "The water was incarnadined with blood:" he could not say "reddened with blood," for that would have been tame. Other things being equal, it adds much to the transparency of style if the resultant words, in which the emphasis of the idea lies, or the hinges on which the connection turns, be Saxon. The people take in the force of such words easily and quickly.

"Lethal weapons."

The thinking and the reading of the great body of the people are in Saxon dialect. Their conversation is almost entirely Saxon. Hence, as hearers, they feel more at home with Saxon speech than with any other. Note one or two illustrations of a Saxon and a Latin dialect in contrast. When Noah had entered the ark, the sacred narrative, as given by our translators, reads, "The Lord shut him in." Suppose they had translated it, "The Lord incarcerated him." Contrast such a word as "inculpate" with its synonym "blame:" is there any doubt which would be most perspicuous to the popular thought? Dr. Chalmers once said in the General Assembly of the Church of Scotland, "Mr. Moderator, I desiderate to be informed," etc. Can it be questioned that he would have been more promptly understood if he had been content to say, "I wish to know"?

Noah entering the ark.

You will often find that a sentence, every word of which may be authorized English, has a sickly haze hanging over it, as you imagine your utterance of it to hearers, which is entirely due to its Latin vocabulary. It becomes transparent the instant that you strike out Norman words from the points of emphasis, and put Saxon words in their place. This suggests a means of cultivating a perspicuous style which is of

Means of removing obscurity from composition.

special moment to public speakers who, as Wesley used to say to his clergy, "though they think with the learned, must speak with the common people." In oral address to the people, use, as far as possible, their Saxon vernacular.

2. Perspicuity of style may very obviously be impaired by the habitual use of ambiguous words. Every highly finished language like our own abounds with words which have divergent and even contrasted meanings. We speak, for example, of a "nervous writer," meaning a strong writer; we speak of a "nervous woman," meaning a weak woman. We say, "He overlooked the transaction," meaning that he gave it his supervision: we say, "He overlooked the error," meaning that he neglected to mark it. De Quincey speaks of the "active forces of human nature;" does he mean those which concern external action, or those which are vigorous, as distinct from sluggish? The confusion arose from the ambiguity of one word. Dean Swift spoke of "the reformation of Luther." His opponent understood him to mean the personal revolution in the character of Luther. Ambiguity caused by the location of so insignificant a word as the preposition "of" clouded a page. In the eighth chapter of the Epistle to the Romans, St. Paul is represented as saying, "Neither death nor life . . . shall separate us from the love of God." Commentators tell us that this may mean the love of God to his people, or their love to him. Here, again, the insignificant preposition becomes the emphatic hinge on which the meaning turns. "What I *want*," said a pompous orator, "is common sense."—"Exactly so!" said his antagonist.

3. Obscurity of style may be caused by an excessive use of general and abstract words. Oral discourse especially demands a specific and concrete vocabulary. An inordinate use of philosophic terms, however intelligible each one

may be, will often obscure an idea by the number of such terms. Be wary in multiplying such words as "organic," "relations," "proportions," "unison," "cau- sality," "potential," "transcendent," "subsid- iary," "correlative," "objective," "subjective." A style in which such words are the staple of expression may throw a fog over a subject which would otherwise lie in sunlight. *General for specific words.*

4. Affectation in style may take the form of an evasion of concrete expression. Simple, homely, specific words, which a man's good sense first suggests to him, are then abandoned, and he seeks to lift up his thoughts by the leverage of grandiose phraseology. Says one writer of this sort, "There is some subtle essence per- meating the elementary constitution of crime, which so operates, that men become its involuntary followers by the sheer force of attraction, as it were." One can "expis- cate" an idea from this language (to use one of Hugh Miller's ambitious words); but we cannot catch it as it flies in oral speech. A recent political writer describes a cele- brated contemporary as a "republican of progressive integ- rity." What does he mean? If a critic may extort an idea from the language, can a hearer do so on the spur of a moment? *Abstract for concrete words.*

5. Another occasion of obscurity in the use of language is an excessive diffusiveness. Ben Jonson speaks aptly of a "corpulent style." Such a style weakens the momentum of thought. An idea some- times depends for its clearness on the stimulus to attention which springs from quick movement. The corpulent dic- tion is ponderous and slow. Is your thought abstract, and therefore, not easily comprehended? Then let it be packed into few words, and discharged upon an audience like the load of a musket. Perspicuity depends on the state of the hearer's thinking as much as on the speaker's thought. Some thoughts we cannot make clearer than they are by the *Excessive diffuseness.*

mechanism of style: something is needed to quicken the hearer's faculty of perception. Laconic utterance will often do this. You can be hit by a puff-ball and not know it; not so if you are hit by a bullet. Similar is the difference between the diffuse and the condensed style as a means of stimulus to the hearer's thinking power.

Preambles, reports of committees, diplomatic resolves, are often obscure through mere distention of style. The authors beat about the bush in fear of saying a thing shortly. A committee on street railways reports to the Legislature of New York in this manner: "It is not to be denied, that any system which demands the propulsion of cars at a rapid rate, at an elevation of fifteen or twenty feet, is not entirely consistent, in the public estimation, with the greatest attainable immunity from the dangers of transportation." No style deserves to be called perspicuous which needs a second reading. This specimen does so. What is the sense of it expressed shortly? Abandon the negative circumlocution, exchange long words for short ones, and speak without indirection. Then the statement is reduced to this: "It is true that people think that a railway twenty feet above the street is dangerous." That is all that the honorable committee meant. But it does not sound elaborate: therefore, the idea was bloated into the aldermanic diction.

Report of a street railway committee.

Herbert Spencer founds the whole theory of style on the principle of economizing the mental force of hearers. Anything that economizes attention without loss of perception adds to the clearness of an idea. Therefore a style which taxes attention by needless circumlocution tends to produce obscurity. The power of attention in the most willing audiences is limited: beyond its limit, speech to them is nothing but words.

Herbert Spencer.

6. A certain cause of obscurity in style is the opposite of the one last named. It is excess of conciseness. In mod-

erate degree, as we have observed, conciseness is an aid to precision, but in excess impairs it : so, in moderate degree, conciseness promotes perspicuity, but in excess clouds it. Hence arises the difficulty of translating sententious authors. *An excessive conciseness.* In all languages is found a class of authors, who, like Tacitus, lay too heavy a tax upon interpreters by the multitude of their suppressed words. An excessively elliptical style cannot be a very clear style.

But it should be remarked that in oral speech, the perspicuity of laconic utterance depends partly on elocution. Aided by an animated delivery, complete thoughts may be conveyed by hints. A shrug of the shoulder may express a thought without words. Pantomime may be made transparent. An Italian talks with his fingers. Some speakers can express more by their eyebrows than by their tongues. This effect cannot be *put on* tame discourse ; but, if the force of thought admits it, delivery becomes the complement of language. The hearer's receptive power is quickened. Tone, look, gesture, attitude, mean as much to him as words. Bold words, unqualified words, extravagant words, the extreme of hyperbole, may not be misunderstood with such a commentary of action. False words may not deceive : contradictions may be true. Of American speakers on the platform, John B. Gough presented a notable example of this tribute of elocution to style. Mr. Gough in pantomime could express more than some public speakers who read without delivery.

ANALYSIS.

PERSPICUITY OF STYLE (CONTINUED).

I. **Perspicuity as Affected by the Use of Imagery.**
   1. Incongruous Imagery.
   2. Mixed Imagery.
   3. Learned Imagery.

4. An Excess of Imagery.
5. Entire Absence of Imagery.

II. **Perspicuity as Affected by the Words of Discourse.**
1. By Absence of a Saxon Style.
2. By Use of Ambiguous Words.
3. By Use of General for Specific Words.
4. By Use of Abstract for Concrete Words.
5. By Excessive Diffuseness.
6. By Excessive Conciseness.

CHAPTER XIII

PERSPICUITY OF STYLE (CONTINUED)

I.—PERSPICUITY AS AFFECTED BY CONSTRUCTION.

A STUDIOUS writer, and especially one whose work compels a careful adjustment of language to the receptive powers of a mixed assembly, soon learns that the perspicuity of style is vitally dependent on *clearness of construction*. Construction is as vital to style as to architecture.

1. MONOTONY of construction tends to obscurity. It lulls the thinking power. It almost necessitates monotone in delivery.

2. CIRCUMLOCUTION in construction tends to obscurity. Did you never discover the cause of a certain dimness of impression in the want of quick movement of discourse? The speaker's thought is a stone in a sling from which it is never ejected. He talks around, and around, and around; yet you do not see the upshot of the business.

3. ABRUPTNESS of construction tends to obscurity. Why is Carlyle's "French Revolution" hard reading? Mainly because of the jerks in style, by which English syntax is so rudely dealt with that half your mental force is expended in re-adjusting words to sense. Any defect which is pervasive in style tends so far to defeat the object of speech. Yet very little is achieved if criticism ends with such general observations as these. Some specifications in detail are, therefore, necessary to illustrate the kind of criticism to which every man should subject his own productions.

II.—Special Defects in Perspicuity of Construction.

1. Recalling the fact observed in a former Chapter, that defects in precision of construction, and defects in perspicuity of construction, are the same in kind, differing only in degree, we may profitably note as one source of obscurity a defective arrangement of *pronouns* and their *antecedents*. Alison the historian says of the Russian soldiers, upon their entry into Dresden, "They lay down to rest behind their steeds, picketed to the walls, *which* had accompanied them from the Volga to the Don." "Which" logically refers to "steeds," grammatically to the "walls." Immediate proximity does not always decide the natural connection between a pronoun and its antecedent. A distant antecedent sometimes by its prominence may displace the nearer and the true one. Prior, in his "Life of Burke," writes, "The war then exciting attention to the American Colonies as one of the chief points in dispute, *they* came out in two volumes octavo." Who are "they"? He means that the chief points in dispute were then published; and so grammatical connection would indicate. But the construction leads one to suppose that the American Colonies were the publishers; yet the word "colonies" is the more remote antecedent. Proximity, then, cannot always be trusted to determine the question. Dr. Chalmers, in a speech on Christian union, says, "I am not aware of any topics of difference which I do not regard as so many men of straw; and I shall be delighted if these gentlemen get the heads of the various denominations together, and make a bonfire of *them*." Bonfire of what, or of whom?—of the "men of straw," or of the "heads of the denominations"? Here, again, proximity does not settle the question. The more remote antecedent is the true one.

[Marginal notes: Pronouns and antecedents. Alison. Prior. Dr. Chalmers.]

2. Sometimes confusion is created by the repetition of the same pronoun with different antecedents. Archbishop Tillotson writes: "Men look with an evil eye upon the good that is in others, and think that *their* reputation obscures *them*, and that *their* commendable qualities do stand in *their* light; and therefore *they* do what *they* can to cast a cloud over *them*, that the shining of *their* virtues may not obscure *them*." Who are "they"? Who are "them"? What is "their"? What, who, which, is anything in this round-robin of pronouns? A burlesque on grammatical antecedents could not be more adroitly executed.

<small>Repetition of the same pronoun with different antecedents.</small>

Sometimes this defect amounts to a blundering obliviousness of all antecedence. The following tearful reproof was given by a judge of the State of New York to a prisoner just convicted: "Prisoner at the bar, nature has endowed you with a good education and respectable family connections, instead of *which* you go around the country stealing ducks." This is found among the "Humors of the Day." But in what is it essentially less elegant or accurate than the following, from Loring's "Hundred Boston Orators"? "William Sullivan was grandson of John Sullivan, who came from Ireland in a ship *which* was driven by stress of weather into a port on the coast of Maine, and settled at Berwick." How did John Sullivan's ship reach Berwick? Is Berwick one of the ports on the coast of Maine? Again he writes: "His oration produced such a strong impression that *it* led to his election to the House of Representatives, and was afterwards elected to the Senate." Are orations eligible to the Senate in Massachusetts?

<small>A judge's reproof.</small>

<small>"Hundred Boston Orators."</small>

This blundering in antecedence is often burlesqued by Dickens. His colloquial pictures of low life are full of it. In the extreme it marks the absolute absence of culture. Bret Harte illustrates this in the "Heathen Chinee."

"Which I wish to remark," says "truthful James;" and again, "which we had a small game."

This defect sometimes destroys, not only the finish of an elegant style, but the very substance of the speaker's meaning. The following incident in the history of the United States Senate will illustrate this:

The 7th of March, 1850, was a critical date in the career of Daniel Webster. He then delivered his last great speech in the Senate. It was in defence of the Fugitive Slave Law. The country rang with denunciations and defences of that speech till he died. One of the most effective anathemas upon it depended on the antecedent of a pronoun. As reported at first, the speech read thus: "Mr. Mason's bill, with some amendments, *which* I propose to support to its full extent." This committed Mr. Webster to the bill as it then stood with amendments then before the Senate. Some of those amendments were deemed by antislavery men the most atrocious feature of the bill. "But," said Mr. Webster, "I have been misreported. What I said was this, 'Mr. Mason's bill, which, with some *amendments*, I propose to support in its full extent.'" This committed him to the bill indeed, but with amendments of his own, which might ameliorate the bill, and render it less objectionable to his constituents. His reputation with them hung for a time upon the syntax of that one sentence. The death of the great statesman two years later was attributed by many to his loss of the nomination and election to the Presidency. If this was true, his epitaph might have been inscribed, with more truth than is common to epitaphs, "Died of the dislocation of a relative pronoun."

Daniel Webster.

Few writers exist who do not sometimes blunder in the adjustment of pronouns to their antecedents. Says Reinhard, in his "Memoirs and Confessions," " I have always had difficulty in making a proper use of pronouns. Indeed, I have taken great pains so to use

Reinhard.

them that ambiguity should be impossible, and yet have often failed in the attempt." If a careful writer and a practised critic often failed, what can be expected from a reckless writer, to whom study of style appears contemptible?

3. A similar source of obscurity in construction is a defective arrangement of *adjectives* and *adverbs*. Adjectives and adverbs are qualifying words. This is their sole use. What do they qualify? is often a capital inquiry, on which the whole sense depends. "Such was the end of Murat at the premature age of forty-eight:" so writes Alison. His construction does not make sense: Murat's age could not be "premature." Did he reach the fatal age of forty-eight in less time than his contemporaries? Alison means to say, Such was the premature *end* of Murat," etc.

Adjectives and adverbs.

"The command was reluctantly forced upon Prince Eugene," he writes. Did Napoleon, then, act against his own will? The historian says that, but the connection shows that he did not mean that. He meant to say, that the command was received with reluctance. Again he writes, in speaking of Napoleon: "He could only live in agitation; he could only breathe in a volcanic atmosphere." That is to say, in agitation and in a volcanic atmosphere, all that he could do was to live and to breathe. Good sense is this, but just the sense which Alison did not mean. Change the location of the adverb, and you perceive what he did mean, "He could live only in agitation; he could breathe only in a volcanic atmosphere." Once more: "When Napoleon's system of government became unfortunate alone, it was felt to be insupportable." Does he mean that it became insupportable when misfortune found it without allies? Not at all. He means to say, "*Only* when Napoleon's system of government became unfortunate, it was felt to be insupportable."

Alison.

The location of an adverb is one of the most perplexing details of composition. One must have a very well trained and quick taste to decide upon it intuitively with uniform accuracy. Take, for example the word "only," which is sometimes adverbial, and sometimes adjective, in its qualifying force. Notice in Gibbon's History a sentence of moderate length, which contains the word. Observe how many distinct meanings may be obtained by simply sliding it gradually from the beginning to the end of the sentence.

Only.

First. "*Only* they forgot to observe, that, in the first ages of society, a successful war against savage animals is one of the most beneficial labors of heroism;" that is, they did some things well, but one thing not well—"they forgot to observe," etc. Secondly, "*They* only forgot to observe," etc., that is, either they were the only persons who did so; or, thirdly, they did not intentionally neglect the fact, they only *forgot* it. Fourthly, "They forgot to observe, that only in the *first* ages of society," etc.; that is, there is but one period in the history of society in which the fact observed is true. Fifthly, "They forgot to observe, that, in the first ages only of *society*," etc.; that is, it is not true in the ages preceding organized social life. Sixthly, "They forgot to observe, that, in the first ages of society, only a *successful* war against savage animals," etc.; that is, not war which is a failure. Seventhly, "They forgot to observe, that, in the first ages of society, a successful war only *against* savage animals," etc.; that is, not a war for their preservation. Eighthly, "They forgot to observe, that, in the first ages of society, a successful war against only *savage* animals," etc.; that is, not a war against animals of domestic use. Ninthly, "They forgot to observe, etc., war against savage animals is only *one* of the most beneficial labors;" that is, there are other such

Example from Gibbon's History.

labors of heroism. Tenthly, "They forgot to observe, etc., a successful war against savage animals is one of only the *most* beneficial labors of heroism;" that is, it is not to be deemed a labor of inferior worth; or, eleventhly, "They forgot to observe, etc., that such a war is one of only the most beneficial *labors* of heroism;" that is, it is not to be regarded as a pastime. Twelfthly, "They forgot to observe, that, etc., is one of the most beneficial labors of *heroism* only;" that is, no virtue inferior to heroism is competent to the task.

Here are no less than twelve distinct shades of thought, not all of them elegantly, not all precisely, but all perspicuously, expressed, with the aid of emphasis in the reading, by simply sliding one word from point to point from the beginning to the end of a sentence of but twenty-seven words.

It is said in one of our standard text-books on rhetoric, that it has been proved by experiment, that the line in one of Gray's poems,

"The plowman homeward plods his weary way,"

can by transposition be read in eighteen different ways without losing good English sense. The words of the line are susceptible of over five thousand different combinations. One writer adduces a sentence of which the words are susceptible of four hundred and seventy-nine millions of distinct combinations. A curious writer transcribing them at the rate of a thousand a day would complete the record in thirteen hundred and twelve years. In the same proportion of grammatical constructions to alphabetic combinations which exists in the possibilities of the line from Gray, the elements of this sentence would admit of more than seventeen

Different readings of a line of poetry.

Different readings of a single sentence.

hundred thousand grammatical sentences. This illustrates the degree of peril to which a careless writer is exposed, of saying what he does not mean. It illustrates also, the difficulty which a critical writer may experience in saying with perfect perspicuity what he does mean.

De Quincey confirms this view. In some remarks on the writings of St. Paul he observes: "People who have practised composition as much and with as vigilant an eye as myself know also, by thousands of cases, how infinite is the disturbance caused in the logic of a thought by the mere position of a word so despicable as the word 'even.' . . . The station of a syllable may cloud the judgment of a council."

4. Obscurity in construction may be caused by a defective arrangement of the *qualifying clauses* of a sentence. The laws which govern qualifying clauses are the same with those which govern qualifying words. The danger of obscurity is therefore the same. "When the foundation of the Pagan mythology gave way the whole superstructure, of necessity, fell to the ground:" thus writes that "vigilant" writer De Quincey, in one of his philosophical essays. Did the Pagan doctrine of "necessity" depend on the Pagan mythology? and did he mean to say that? He does say it. "I know not how they can be saved from perishing there by famine, without parliamentary assistance;" so writes Robert Southey, in one of his letters. Did the absence of parliamentary aid aggravate the evil of death by starvation? and did he mean to imply that? He does imply it. An affectionate farewell was that recorded by an editor in Connecticut, who published the item of local news, that a man down there "blew out his brains, after bidding his wife good-by, with a shot-gun." But enough: such constructions doom themselves.

ANALYSIS.

PERSPICUITY OF STYLE (CONTINUED).

I. Perspicuity as affected by Construction.
    1. Monotony of Construction.
    2. Circumlocution of Construction.
    3. Abruptness of Construction.

II. Special Defects in Perspicuity of Construction.
    1. Defective Arrangement of Pronouns and Antecedents.
        (a) Blunders by Alison, Prior, Dr. Chalmers.
    2. Repetition of Pronouns with Different Antecedents.
        (a) Examples from " Hundred Boston Orators."
        (b) Daniel Webster and Mr. Mason's Bill.
    3. Defective Arrangement of Adjectives and Adverbs.
        (a) Alison writing of Murat and Napoleon.
        (b) Use of Only, and Example from Gibbon's History.
        (c) Different Readings of a Line of Poetry and of a Single Sentence.
    4. Defective Arrangement of Qualifying Clauses.

CHAPTER XIV

PERSPICUITY OF STYLE (CONCLUDED)

I.—Special Defects in Perspicuity of Construction, Continued.

1. Another occasion of obscure construction may be a failure to express the true order of thought in the *emphatic portions* of a sentence. We have just been considering obscurity in secondary clauses. The same evil often pervades the whole structure. The order of succession is no order; it jumbles the sense; it is chaos. Dr. Johnson writes: "This work in its full extent, being now afflicted with the asthma, he had not the courage to undertake." Who, what, which, had the asthma? An express company advertises that it "will not be responsible for loss by fire, or the acts of God, or Indians, or other enemies of the government." East Tennessee has a tombstone on which is inscribed this epitaph: "She lived a life of virtue, and died of cholera-morbus caused by eating green fruit in the hope of a blessed immortality. Go thou and do likewise." On a tombstone in a churchyard in Ulster, Ireland, is the following: "Erected to the memory of John Phillips, accidentally shot, as a mark of affection by his brother." Who can solve the enigma, that epitaphs are such a storehouse of rhetorical blunders? Is the world of the living in conspiracy to burlesque the dead? It is no sufficient apology for such errors that they are detected as soon as seen. That is the acme of the evil: hearers detect them as well. A public speaker needs

[margin: Wrong order of thought in the whole structure.]

such a habit of mental command of construction, that he shall unconsciously eject such blunders from his style in the heat and swift movement of composition. Style must be as nimble as thought.

2. Obscure construction is often due to an *excessive or careless use of ellipsis.* "He must be an irreparable loss to his family:" so writes Dr. Arnold, in a letter of condolence. The error is not infrequent in the colloquial style of cultivated people. *Excessive or careless use of ellipsis.* The ellipsis is unwarrantable, for some such construction as this: "His decease occasions an irreparable loss to his family." "The French Government made great exertions to put their navy on a respectable footing; but all their efforts on that element resulted in disaster." On what element? The writer, Alison, has named none in the context. Alison's History abounds with such misconstructions: search for them anywhere; you cannot go wrong.

A common instance of a careless use of ellipsis, which calls for reconstruction, is found in certain forms of inverted sentence. "Conscious of his own importance, the aid of others was not solicited." *The inverted sentence.* The biographer of Curran writes of him: "Eminent at the bar, it is in Parliament we see his faculties in full development." You cannot parse these sentences by the rules of English syntax. When the Rev. Dr. Harris was inaugurated to the presidency of Bowdoin College, the clergyman appointed to deliver the address of induction began thus: "Rev. Dr. Harris, sir, having been elected president by the unanimous vote of the boards of trustees and overseers of Bowdoin College, I come on their behalf to induct you," etc. *An address of induction.* Grammatically this implies that the orator appointed to give the address was the president-elect. To express the real meaning with grammatical precision, the whole sentence must be reconstructed, or broken into two.

A frequent form of careless use of ellipsis occurs in cases in which the phrases "the one" and "the other," or "the former" and "the latter," are employed. Not always are these forms obscure, but they always need to be scrutinized. Specially if they are repeated in a series of antithetic declarations, they need extreme care.

The one and the other.

Another form of ellipsis which may easily degenerate into obscure construction is that of a hypothetical expression of an alternative. An example must explain this.. "If this trade be fostered, we shall gain from one nation; and if another, from another." "If we hold to the faith of the church, we shall have the confidence of the church; and if not, not." Such ellipses as these carry the idiom to its extreme. The subject must be very simple, and the thought very direct, to render them perspicuous. We cannot, for this reason, exclude all extreme ellipses: we can only say that they should be studiously, and not abundantly used. If such a construction suggests a doubt of its clearness, let it be abandoned.

Alternative hypothetically expressed.

In Froude's "History of England" we find this sentence: "Had Darnley proved the useful Catholic which the Queen intended him to be, they would have sent him to his account with as small compunction as Jael sent the Canaanite captain; or they would have blessed the arm that did it, with as much eloquence as Deborah." Grant White indicates the excessive omission of needed words in this example by inquiring, "How small compunction did Jael send the Canaanite captain? What degree of eloquence did the arm attain that did *it* with as much as Deborah? What was *it?* How much eloquence was Deborah?" Style which suggests such blind queries is slovenly. The connection may prevent obscurity, but not a loss of precision. Style in which such looseness is in-

Froude.

dulged will often degenerate from the loose to the obscure. The step between is not so long as that between the sublime and the ridiculous.

3. A still further cause of obscurity in construction is an *abuse of the parenthesis*. Parenthesis may cause obscurity by its position. It may be so located as to break the flow of sense. It may separate a verb from its nominative by too large a hiatus. Some writers thus put into an English sentence the peculiarities of Latin syntax. A Roman ear could bear in this respect what an English ear cannot. A parenthesis is a *chasm*: the hearer must be able to vault over it. Not all hearers are agile enough to do that, if the position of the parenthesis holds asunder vital and emphatic fragments of the thought. Abuse of the parenthesis.

Chasm.

Parenthesis, again, may cause obscurity by its length. It is a *digression*. If it be of excessive length, it may impair the recollection of that which went before, and attention to that which comes after. One of the difficulties in interpreting the style of St. Paul in his Epistle to the Ephesians is the abundance of parenthetical enclosures of the inspired thought. Parenthesis may also obscure the sense by the form of parenthesis within a parenthesis. An amendment to an amendment, a patch upon a patch, a wheel within a wheel, are bewildering. Rarely is such an involuted style suited to oral speech. Digression.

Abuse of parenthesis is one cause of the obscurity of German constructions. A German sentence is often a conglomeration, rather than an arrangement of materials. It is voluminous rather than lucid. One critic says that there are books in German which consist of one or two enormous, overgrown, plethoric sentences. De Quincey criticises the German sentence as an arch between the rising and the setting sun. He declares that a sentence by Kant was once measured by a car- German constructions.

penter, and found to be a foot and eight inches long. When not parenthetic in form, a sentence may be so in fact. A reader of it must make it so in order to deliver the sense well. A multiplication of interdependent yet loosely jointed clauses may have the effect of the extreme abuse of parenthesis. To recur once more to the most affluent source of rhetorical blunders, Alison's History, observe the following, viz.:

"Nations, like individuals, were not destined for immortality." This is the thought in a nutshell. Now observe how he expands it. "In their virtues equally as their vices, their grandeur as their weakness, they bear in their bosoms the seeds of mortality; but in the passions which elevate them to greatness, equally as those which hasten their decay, is to be discerned the unceasing operation of those principles at once of corruption and resurrection, which are combined in humanity, and which, universal in communities as in single men, compensate the necessary decline of nations by the vital fire which has given an undecaying youth to the human race." This passage has not one mark of parenthetic structure in punctuation, and it needs none; but its burden of dependent clauses with suspended sense has the dead weight of parenthesis of the most cumbrous form. The thought is obscure. Nothing else gives to English style such a leaden weight of words as this packing of suggested clauses into all the interstices of a sentence.

Alison.

4. Obscurity of construction may be caused also by that figure of rhetoric which is technically termed "*anacoluthon.*" Says Daniel Webster, in his apostrophe to General Warren, in the first oration at Bunker Hill, "Ah, Him! How shall I struggle with the emotions which stifle the utterance of *thy* name?" So in the well-known invective of Cicero, in his oration against Verres: "It is an outrage to bind a Roman citizen, etc.

Use of "anacoluthon."

... to crucify him—what shall I call it?" The idioms of all languages permit this figure of rhetoric when the sentiment calls for it and the speaker means it. The philosophy of it is clear. It implies a sudden overflow of emotion beyond the confines of orderly grammatical speech. Eloquence, in such examples, is like the torrent of the Mississippi: it forces for itself abnormal channels. But let the same license of speech be adopted as a grammatical blunder, and it must pass for that. If no emotion compels its use, no canons of good taste tolerate its use. Few things are so fatal to the transparency of style as the adoption of the impassioned figures of speech when nothing in the thought demands them. Such a style is oratorical abortion.

5. Finally rhetorical construction may be made obscure, or if not obscure, not precise, by the combination, in one sentence, of *materials irrelevant to each other*. Proximity of thoughts in one sentence implies mutual relationship. If none exists, that instinct of good hearing which expects it is balked. It looks for the point of connection, and cannot find one. Through sheer misdirection of attention, the thought escapes. Says a reporter in giving an account of a case of suicide, "His head was supported by a bundle of clothing, *but* all efforts to revive the vital spark were fruitless." This is ludicrously inconsequent. But is it more so than the following, from a certain historian who shall be nameless? "Tillotson was much beloved by King William and Queen Mary, who appointed Dr. Tennyson to succeed him." Were Tillotson and Tennyson first-cousins? If not, why should the two facts be recorded in the same breath? A reader instinctively searches for the latent connection.

Introduction of irrelevant matter.

Tillotson.

Artemus Ward burlesques this error by saying, "I am an early riser, *but* my wife is a Presbyterian." A passable jest is this for Artemus Ward. But is it any more inconsequent than the following? "Their march was through an uncultivated country, whose savage inhabitants fared hardly, having no other riches than a breed of lean sheep, whose flesh was rank and unsavory by reason of their continual feeding upon seafish." Here we begin with the tramp of an army, and end with the effect of a fish-diet on the quality of mutton. Let an abstract and dignified subject be treated in a public address in a style composed of a succession of such sentences as these, and you can easily imagine the effect on the search of a hearer after latent connections. Herbert Spencer's theory of style is so far true as this, that all attention of the hearer which is absorbed in the search for relations which do not exist is so much abstracted from relations which do exist. The result is a waste of both thought and interest. We are never more sightless than when we are looking at nothing, yet struggling to see something.

Herbert Spencer's theory of style.

A single remark is suggested by this review of the causes of obscurity in construction. It is that the most laborious and original thinkers have been the most faithful critics of construction. Profound thought finds such study a necessity to an expression of itself. John Foster used to spend days on one sentence. He wrote, rewrote, enlarged, contracted, transposed, till he satisfied his thought. He often discussed construction in his correspondence with literary friends. He pursued the study of style with an artist's enthusiasm. True, that enthusiasm was excessive: he injured his style by extreme elaboration. Yet it is doubtful whether much of his thinking could have found expression otherwise. The more he labored for exact expression, the more thought he found which was worth expression. To this is attributable the marvellous richness of some of his essays.

Faithful critics of construction.

On the contrary, negligent critics of construction become

by that very negligence indolent thinkers. The habit soon grows of trying to express none but thoughts which can be expressed with ease. One's thinking tends always to the level of one's habit of utterance. First thoughts in first forms become the staple of such a one's productions. That is the very essence of commonplace. It cannot be too deeply impressed on a youthful writer, that *style is thought.* In the long run, each will be the gauge of the other. The study of style is the study of thought. Original thought demands original style, neither of which will come unbidden to a dormant or an indolent mind.

<small>Negligent critics of construction.</small>

ANALYSIS.

PERSPICUITY (CONCLUDED).

I. **Special Defects in Perspicuity of Construction, Continued.**
  1. Wrong Order or Thought in the Whole Structure.
  2. Excessive or Careless Use of Ellipsis.
      (a) The One and the Other.
      (b) Alternative Hypothetically Expressed.
  3. Abuse of the Parenthesis.
      (a) The Parenthesis a Chasm.
      (b) The Parenthesis a Digression.
      (c) The Construction of German Sentences.
  4. Use of "Anacoluthon."
      (a) Examples from Daniel Webster and Cicero.
  5. The Introduction of Irrelevant Matter.
      (a) Faithful Critics of Construction.
      (b) Negligent Critics of Construction.

CHAPTER XV

ENERGY OF STYLE

Is energy of style susceptible of definition? Not otherwise than by the use of its synonyms or by illustrative emblems.

I.—Energy Distinguished from Other Qualities of Style.

1. Energy is not, as Dr. Campbell defines it, *vivacity* of style. A lamb or a kitten may be vivacious, but neither is

Not vivacity. a symbol of energy. There is a style which may aptly be called a frisky style, but that is not a vigorous style.

2. Again: energy is not merely the superlative of *perspicuity*, as it seems to have been regarded by Dr. Lindley

Not perspicuity. Murray. Perspicuity underlies energy as it underlies other qualities, but it is not the equivalent of energy. The style of the multiplication table is clear, but it is not forcible. Light is the emblem of perspicuity: lightning is the emblem of energy.

3. Further: energy is not merely *impressiveness* of diction. Some writers contend that all eloquence consists in impres-

Not mere impressiveness of diction. sion. A mathematical demonstration, then, is eloquent in that it produces an effect. An oration of Demosthenes is its kindred in producing impression. Starlight, a lily-of-the-valley, the song of a nightingale, an æolian harp, are all eloquent in the same sense that this quality is attributable to a volcano or an earthquake. Those diversities of diction, therefore, of which these objects are symbols, are all alike. When you have said that they are impressive, you have said all there is to be said of them in the way of definition.

This theory is either a play upon words, or it is a false conception of things. It leaves no room for distinguishing energy from any other kind of impression produced by language. On such a principle you cannot distinguish an oration from a song, not even a comic song from an elegy. These words, which have their synonyms in all languages—energy, strength, force, vigor—do certainly express an idea not otherwise definable than by interchange of these words. They convey an idea which the common-sense of men never confounds with the impressiveness of a mathematical theorem, or that of a bird-of-paradise, or that of the tail of a peacock. These words are ultimate in all languages; so that we cannot add to their significance, except by material emblems. We can only say that energy is a *peculiar kind of impressiveness:* it is the impressiveness of *strength* as distinct from that of clearness; it is the impressiveness of *force* as distinct from that of beauty; it is the impressiveness of *vigor* as distinct from that of vivacity. Leaving it thus undefined, except by interchange of synonyms, we are in no more danger of mistaking it for either of the impressive qualities from which it differs than we are of mistaking an elephant for a humming-bird.

Peculiar kind of impressiveness.

II.—Forcible Composition Dependent on Forcible Thought.

Let it be observed that a forcible writer must have *thoughts* to which forcible expression is appropriate. Energetic expression is not apt to all varieties of thought. Some thoughts as existing in the speaker's mind are too feebly conceived to be naturally put forth with energy. Words cannot put on them by authority of the dictionary a quality which is not in them.

1. *Unimportant thought,* however clear, is not the proper subject of energy of expression. Speakers who ignore this create in their style a gap between expression and thought which commonly results in bombast. This is only another mode of putting upon a thought a quality which is not in it. You cannot speak with energy of an infant's rattle or a tuft of thistledown, without uttering burlesque. Rufus Choate once poured out an impassioned strain of eloquence, in a vocabulary which no other man could equal, in defence of his client's right to a side-saddle. It convulsed the Boston bar with laughter.

<small>Unimportant thought.</small>

2. Some thoughts are important, and as clear as they can be, and yet are not becoming subjects of an energetic utterance. Some thoughts are necessarily *indefinite* in any truthful conception of them by a finite mind. They depend, for all the impressiveness of which they are susceptible, on a certain degree of vagueness. Define them sharply, and they are no longer true. All thoughts suggestive of the infinite in time or space must be clouded to finite vision in order to be truthful. They must be felt, if at all, through a remote perspective—so remote as to create a certain dimness of outline which gives room for the imagination to play. You cannot drag them out of their sublime reserve by the mere enginery of style.

<small>Indefinite thoughts.</small>

A French preacher, endeavoring to illustrate the certainty with which death must swallow up all men in oblivion, remarks, in substance, taking the hint probably from Saurin, "This audience may number about eighteen hundred souls. Between the ages of ten and twenty years, there may be about five hundred and thirty; between the ages of twenty and thirty years, about six hundred and fifty; between the ages of thirty and forty

<small>Illustration by a French preacher.</small>

years, about four hundred and sixty." So he proceeds to classify and count his audience, as if the national census were before him; and then he goes on to say, "According to the national bills of mortality, only twelve hundred and seventy of my hearers will be living in ten years; in twenty years only eight hundred and thirty." Thus he reckons the prospect of life, as if he were constructing tables for life-insurance; and the conclusion of his elaborate computation is, "So you see, my brethren, that human society is in one continual flux." The flatness of the inference is a caustic satire on the rhetorical method of the discourse. It is as eloquent as a table of logarithms.

Compare the foregoing with a passing hint at the tears of Xerxes at the thought that his army of a million of men would be in the grave in a hundred years. Which of the two is the more impressive? The fact was once affirmed in a sermon, that if the whole past population of the globe had been buried in regular order, side by side, its surface would have been twice covered over with graves. *Vastness of the whole past population illustrated.* That brief hint at the number of the dead produced a powerful effect so long as the truth of it was unquestioned. But unfortunately a hearer of mathematical taste set himself to reckoning the facts geometrically, and found that the highest probable number of the earth's past and present population might have been buried with room to spare, within the area of Worcester County in Massachusetts. So long as the preacher's statement was believed, however, the hearer's imagination gave to it more than the force of demonstration.

These are specimens of truths which must be left in some indeterminate form, and given over to the hearer's imagination, in order to be forcible. Dwell upon them by an attempt to define them, and the effect is that you flatten them. Milton recognizes this principle in the fact that he makes no attempt to describe minutely the angels who appear in the "Paradise Lost." He leaves them in shadowy outline, in which we see their differences enough to know them apart, and no more.

3. *Some thoughts not unimportant, and not necessarily indefinite*, are still not the proper subjects of energetic expression. Thought in which beauty or pathos is the predominant element does not admit of energy in its utterance. Forceful words and metaphors may be thrust upon it, but do not express it.

<small>Other kinds of thoughts not proper subjects of energetic expression.</small>

This suggests the most common defect, in point of energy, in otherwise good composition. It is that the speaker is not content with a style which fits the thought, but must strain to force into it strength which is foreign to the thought. Be it an earthquake or a summer twilight which is to be represented, it must be clothed with strength, like the neck of a war-horse. Evidently, then, the first thing requisite to a genuine energy of speech is the possession and the mastery of materials which demand energy of speech.

III.—Forcible Composition Dependent on the State of Mind of the Writer while in the Act of Composing.

In the same line of thought, a second requisite is that one should speak or write *with enthusiasm*. "Logic set on fire" is one of the recorded definitions of eloquence. "Heat is life, and cold is death," says a living scientist. The absence of the element of heat in all things tends to stagnation. One may be uplifted by emotional fervor in the abstract contemplation of the work, yet not in the discussion of the present theme. One may be inspired by a present theme as a subject of meditation, yet not inspired by it as a sub-

<small>One must write and speak with enthusiasm.</small>

ject of discourse. One may be eloquent on the present subject to some audiences, yet not eloquent in discourse to a present audience. *Enthusiasm of communication on a present theme to present hearers is the power of movement in public speech.*

Some who extemporize with fire cannot write with fire. All conditions must be favorable to the generation and the emission of heat in order to secure the superlative force in expression. *It is an invaluable mental habit, therefore, to picture an audience in the solitude of one's study.* This gives reality to the written discourse as nothing else can. It makes a living thing of it: it turns soliloquy into discourse —two things which are very unlike, and which characterize two very dissimilar styles of composition.

Nothing else can take the place, or do the work, of this force of feeling. Energy and enthusiasm coexist in character; they must coexist in style. Men of science tell us, that the force of the pulsations of the human heart is measured by the weight of tons in twenty-four hours. If all the beats of your heart in one day of time could be concentrated into one huge throb of vital power, it would suffice to throw a ton of iron a hundred and twenty feet into the air. A fitting symbol is this of the spiritual power which a human mind may put forth in its great moods of inspired emotion. Faith then hurls the mountain into the sea. One reason, the chief reason, why some speakers exhibit power on great occasions only, is that their emotive nature is roused by great occasions only. Energy and enthusiasm. An illustration from science.

2. The materials to which energy of expression is apt, being in possession, and these being projected in the style by the force of personal enthusiasm in the speaker, energy requires still further, that, in the act of composing, he shall write or speak *with an immediate object in view.* One must write and speak with an immediate object in view.

Oral discourse is sometimes soliloquy in its nature. If not such as a whole, it often is such in unwary passages. It may degenerate even into revery, or rise on the wing into rhapsody. Then, the speaker is only thinking aloud. The whole power of his discourse is expended on himself. No audience is pictured in his imagination: therefore no projecting force aims the discourse at an object outside of his own being. Such discourse is apt to appear to a hearer indolent. Its movement is laggard. Time hangs heavy in listening to it. A short discourse thus constructed is tedious, and a long one intolerable. This must be so, for the reason that the hearer is not sensible of being made the object of the address. Least of all does the discourse create the sense of its having been created for him, and predestined to reach him.

Oral discourse when a soliloquy.

On the contrary, discourse which has an object—a palpable object, an immediate object, an urgent object, an object incessantly present to the speaker's thought, to which he hastens on for the hearer's sake—is sure to be in some degree energetic discourse. Why does everybody spring at a cry of "Fire"? For the same reason, direct writers are almost always energetic speakers.

Oral discourse with an object in view.

Vigorous materials, enthusiasm in composing, and an immediate object in view, will not of necessity and always secure the supremely forcible expression. One other element is requisite.

3. It is, that, in the act of composing, a writer or speaker *should be self-possessed.* A French critic says that eloquence is not delirium. Carlyle adds: "We do not call a man strong who has convulsions, though in the fit ten men cannot hold him." For superlative force in style a man must be master of his *subject,* his *audience,* his *occasion.* He must not permit them to be master of

One should be self-possessed.

him. Enthusiasm must be so under control as to be susceptible of use at the speaker's will.

Shakespeare had in mind the element of oratory corresponding to this when he said, "In the very torrent and tempest, and, as I may say, whirlwind, of his passion, he must acquire and beget a *temperance* that may give it smoothness." Fury in speech is not energy. *Shakespeare.*

Uncontrolled enthusiasm is founded on a partial mastery of thought. It is necessarily one-sided. So far, it is ignorant. Absolute mastery of a truth never puts a man out of reason. By seeing a truth all around, we see it as modified by other truth. We see it as balanced by its opposites. The loss of a balanced mind is always the loss of something true. Therefore unbalanced enthusiasm leads to false assertions in style. It prompts to inconsiderate superlatives. Qualifications are ignored. Metaphor ceases to be auxiliary to truth: it becomes intemperance of speech. An intemperate style thus formed invites and is aggravated by an intemperate delivery. The utterance of such a style demands vociferous tones. A severity of countenance approaching to a scowl is becoming to it. Gesture with the fist becomes instinctive in place of gesture with the open palm. The entire physical magnetism of the speaker is perverted to exaggerated and repellent uses. *Unbalanced enthusiasm.*

A passionate style, therefore, tends always to defeat itself. Like anything else that is overwrought, it invites reaction. It disgusts, it shocks, it wearies, it amuses, according to the mood of the hearer. *A passionate style.*

Practically it is weakness, not strength. Why is it that we are often inclined to laugh at an angry man? Shrewd politicians understand that one way to defeat an opponent is to fret his good nature, and let him defeat himself. Make a man furious in debate, and you make him harmless. Entice a man into a duel, and he is politically dead, whether the bullet reaches him or not.

Daniel Webster in middle life was a model of self-possession, and therefore of power. His habit was to restrain himself under the provocations of debate ; never to be tempted by them into petty skirmishes with opponents ; to wait till the great principles involved could be reached, and then to handle them, rather than the men who denied them. In his old age he lost prestige in this respect, and with a corresponding loss of power. The English Parliament used to laugh at Edmund Burke's most solemn adjurations, because they exceeded the dignity of self-collected speech. Lord Brougham was more frequently defeated by his own petulance than by the argument of his opponents.

Daniel Webster.

One of the most remarkable examples of intemperate style among modern essayists is that of De Quincey. His is a most fascinating style to young writers ; excellent, therefore, for the purpose of mental quickening. But you will find that it will not wear well to your maturer tastes, and that its most serious defect is its want of the dignity of self-possession. The following will illustrate my meaning : " Any man of sound sense might take up the whole academy of modern economists, and throttle them between heaven and earth with his finger and thumb, or bray their fungous heads to powder with a lady's fan." Again : he writes of " a dilemma, the first horn of which would be sufficient to toss and gore any column of patient readers, though drawn up sixteen deep." Fortunate is it for the future of the English language that he did not tax it with a description of the other horn. Yet you will observe that no personal ill-will is expressed in these invectives, no anger, no petulance, no malign hostility. The strain of the style is jocose rather. Still it is intoxicated style. It is reckless threshing of language, in

De Quincey.

which you lose the sober thought in its sober truthfulness, and are only astounded at the words.

ANALYSIS.

ENERGY OF STYLE.

I. **Energy Distinguished from Other Qualities of Style.**
   1. Not Vivacity.
   2. Not Perspicuity.
   3. Not Mere Impressiveness of Diction.

II. **Forcible Composition dependent on Forcible Thought.**
   1. Unimportant Thought not the Proper Subject of Energetic Expression.
   2. Indefinite Thought not the Proper Subject of Energetic Expression.
   3. Other Kinds of Thought that are not the Proper Subjects of Energetic Expression.

III. **Forcible Composition dependent on the State of Mind of the Writer while in the Act of Composing.**
   1. One must Write and Speak with Enthusiasm.
        (a) Vital Relations of Energy and Enthusiasm.
   2. One must Write and Speak with an Immediate Object in View.
        (a) Effect of Oral Discourse when a Soliloquy.
        (b) Effect of Oral Discourse with an Object in View.
   3. One should be Self-possessed to Write or to Speak with Force.

CHAPTER XVI

ENERGY AND LANGUAGE

I. ENERGY DEPENDENT ON THE KIND OF WORDS USED.

WE have thus far considered energy of style as having its foundation in the state of a writer's mind in the act of composing. We now advance to regard it *as assisted by certain means which are common to the literal and the figurative uses of language.*

1. First, energy is promoted by the *use of pure words.* Purity of style assists energy, partly because it assists perspicuity, but more directly because it tends to make style intelligible at the moment of its utterance. Labyrinthine style tends to feeble impression. Slow evolution of the meaning is, for that reason, weak. But rapidity in a hearer's discovery of thought enlivens, and therefore enforces, thought. This is the working of a pure English vocabulary. The force of it is augmented by the silent sympathy of a hearer with his vernacular tongue. That which energy adds to perspicuity is chiefly movement of the sensibilities of hearers by the aid of their imagination. Of this power vernacular style must be the chief medium; and the most perfect vernacular is the purest English.

<small>Pure words.</small>

On a similar principle, energy is augmented by the preponderance of a Saxon vocabulary. The strength of a Saxon style has become one of the truisms of literature. It is worthy of remark, that public speakers often talk Saxon who do not write it, nor

<small>Strength of a Saxon style.</small>

employ it predominantly in public address. A man's colloquial style often discloses his Saxon birthright, when a Latinized dialect prevails in his continuous discourse. This is sometimes the explanation, in part, of the fact that a speaker produces more impression by his extemporaneous than by his written discourses. It is, that, in extemporaneous discourse, he speaks as he talks ; and he talks Saxon. His extemporizing is thus homely, as distinct from stately speech. It is speaking *home* to the sympathies of hearers. A stereotyped criticism on a bookish speaker is, ' You should speak more as you talk." This means, in part, " Use more liberally a Saxon vocabulary." {*Extemporaneous and written discourse.*}

Perhaps the most remarkable illustration in literary history of the contrast between extemporaneous and written styles is found in Dr. Samuel Johnson. Johnson the conversationalist and Johnson the essayist were two different men. In writing he was a Latin slave : in conversation he was a Saxon prince. Short, crisp, blunt monosyllabic words abounded in his colloquial style ; and such words in our language (those, at least, which are naturally used colloquially) are almost all Saxon. Dr. Johnson ruled English letters in his day mainly by what he talked, not by what he wrote. His fame grew out of what we speak of as the Johnson Club. Goldsmith, Sir Joshua Reynolds, Edmund Burke, and Boswell knew him at his best, because they heard him talk. In our own day his works are little read. If he could have respected his Saxon vocabulary enough to have made it the warp of his written style, his works might have lived another century beyond us. But no ; he could talk Saxon, but he must write Latin. The ghost of Cicero haunted him when he took to his pen. His first conception of a thought was commonly in Saxon forms ; and he then deliberately set to work, as other sophomores have done, to translate it into an English mimicry {*Dr. Johnson's two styles.*}

of the Ciceronian. Macaulay has made you familiar with amusing instances of this.

Every speaker may find it worth his while to search his own colloquial style, to see if he has not already at his command there resources of Saxon vigor which he is not using in his public speech, but which are perfectly pure, racy English, and therefore as well fitted to public speech as to the table-talk.

A suggestion to speakers.

Yet the claims of a Saxon style must be qualified. Lord Brougham lays down the rule, to which in theory he makes no exception, "Always prefer the Saxon word." But in practice he constantly disregarded the rule, as every writer will do who indulges much in contemplative or philosophic thinking. The Greek and Latin importations into our language are indispensable to such thinking. They are more varied and more precise than the words of Saxon stock. We are safe in saying, that a Saxon vocabulary should be chosen when strength of style is the chief quality which the thought demands. But often the thought requires not so much strength as precision. Then the Saxon must give place to the Latin or Greek derivative. The thought, again, may require beauty or pathos of expression. Then one instinctively chooses the word which is capable of mellifluous utterance ; and that most surely is not the Saxon word. For some conceptions a sensitive writer will long for a liquid dialect like the Tuscan. But such qualifications leave the general principle intact, that a Saxon vocabulary is a strong vocabulary. It should, therefore, predominate in the expression of strength of thought.

When Saxon English is not to be used.

2. Energy of style is further augmented by the *use of specific words*. "Thou art my rock," "my fortress," "my tower," "my shield," "my buckler." Why does the Psalmist use these specific emblems, instead of saying, "Thou dost preserve me," "protect me,"

Specific words.

"befriend me"? It is because the specific quality of the symbols gives reality to the thought by their appeal to the imagination. In like manner, the Scriptures discourse upon the two future worlds, heaven and hell. Rarely, if ever, does the Bible present these as states of being, and never as qualities of character. The inspired thought conceives of them as places: the inspired style therefore paints them as things. It describes persons in them. Heaven is a city, a country, a building, mansions: music is there; harps are there, crowns, palms, robes, rivers, thrones, gates, walls. So the Bible represents hell as a place of fire, a lake of brimstone, prepared for the Devil. Its population is personal. The scriptural manner of speaking of the future worlds is, in the main, not didactic, it is picturesque. The force of it is due largely to the specific element in the style.

The Bible.

3. Energy is still further promoted by the *abundant use of short words*. Run over in your minds such synonyms as these: "wish and desire, breadth and latitude, joy and felicity, sure and indubitable, height and altitude, law and regulation, guess and conjecture." Are we not sensible of a difference in the force of these words, which is due almost wholly to their diversity in length? The chief defect in the vocabulary of Dr. Chalmers is the preponderance of long over short words. Vigor of expression often depends on surprises in thought, and therefore on quick turns in style. There is said to be even a painful force in the strokes of the wing of a humming-bird, arising from the almost inconceivable rapidity of their succession. Force in style may be due to a similar cause; but a style in which long words greatly preponderate can have no quick strokes in utterance. The intent of the author is often disclosed prematurely. The plot of a sentence, if the figure may be used, is detected before it is ripe.

Short words.

The humming bird.

Analyze your own sentences sharply, and you will often find that you have, in the heat of composition, written with unconscious guile. Your style here and there is a trap. It is so constructed as to catch the listener in surprises: you detect in it a series of ambuscades. If, then, it be so constructed, by a large preponderance of long words, as to give the hearer time to discover the catch prematurely, it defeats itself. An unwieldy style, through excess of this long-winded structure, resembles the movement of a crocodile in chasing its prey. An agile boy, it is said, can keep himself out of its way by running in a circle. Recall the familiar example which Macaulay gives from Dr. Johnson. Said Johnson, speaking of "The Rehearsal," a production then fresh to the critics of London, "'The Rehearsal' has not wit enough to keep it sweet." This is brief, quick, Saxon strength. But, after a pause, he summoned to his aid the dignity of autocratic criticism, and remarked, "I should have said, 'The Rehearsal' has not vitality sufficient to preserve it from putrefaction." This is the style of the crocodile.

<small>Suggestion to writers.</small>

<small>Dr. Johnson.</small>

It needs hardly to be said that the choice of short words may be easily abused. A style made up of monosyllables would be the extreme of affectation. "Robinson Crusoe" was, some years ago, translated into monosyllabic words. But "Robinson Crusoe" is addressed to a juvenile taste. Even children will not long patter through a story of that length in monosyllabic slippers. The man must have been a wiseacre who is said to have read fifteen pages of it without discovering that it was not the original.

<small>Exclusive use of short words.</small>

4. Energy is also aided by the *choice of words whose sound is significant of their sense.* "Hiss, rattle, clatter, rumbling, twitch, swing, sullen, strut," are specimens of words not relatively numerous in our language, but very

forcibly expressive, because their sound reduplicates their sense. Ought onomatopoetic words to be chosen studiously? Will not the deliberate selection of them cultivate an affected energy? Doubtless it may do so; but the instinct of speech has created such words in all languages, and that which the human mind thus sanctions, literary taste may wisely select. Why not, as well as other elements of speech which carry the same authority? They do not constitute a sufficiently large proportion of any language to form a strong temptation to an affected use.

<small>Words whose sound is significant of sense.</small>

II.—Energy Dependent on the Number of Words Used.

One of the means of augmenting energy of expression, which concerns both the literary and figurative uses of language, relates to the number of words. It is conciseness of style. Conciseness has been already considered as tributary to perspicuity and to precision: it is more conducive to energy than to either. It has passed into an axiom in criticism, "The more concise, the more forcible." Many years ago Kossuth, the Hungarian patriot, in an address in the city of New York, expressed the idea that the time had gone by when the people could be depended on for their own enslavement by standing armies. He compressed it into two words. Said he, "Bayonets think." The words caught the popular taste like wildfire. They took rank with the proverbs of the language immediately. The idea was not new but the style of it was. It had been floating in the dialect of political debate ever since the battle of Bunker Hill, but never before had it been condensed into a brace of words. The effect was electric. Millions then, for the first time, felt it as a fact in political history. Within a month the newspapers of Oregon

<small>Conciseness as an element of force.</small>

had told their readers that bayonets think. Everybody told everybody else that bayonets think. In style it was a minié-bullet: everybody who heard it was struck by it. Such is the force of a laconic dialect.

A. The most important violations of conciseness as affecting energy are three. One is *tautology*. A weak style is some-

Tautology a violation of conciseness.

times due to no other cause than repetition of ideas in varied language. This is toil without progress. A tendency to tautology was created in English style by the Norman Conquest of England. As you are aware, from the time of William the Conqueror, the Norman was made by law the dialect of the court, Saxon remaining the vernacular of the people. The usage, therefore, grew up of expressing thought consecutively by the use of words from both dialects, and mean-

Book of Common Prayer.

ing precisely the same thing. In the Book of Common Prayer, which was constructed for court and people alike, this tautology is still discernible in such phrases as "assemble and meet together," "dissemble and cloak," "pure and holy," "confirm and strengthen," "joy and felicity." Traces of the same feature still exist among us, especially in the dialect of extemporaneous prayer. Diffuse writers commonly betray their diffuseness in this yoking of Saxon and Norman synonyms together.

Do you not recognize the following words in couples as having become standard yokes in style of the second and

Saxon and Norman synonyms.

third rate?—"Null and void, clear and obvious, pains and penalties, forms and ceremonies, bounds and limits, peace and quiet, sort or kind, weak and feeble, mild and gentle, just and righteous, rules and regulations, trust and confidence"? Some of these do not illustrate strictly the contrast of Saxon and Norman roots; but, of these couples, in every instance one word was familiar to the Saxon mind, and the other to the Norman. In the first blending of the two dialects hundreds of such twins found their way into the usage of writers. For a time they were a necessity. But, now that the two dialects are welded into one, such couples are no longer needed. They encumber style by needless synonyms. Yet that usage has infected the entire history of English diction from that day to this. It has led to the duplication of a multitude of words not distinguished by that diversity of origin. One of the first acts of a young writer, therefore, in the criticism of his own discourses, should be to examine the braces of words, and see if they do not comprise needless synonyms.

B. Similar to the tautological sacrifice of conciseness, and yet distinct from that, is *verboseness*. This occurs when words are introduced which express unimportant shades of thought. Sentences, the gist of which might be compressed into half their length, are extended to make room for hints which add a little, but not much, to the weight of thought. They do not add enough to compensate for the increase of bulk and the labor of carriage. Complex sentences are needlessly preferred to simple ones. *[Verboseness a violation of conciseness.]*

In prose, and specially in inexperienced writers, the error is most frequently committed by piling together qualifying words and clauses. Adjectives, adverbs, and adjective and adverbial clauses, if they do not add force enough to support them by their intrinsic worth, must of course be carried by the rest of the sentence. They may, therefore, make all the difference between heavy and sprightly movement. The more weighty the thought, the less force it may have, if, relatively to the main idea, it is a dead weight. Style, to be forcible, must have celerity of movement. Thought thus borne on words must be capable of quick utterance. Words must be wings. Rapid succession, if coherent, is the token of energetic *[Qualifying words and classes.]*

thinking. Thought is a quick process, the most nimble that we know of. "As quick as thought," we say, and we can say no more, to express rapidity. Energy of expression must always convey that quality in thought. Yet to do this it must have buoyancy proportioned to the weight it carries. Without this, we say of style that it drags, no matter how solid the materials.

Verboseness is often the peril of the scholastic as opposed to the popular style. A scholar commonly writes in retirement and at his leisure. He writes under the influence of tastes and habits which keep him aloof from real life. He is apt, therefore, to take his time for it. The mere sense of leisure will often make a man plod. He involves, he complicates, he twists, he tangles his thought, merely because he has the time to do it. A pressure from without which should crowd him, would create force of style by compelling him to quicker movement. Dr. Arnold showed a very keen observation of men and things when he said to a friend who urged him to write more for the newspapers, "I cannot write well for the newspapers. A newspaper demands a more condensed style than I am master of, such as only the mingling in the actual shock of opinions can give a man." This is the true ideal of a popular style.

Scholastic verboseness.

Dr. Arnold.

Observe as a specimen of that kind of force which conciseness alone may create in style, the following description of China : " It is a country where roses have no fragrance, and women no petticoats ; where the laborer has no sabbath, and the magistrate no sense of honor ; where the roads bear no vehicles, and the ships have no keels ; where old men fly kites ; where the needle points to the south, and the sign of being puzzled is to scratch the heel ; where the seat of honor is on the left hand, and the seat of intellect in the stomach ; where to

Example of concise description.

take off your hat is an insolent gesture, and to wear white is to put yourself in mourning; which has a literature without an alphabet, and a language without a grammar." This is in style what sketching is in art. The passage contains not one adverb, only one adjective, not one qualifying clause, and nothing expressive of a secondary idea. It reminds one of national proverbs, which are commonly models of that density of thought which the compressed wisdom of ages deserves. Who ever heard of a long-winded proverb?

It is a singular idiosyncrasy sometimes detected in public speakers, that they are verbose in the use of certain favorite parts of speech. One has an unconscious favoritism for adjectives, another for adverbs, another for substantives in apposition. *Peculiarities of public speakers.* The style of Rufus Choate, magnificent as it was in the affluence of its vocabulary, would still have been invigorated if it had been shorn of one-half its adjectives.

But the view here suggested should be qualified by the remark, that sometimes the qualifying word imparts a tonic to the style. One such word may condense the whole emphasis of the utterance. *A tonic to style.* De Quincey, descanting on the falsehoods of Pope as being no indication of recklessness of the feelings of other people, says, "In cases where he had no reason to suspect any lurking hostility, he showed even a *paralytic* benignity." A half-page of description could not so forcibly express the sarcasm which is flung at Pope in this one word.

C. One other method by which the want of conciseness may impair energy of expression is that of a needless circumlocution of thought. Circumlocution of thought is not necessarily tautological nor verbose. No more words may be employed *Circumlocution of thought a violation of conciseness.* than are needful to express thought circuitously. The fault lies in multiplying words by a circumlocutory train of thinking, when direct thinking is equally good, and, if so, better, because it is direct. Says Mr. Disraeli, in a speech on the hustings, "The national debt is nothing but a flea-bite." But in the House of Commons he scruples to repeat the figure in its strong, homely form, but says, "The national debt is nothing but the incision of the most troublesome, though not the most unpopular, of insects." Why this polite euphemism? Circumlocutory thought displaced directness, and that made just the difference between weakness and energy of diction.

ANALYSIS.

ENERGY AND LANGUAGE.

I. Energy dependent on the Kind of Words Used.
   1. Energy is promoted by the Use of Pure Words.
      (a) Strength of a Saxon Style.
      (b) Why Extemporaneous is more Effective than Written Discourse.
      (c) The two Styles of Dr. Johnson.
   2. Energy is promoted by the Use of Specific Words.
   3. Energy is promoted by the Use of Short Words.
      (a) Suggestion to Writers.
      (b) Exclusive Use of Short Words.
   4. Energy sometimes promoted by Words whose Sound is significant of their Sense.

II. Energy dependent on the Number of Words Used.
   1. Conciseness as an Element of Force.
      A. Tautology a Violation of Conciseness.
      B. Verboseness a Violation of Conciseness.
      C. Circumlocution of Thought a Violation of Conciseness.

CHAPTER XVII

ENERGY AND LANGUAGE (CONTINUED)

I.—Exceptions in which Conciseness is not Favorable to Energy.

THE last chapter closed with a consideration of conciseness of style as generally tributary to energy. The view there presented is subject to exceptions in which conciseness is the reverse of energy.

1. Exception occurs where conciseness is obviously affected. Affectation of anything is never other than a weakness. A friend of Dr. Johnson died, and he wrote to his widow a note of condolence, thus: "Dear madam, oh!" In less than a year she married again, and he wrote a note of congratulation thus: "Dear madam, ah!" This would satisfy Lacedæmonian taste in respect to brevity, but what is the effect of the laconics rhetorically? Would the first note comfort a disconsolate widow? Would the second please a comforted widow? Neither. Both are extremes of affectation, in which the doctor was thinking of his very smart style. No style is impressive which is not sincere. *[sidenote: Conciseness affected.]*

2. Again: exception obviously occurs where diffuseness is necessary to perspicuity. For some audiences, on some subjects, as we have seen, perspicuity demands diffuseness. In such cases, energy, of course, demands the same. Perspicuity always lies back of energy. The form of concise force is delusive if the thought is not clear. It is not entirely fair to criticise an author by fragments of his composition dis- *[sidenote: Diffuseness necessary to perspicuity.]*

located from their connections; but the following are examples, which, read in their connections, would still represent obscure conciseness. They are taken from the earlier essays of Ralph Waldo Emerson. "The way of life is by abandonment." "With the geometry of sunbeams the soul lays the foundation of nature." "I, the imperfect, adore my own perfect." "The soul knows only the soul." "The world globes itself in a drop of dew." "The great genius returns to essential man." "Prayer is the spirit of God pronouncing His works good." "The devil is an ass."

<small>Examples from Emerson.</small>

Such aphoristic sentences abound in the style of Emerson in his early manhood. They are laconic, but they are not forcible. The question is not whether they convey any meaning, but do they convey any such force of meaning as that professed by their extremely laconic form? Their compactness promises a great deal: does the reader realize the promise? Who is sure that he understands them? How many of these sage proverbs, which by their form put themselves by the side of the apothegms of the ages, will you remember in a week? Probably none but the compliment to Satan, and that is asinine in more senses than one. It will cling to your memory rather as a rude jest than as the utterance of an axiomatic truth.

3. Exception to the principle that conciseness is energy occurs in some examples of descriptive writing. Edmund Burke, in his speech on the nabob of Arcot, describes the effects of the war carried on by the East India Company in the Carnatic territory. An unimaginative speaker, seeing things in what Bacon calls "dry light," would have said, "The war was a war of extermination:" this was the whole of it. An indignant and diffusive speaker, boiling over with his wrath, would have said, "The war was murderous, inhuman, devilish." His invective would have spent itself in epithets. But Burke,

<small>Descriptive writing.</small>

more forcible than either, compresses his indignation, has not a word to say of the character of the war, but describes the facts, and leaves them to speak for themselves. He says, "When the British army traversed, as they did, the Carnatic for hundreds of miles in all directions, through the whole line of their march they did not see one man, not one woman, not one child, not one four-footed beast of any description whatever." Energy of thought here requires particularity of detail: therefore energy of expression requires many words. *Edmund Burke.*

Sometimes a descriptive speaker needs to gain time for a thought to take hold of an obtuse hearer. Macaulay says of the effects of the French Revolution, "Down went the old church of France, with all its pomp and wealth." This is forcible fact forcibly put. But he intensifies it by saying, "The churches were closed; the bells were silent; the shrines were plundered; the silver crucifixes were melted down; buffoons dressed in surplices came dancing the carmagnole, even to the bar of the Convention." By these details, time is gained for the imagination to realize the main truth that the church was destroyed. Longinus illustrates the two styles here contrasted by the examples of Demosthenes and Cicero. He says, "Demosthenes was concisely, Cicero diffusely sublime. Demosthenes was a thunderbolt: Cicero was a conflagration." *Time needed in description to interest.* *Demosthenes and Cicero.*

4. Exception to the general principle before us takes place, also, in certain momentary utterances of intense emotion. Profane men in a fit of passion do not swear concisely. Intense emotion may express itself, on the spur of the moment, by a volume of words. Passion heaps words on words, piles epithet on epithet, repeats itself once and again, and thus creates in style that kind of energy which a torrent symbolizes. A *Expression of intense emotion.*

volley of oaths is the transient utterance of overwhelming wrath. The single tremendous oath of studied force is the expression of cool purpose and self-collection. Dignified discourse sometimes admits a style which transiently resembles that of overpowering passion. Style, then, does not condense, but expands thought, pours it forth in a volume of sound. Words at best are but hints. They are but symbols of ideas. The sum total of them is a symbol as well as the units. A flood of words may have the same kind of force as that of a flood of tears.

But is not this contradictory to the principle we have considered, that energy demands self-possession? Yes, it is so in appearance, but not in fact. Did you never pause in the street to watch a horse at the top of his speed, when at first you doubted whether he was not a runaway? And, when you saw that his rider had him well in hand, did not your first thought enhance your sense of power in the second? There is in style a phenomenon which resembles that. Speech carried to the verge of frenzy, but indulged only for the moment, then reined in, and used for a purpose, becomes an evidence, and therefore an instrument, of power. Disorder ruled and utilized is the exponent of superlative power.

Self-possession as affected by this exception.

II.—Construction of the Sentence an Element of Energy.

Not only does energy of style concern words considered singly; not only the number of words; but there is a class of tributaries to it which concerns the construction of sentences. We cannot wisely carry criticism of construction beyond a few simple principles. For the most part, in practice, it must be left to the bidding of the oratorical instinct. But in written composition especially, the three following principles of rhetorical mechanism may be applied without detriment to freedom in composing.

1. One is, that emphatic words be so located that their force shall be obvious. Observe, this criticism does not concern the choice of emphatic words: it concerns location only. The *where* is often more significant than the *what*. The distinction often made between the natural and the inverted order of a sentence is fallacious. Any order is natural which makes obvious the full force of the language. The oratorical instinct needs to be so trained, that in practice it will spontaneously choose the natural order, be it inverted or direct Yet one may deliberately apply this as one principle of mechanism in style, that a sentence should not commonly end or begin with an insignificant word.

Emphatic words.

The ending and the beginning of a sentence are the only two localities with which criticism can consciously concern itself, in the act of composing, without loss of freedom. But so far, conscious vigilance may direct the pen. Therefore we should not end a sentence with a little word, unless the connection gives it emphasis. One writer, who probably means no more than this, lays down the rule (so the text-books tell us) that a preposition ought not to close a sentence. The most conclusive answer to such a rule is the very form in which the rhetorical instinct of the critic cast the statement of it. He puts it thus: "A preposition is a feeble word to end a sentence *with*." This rule, though in more adroit form of statement, has long encumbered the books on rhetoric. It is indefensible in any form. A preposition as such is by no means a feeble word. What can be finer than this from Rufus Choate? "What! Banish the Bible from our schools? Never, so long as there is left of Plymouth Rock a piece large enough to make a gun-

Rules for the ending of a sentence.

Prepositions ending sentences.

Rufus Choate.

flint *of!*" This is purest idiomatic English. Our Lord's rebuke to His disciples is fashioned, in our translation, on the same model. "Ye know not what manner of spirit ye are *of.*" The old Scotch interrogative, "What for?" is as pure English in written as in colloquial speech.

The true principle, and the only one which the oratorical instinct can use in the act of composing, respecting the ending of a sentence, is the one already named—*that a sentence should not needlessly be ended with an unimportant word of any kind.* A similar rule holds good, but with more frequent exception, respecting the beginning of a sentence. When energy of expression is required, we should not, if we can avoid it, locate at the beginning insignificant words. Certain declarative phrases, such as "it is," "there is," are employed to start the movement of sentences when often they are not emphatic; they are only mechanical expedients for setting the ball in motion. Among inexperienced writers, the word "and" probably begins more sentences than any other word in the language.

<small>The true principle.</small>

2. The mechanism of sentences may assist energy further by the conscious use or omission of the conjunctive beginning. It has just been observed that the word "and" probably begins more sentences in the productions of inexperienced writers than any other in the language. This fact gives importance to intelligent criticism of all forms of conjunctive beginning. Let it be noticed, then, that the conjunctive beginning is forcible if the succession of thought requires it. Often it does so. Something is needed to express or to hint the fact of continuity. The idea of inference, or of other sequence, or of qualification, or of contrast, is to the point. Instinctively, then, you link sentence to sentence by beginning the second of two with "but" or "and," or an adverbial term which has a conjunctive effect, like "yet" or

<small>Care in the use and the omission of the conjunctive beginning.</small>

"nevertheless." What is the exact force of this conjunctive beginning? It is to bridge over the period preceding. Sometimes energy requires that.

But, without such demand of thought, the conjunctive beginning is meaningless, and therefore vapid. Did you never hear an inferior conversationalist begin sentence after sentence with the corrupt formula "and-er"? That indicates momentary vacuity of mind. The speaker is on the hunt for something to say. The "and-er" has no conjunctive force. Not once in a score of times does the connection demand a reminder of that which went before. This mongrel expression is only an interjectional expletive, by which the speaker holds on to the right of utterance while his mind is exploring. To compare it with a thing on a level with it in dignity, it is like the travelling-bag which you leave to represent you when you for a moment leave your seat in a railway-car. Precisely such is the needless use of the conjunctive beginning in written discourse. In the succession of thought it has no conjunctive force. Therefore, style it is not. It is language not freighted with sense.

<small>When the conjunctive beginning is meaningless.</small>

Oral delivery may be sadly weakened by the conjunctive beginning. Punctuation may remedy it to the eye in print; but, orally delivered, such sentences lose their only sign of separation. The period is bridged over when you do not mean it, and your style runs together. Two, even three, possibly four, short sentences, which for force of utterance ought to be short, and ought to be uttered with crisp delivery, are stretched into one long one; made long by that most flattering expedient of composition, a mechanical coupling of ideas. The conjunctive beginning, therefore, should be intelligently used. Use it when you mean it. Drop it when it is only the sign of vacuum. Common etiquette requires you to conceal a yawn.

<small>Oral delivery and the conjunctive beginning.</small>

3. Again: energy may be expressed in the mechanical construction of style by the skilful use of the periodic structure. What is meant by a rhetorical period? The period is *a structure in which the completion of the sense is suspended till the close.* The ancient rhetoricians compared it to a sling, from which the stone is ejected after many circuits. A loose sentence is *one in which the end might grammatically occur before the close.* Such a sentence is a chain, from which a link may be dropped from the end, and it will still be a chain, and will have an end. The periodic sentence is a glass ball; to part with a fragment of it is to ruin the whole.

<small>Skill in the use of periodic structures.</small>

<small>Period and loose sentence defined.</small>

(a) One effect of the periodic structure is to throw forward emphasis upon the end. Also, by the suspense of the sense, attention is claimed till the close.

<small>Advantages of the periodic structure.</small>

(b) Further: the period satisfies all the expectation it excites. In the act of attending to discourse, the mind of a hearer always gravitates. Its instinct is to seek a state of rest, and to rest at the first point at which rest is grammatically possible. In listening to the period, it finds but one such point; in listening to the loose construction, it may find many.

(c) Besides, the period permits the disclosure, to the hearer, of the growth of a thought. Here lies its chief advantage. A loose sentence can grow, only as the tail of a kite grows. A period has symmetry: its parts do more than cohere; they are interdependent and interlocked. The construction furnishes scope for that visible evolution and involution of thought which constitute the charm of the most powerful style. Critical description of this is very tame. But look, for examples, at the style of Jeremy Taylor, of Milton's prose-works, and of Edmund Burke. Those passages which will strike you as the most eloquent are the passages of sustained, prolonged intercurrence of ideas by means of the periodic mechanism.

(d) In the most perfect examples of extemporaneous style, thought actually grows thus in the mind of the speaker. He does not know the whole of it when he commences a sentence. Yet, by oratorical instinct, he chooses the broad, circular, periodic inclosure; and in it his mind careers around and across, gathering its materials as it goes. To the hearer that process of inventing thought is made visible, yet without suggesting the weakness of after-thought. A certain loftiness of imaginative thinking cannot be expressed without a skilful and free use of the periodic structure. Short, dense, antithetic sentences will not do for it. Many are masters of these who cannot command the other. Dr. South could not. If he had been able to do it, he would have been a more genial critic of Jeremy Taylor. *The period in extemporaneous speech.*

(e) Once more: the periodic style assists energy of expression by a certain roundness of construction which is favorable to dignity of delivery. Difficult of execution though it be, and requiring certain physical resources which few possess in their perfection, when well matched by a grand physique, in person, voice, attitude, and gesture, it carries everything before it. The Rev. R. S. Storrs, D.D., of Brooklyn, is an example of a speaker whose physique and elocution invite the use of the periodic style; and he often employs it with great power. *The period effective in delivery.*

But it should be observed, as a balance to the view here given, that the periodic structure may be abused. *Abuse of the period.*

The point of this criticism cannot be more briefly expressed than by recalling to you a familiar one from De Quincey on the defectiveness of German construction. The construction which is indigenous to the German mind is the ideal realized of this abuse of the period. De Quincey writes of it thus: "Every German regards a sentence in the light of a package . . . into which his privilege is to crowd as much as he possibly can. Having framed a sentence, therefore, he next proceeds to *pack* it; which is effected partly by unwieldy tails and codicils, but chiefly by enormous parenthetic involutions. Qualifications, limitations, exceptions, illustrations, are stuffed and violently rammed into the bowels of the principal proposition. That all this equipage of accessories is not so arranged as to assist its own orderly development, no more occurs to a German as any fault than that in a package of carpets the colors and patterns are not fully displayed. To him it is sufficient that they are *there*." You doubtless recognize the original, in this caricature, of many sentences in the writings of Kant.

<small>De Quincey on German construction.</small>

Abuse of the period, furthermore, impairs energy in oral address by rendering a forcible delivery impossible. In either form, that of excessive stateliness or that of slovenly crowding, impressive elocution is beyond the reach of art. Try it. Could you deliver well three pages of Sir Thomas Browne? Could you pronounce impressively one of Kant's sentences, covering an octavo page, and packed at that? You must chant the one, and mouth the other. In adopting the resonant periodic structure, a speaker should see to it that the passage be so adjusted as to deliver well. *We must sacrifice an excellence in written style, if it is not also an excellence in oral speech.* A daring exploit is it, under some conditions, to speak the period at all. A double-bass voice in an auditorium whose acoustic proportions put in a claim for a hearing of its own will doom any specimen of the periodic style to ridicule.

<small>Abuse of the period prevents a forcible delivery.</small>

ANALYSIS.

ENERGY AND LANGUAGE (CONTINUED).

I. Exceptions in which Conciseness is not Favorable to Energy.

1. Where Conciseness is Affected.
2. Where Diffuseness is a means of Perspicuity.
3. Sometimes in Descriptive Writing.
4. Sometimes in Expressing intense Emotion.

II. Construction of the Sentence an Element of Energy.

1. Emphatic Words to be placed so that their force shall be obvious.
2. Care to be observed in the Use and the Omission of Conjunctive Beginnings.
3. Skill in the Use of the Periodic Structure.
   A. The Period and the Loose Sentence defined.
   B. Advantages of the Period.
      (a) Throws Emphasis upon End of the Sentence.
      (b) Fully satisfies Expectation.
      (c) Permits the disclosure to the Hearer of the Growth of Thought.
      (d) The Form of the Finest Examples of Extemporaneous Speech.
      (e) An Aid to the Highest Eloquence in Delivery.
      (f) Abuse of the Period.

CHAPTER XVIII

ENERGY AND LANGUAGE (CONCLUDED)

Thus far, energy of style has been treated as depending on the state of a writer's mind in the act of composing, and as depending on certain tributaries which are common to both the literal and the figurative uses of language.

I.—Figurative Language an Element of Energy of Style.

It remains now to consider it *as related to certain means which are peculiar to figurative speech.*

Of these should be first recalled those principles concerning imagery which were named as essential to perspicuity. In treating that branch of our general subject, the chief causes of obscurity in style were mentioned, and discussed at length. They were, *incongruous* imagery, *mixed* imagery, *learned* imagery, *excess* of imagery, and the *absence* of imagery. We need not traverse the same ground again any farther than to observe that the same causes may render style feeble which render it obscure. Indeed, they may do so, by making it obscure. Anything that blurs a thought deadens its force. Good taste is even more sensitive to the force of imagery than to its clearness.

Two preliminaries here will prevent misconception. One is, that figure in speech is not confined to imagery strictly so called. Construction in style admits of figure. This is what the books mean when they enumerate "figures of rhetoric." A sentence by its

Two preliminaries.

very structure may be figurative when its words are not so. By an occult sense, style may be made figurative when its words are as literal as the alphabet. Irony, for instance, is one of the " figures of rhetoric."

The other preliminary is, that the object of naming these " figures of rhetoric " is not to facilitate a mechanical use of them. The use of them ought not to be mechanical. Criticism which should make them so would be worse than useless. Moreover, criticism is useless in assisting the invention of these figures of speech. The invention must come from the instinct of an excited mind, or it cannot be at all. The most that criticism can do is to confirm the oratorical instinct in the use of such resources, and to guard against abuses of them.

1. The instinct of oratory numbers among its simplest figures of rhetoric the *climax*. It is a symbol of cumulation, and cumulation of thought is force. In few expedients is the skill of a writer more constantly put in unconscious requisition than in this of the pertinent use of the cumulative structure. In the order of adjectives, of adverbs, of verbs, of substantives, of clauses, a choice is practicable, which commonly climax should determine. You are heedless of the instinct of oratory, if you say, " he was beloved and respected," instead of saying, " he was respected and beloved," unless the " respect " in question is the point which needs enforcement. Would you say, " he had a good conscience and a Roman nose "? Why, then, reverse the order of climax in any energetic speech? Climax reversed is one form of burlesque. A succession of tapering sentences, advancing from the greater to the less, makes one feel as if one were sitting on an inclined plane. By confusion of order, proceeding from greater to less and from less to greater in succession, style may seem to make a zigzag movement.

Effect of the reverse of climax.

2. The instinct of forcible utterance recognizes the energy of *antithesis* in style. Antithetic structure expresses an idea—that of contrast. Contrast itself is force. De Quincey supposes the whole structure of the "Paradise Lost" to rest, as a work of art, on a designed multiplication of contrasts. That which some have charged to the pedantry of Milton he claims to be the effect of a lurking antagonism of effects. The introduction of architecture into pandemonium, and again into paradise, he vindicates, not by any law of historic probability, but simply by the law of imagination, which invents and delights in reciprocal collision of ideas.

<small>Antithesis.</small>

<small>"Paradise Lost."</small>

It is this intrinsic energy of contrast which inclines deep feeling to express itself in contradictions. St. Paul, with no oratorical theory about it, pours out his profound experience in forms which are false, yet which deceive nobody: "Sorrowing, yet always rejoicing; dying yet we live; having nothing, yet possessing all things." What is the secret of this language from De Bray, the Huguenot martyr?—"These shackles are more honorable to me than golden rings: when I hear their clank, methinks I listen to the music of sweet voices and the tinkling of lutes." Contrast promotes force, also, by augmenting conciseness. Contrast saves words. Of two contrasted ideas, each is a mirror to the other; and a mirror gives you vision, instead of words. Pithy, condensed sayings, which, because of their force, pass into proverbs, and live forever, commonly take the antithetic form. The majority of the proverbs of Solomon are of the antithetic structure.

<small>St. Paul.</small>

<small>De Bray.</small>

3. The intuition of the orator recognizes the *interrogation* as a tribute to energy in style. Few expedients of speech so simple as this are so effective in giving vigor to style. Composition comparatively dull may be made comparatively vivacious, and so far forcible,

<small>Interrogation.</small>

by a liberal sprinkling of interrogatives. Is a declarative utterance of a truth tame? Put it as an inquiry. Ask a question which implies it, and the silent answer may be more impressive to the hearer than any words of yours. Does an antithetic expression disappoint you? Try the mark of interrogation. Put it to the hearer as if he must sharpen it by a response. It is not meant that this is to be put on mechanically, but that you should throw your own mind into the mood of colloquy. Single out one man in your audience, and *talk* with him. Jeremiah Mason, who contested with Daniel Webster the head-ship of the Boston bar, used, in addressing juries, to single out one man in the jury-box, the man of dullest look, of immobile countenance, who went to sleep most easily, and then directed his whole plea to him, keeping his eye upon him till the man felt that he was watched, and that the counsel had business with him. *Method of Jeremiah Mason.* That kind of impression can often be wrought into your style, and made to come out of it again to the one hearer whom it is aimed at. The effect of that mental change in you will be magical. The style which was humdrum becomes alive, because you have come to life. The thought springs, because you spring. There is no mechanism about it : it is an honest expression of a new force within you.

Observe briefly the philosophy of the interrogative. It makes a hearer active in the reception of a truth. An interrogation is *an appeal:* an appeal invites silent rejoinder. Did you never see a hearer's lips move, or his head nod or shake, in answer to an interrogation from the speaker? Again : interrogation is *an expression of confidence.* It is a bold utterance, and therefore forceful. *Philosophy of the interrogative.* The instinct of earnest speech does not put doubtful opinions into the interrogative style. If we doubt, we do not give the hearer a chance to reply, even silently : therefore we say our say, but *Confidence of the interrogative.*

ask no questions. This is the instinct of keen oratory. Interrogation is the electric wire which carries from speaker to hearer the sign of vivid conviction. Hence arises the popularity of interrogatives among earnest talkers. The common people, when roused, spring to the interrogative. Men scold in interrogatives. This is only the vulgar counterpart of the same feature in the philippics of Demosthenes.

Further: the interrogative style invites, yes, commands, an animated delivery. He must be a remarkable speaker who for an hour in succession can deliver well declarative sentences without an interrogative break. No matter how weighty nor how skilfully constructed, a speech gets nothing if it asks nothing. The elocution natural to it flattens it. On the contrary, he must be fearfully and wonderfully made who cannot in public speech put life into a question. Can you drawl a question? Can you sing a question? Can you make humdrum of question? Can you deliver a series of questions without a quickening of your elocution? Try it. Experiment on Shylock's talk with Salarino: "I am a Jew. Hath not a Jew eyes? Hath not a Jew hands? If you prick us, do we not bleed? If you tickle us, do we not laugh? If you poison us, do we not die? And, if you wrong us, shall we not revenge?" *If the interrogative could do nothing else than to energize delivery it would be indispensable to a forcible style for that.*

Effect in delivery.

4. A modification of this figure is found in the *colloquy*. This was formerly employed in public speech more freely than now. Question and answer, with question again and rejoinder, have often given an energetic presentation of argument. This form of discussion by disputation, as you are are aware, was abundantly used by the ancient philosophers. Some of the most impassioned passages of the Bible are in this style.

Colloquy.

5. It scarcely needs a reminder that *hyperbole* is a favorite figure of rhetoric among 'energetic writers.' Anything adds force to style which expresses 'strength of conviction in the speaker. This hyperbole obviously does. It needs only the caution that the speaker should not allow it to pass for reckless assertion. *Hyperbole.*

6. The forcibleness of *irony* needs no illustration. It needs, rather, to be flanked with cautions, of which one is, that it should not be a favorite with a public speaker. As an instrument of serious speech, it is corrosive. In itself it repels good feeling. *Irony.*

7. The figure of *exclamation* deserves a caution rather than commendation. It is very easy composition; it is a facile way of beginning a sentence: therefore we employ it excessively. It is a sign of indolent composing. Our inquiry, therefore, should be, When may we omit it? and our rule to dispense with it whenever we can. Dean Swift commends a reader who said it was his rule to pass over every paragraph in reading, at the end of which his eye detected the note of exclamation. Horne Tooke denied that exclamations belong to language: he said they were involuntary nervous affections, like sneezing, coughing, yawning. *Exclamation.*

8. A speaker who is perfect master of his imagination will sometimes instinctively choose the figure of *vision* to express his most powerful conceptions. The life which it gives to style is splendidly illustrated in some of the prophecies. The strictly prophetic state was a state of vision of the distant future. Yet note how instinctively secular oratory adopts the same expedient. Napoleon, to his soldiers in Italy, says, "You will soon return to your homes; and your fellow-citizens will say of you, as you pass, 'He was a soldier in the army of Italy.'" So the inspired writer says, "Of Zion it shall be said, This and that man was born in her." But, because it is so pow- *Vision.*

erful, it needs a master of speech to execute it well. It is one of the expedients of style which lie on the border-line between the sublime and the ridiculous. Less than the proverbial "step" separates them.

9. The most passionate forms of eloquence employ the *apostrophe* with power. The most notable example of this figure in secular literature is Mark Antony's apostrophe, as represented by Shakespeare over the dead body of Cæsar.

Apostrophe.

Is the exclamatory use of the name of God to be vindicated as rhetorical apostrophe? "My God!" "O God!" "Good God!" "In God's Name!"—are these apostrophes? The Rev. Dr. Nott, the celebrated president of Union College, defended and used them. The piety of the American Congress often utters its devout aspirations in this form. But these expressions are exclamatory, not apostrophic. The use of them in oratory is of pagan origin. Greek poetry is full of them: we owe them primarily to Homer. They were in perfect keeping with the Greek idea of the gods: rhetorically, therefore, they were not a blemish in Greek oratory. Christian theism, however, condemns them morally, and therefore Christian taste condemns them rhetorically.

Use of the name of God as apostrophe.

These are the chief of the figures of rhetoric which the oratorical instinct has originated to assist its most forcible utterances. The charm of them lies in their variety: no one should be a favorite with a writer or speaker. The thing needed is the cultivated instinct, which shall choose them wisely. But the chief observation which criticism has to make upon them is, *that they all imply force of emotion on the part of the speaker.* Manufacture them, and they are but wooden playthings. They reflect significance back upon the principle with which these discussions began—

The charm of these figures.

The power of these figures.

that a writer must write, and a speaker must speak, from the honest state of his own mind. That state must be such that he *can* write, and *can* speak, with honest enthusiasm. Nothing is powerful in speech which is not sincere. The inspiration which shall command and use these expedients of style must be, as one critic has expressed it, "not put on from without, but put out from within."

ANALYSIS.

ENERGY AND LANGUAGE (CONCLUDED).

I. **Figurative Language an Element of Energy of Style.**
    A. Two Preliminaries to the Discussion of Figurative Language.

II. **Kinds of Figurative Language.**
1. Climax.
2. Antithesis.
3. Interrogation.
4. Colloquy.
5. Hyperbole.
6. Irony.
7. Exclamation.
8. Vision.
9. Apostrophe.

CHAPTER XIX

ELEGANCE OF STYLE

I.—Definition of Elegance of Style.

A VERY vital quality, which is in many respects the opposite of energy, is elegance of style. It may be concisely defined *as the quality by which thought as expressed in language appeals to our sense of the beautiful.*

Beauty, like strength, is one of our ultimate conceptions. We cannot define it but by the use of synonyms, which, in return fall back upon it for their own meaning. Ruskin says, that the question why some material objects seem beautiful to us, and others not, is "no more to be asked than why we like sugar, and dislike wormwood." Sir Joshua Reynolds declares, that, if an African artist were to paint his ideal of beauty, he would produce a person of black glossy skin, flat nose, thick lips, and woolly hair. He also affirms that the artist would be right : so greatly does the conception of beauty depend on association.

An ultimate conception.

Beauty in style, however, admits of partial analysis. In it are found three distinct elements, one or more of which exist in all elegant composition, and all of which are discoverable in the most perfect forms of elegant speech. These elements are *delicacy, vividness,* and *variety.*

A partial analysis.

II.—Delicacy an Element of Elegance of Style.

Elegance of style, then, may be first considered as dependent on the element of *delicacy.*

1. And, first, it has its foundation in *delicacy of thought.* In "The Essay on the Sublime and the Beautiful," Edmund Burke approaches this view by claiming that *smallness* in an object is essential to its beauty. Smallness of object. He observes, "When nature would make anything specially rare and beautiful, she makes it little. Everybody calls that little which they love best on earth." An affectionate husband is apt to call his wife little, though she may weigh two hundred pounds. Dr. Johnson's wife was of nearly twice his own age at the time of their marriage; she was coarse and stout in person; she was affected in manners, and petulant in disposition; and he was far from being a man of refined feeling: yet he used to speak of her as his "dear Letty," as a child might speak of a pet kitten. The diminutive he coined out of her name, "Elizabeth."

2. Of beauty in style, that element which most nearly resembles this of smallness in Burke's analysis is delicacy. It is, if it may be so called, the *feminine* quality in thought. Delicacy the feminine quality in thought. Is there not a diversity in truth corresponding to diversity of sex in human character? Truths are masculine and feminine in their affinities. Woman originates certain conceptions more readily than man, and appreciates them more keenly. Other conceptions the masculine mind grasps the more profoundly. The literature produced by the two sexes will bear traces of this diversity, except in sporadic cases in which the one sex is rabid with the craving to *be* the other. Certain discoveries in science, certain works of art, certain truths of religion, woman will not naturally originate, any more than she will naturally be a drummer, or choose a trombone as the accompaniment of her songs.

Elegance of style, to repeat, groups within its range of expression these feminine qualities of thought. No genuine beauty can exist in literary expression without them. Can you by any description of it in language make chain-lightning beautiful? Can you so describe in words the boom of a cannon that it shall appear in gentle undulations of beauty? But can you, in descriptive style, so represent a moss-rose, or the airs of a flute, that they shall seem other than beautiful?

Diversities in style.

III.—PREJUDICES AGAINST AN ELEGANT STYLE.

The principle in question refutes a certain prejudice against an elegant style. Elegant taste in anything lives at the risk of being despised. Even among able writers, elegance and effeminacy are often treated as synonyms. The Jewish prayer of thanksgiving, "Lord, I thank thee that I was not born a woman!" finds its kindred among literary tastes and canons of criticism. Such is the reverence often felt for Gothic strength in speech, that elegance of diction is condemned without a hearing. We study to be perspicuous, because we must be understood. We study precision, purity, and, above all, force in style, because these add power to clearness. But of an elegant style we are apt to think as Wesley did of the manners of a gentleman, when he told his youthful preachers that they "had no more business to be gentlemen than to be dancing-masters."

Prejudice against an elegant style.

1. This prejudice is *intensified by our English temperament.* The English mind, and, as an offshoot of it, the American mind as well, are not partial to the elegant qualities, specially in public oral address. We are jealous for our strength. We are proud of our Saxon stock. We are, therefore, morbidly afraid of imposing on ourselves by elegant literary forms. We are in this respect what our language is, hardy, rough, careless of ease. The languages and temperaments of Southern Europe are in this

Our temperament.

respect our opposites. We have cultivated learning at the expense of taste; they, taste at the expense of learning.

2. This prejudice, moreover, is *often aggravated by affectations of the beautiful in literary expression.* Affections create caricatures of beauty: these repel taste, as they repel good sense. Literary affectations.

3. All this, and more, might be said in defence of the prejudice against elegant discourse. Still, what is to be said in view of the immense preponderance of beautiful thought within the compass of language. Does not the material world present an obvious ascendency of beauty over force, over sublimity even? The Answers to this prejudice. profusion of creative energy is nowhere else seen so clearly as in the sportive production of objects beautiful to the eye. So far as we know, many of them have no other reason for their creation than their passive beauty. Naturalists have conjectured that the more gorgeous species of the butterfly have a sense of beauty which The beautiful in nature. enables them to enjoy the variegated coloring of their own forms. They are believed to rest from their foraging expeditions, on the cool surface of a leaf, in silent and tranquil joy at the magnificence of their expanded wings. So lavish is Nature in its creation of the beautiful, and its provision of the sense of beauty to respond to it through the sentient universe. Is not this emblematic of a similar profusion in the spiritual world? How is it with perfected forms of human character? Which is there in the The beautiful in human character. ascendent—beauty, or strength? To ask this question is to answer it. Energy we find in savage mind. The ultimate fruitage of culture we sum up under the title of the "refinements of civilization." A ripe mind of evenly balanced sensibilities will discover in the world of thought, which is its mental atmosphere, more of beauty than of any other single quality.

The dependence of elegance on delicacy of thought suggests, further, the true reply to that theoretic error which restricts elegance to ornament. Beauty in discourse interests in proportion to its expression of character. That is not beauty of high order which is not full of character of high order. Often, therefore, the thing which juvenile discourse chiefly needs is to diminish its adornment. Its elegance needs to be brought down to a level with its real character as the herald of thought. Some passages in Wordsworth's poetry, in which he dwells fondly on natural scenery, are dull. They are true to fact; they are polished in form; they are melodious on the lips. A good rehearser of them, on a calm summer's day, would give them in tranquil recitative, which would soothe a tired hearer; but they would not interest an alert one. To such a one they are dull. Why? Because they lack thought proportioned to their elaborateness of form. They fondle commonplaces in the works of Nature: they make as much of an apple-blossom as of a tropical garden. Nothing in literary forms makes the impression of beauty which does not carry thought enough to constitute a certain ballast to the form. Ornament achieves nothing above its own weight in thought.

Elegance not simply ornament.

Poetry of Wordsworth.

Nevertheless, profusion of ornament is beautiful if demanded by thought. If the nature of a subject be such that the most characteristic expression of it requires elaborate adornment, that elaborate adornment is beauty. As the material world abounds with such forms of beauty, and as the fine arts are immortalized by them, so does style often express them in language.

Ornament beautiful when demanded by thought.

Again: that is not an elegant style in which beauty of form is excessive in degree. Often, as has been before remarked, a speaker's thought is not weighty enough to sustain elaborated style of any kind, and, least of all, elaborated imagery. Architects tells us, that a small specimen of the Gothic architecture is of necessity in bad taste. No matter how perfectly finished, it cannot be good art. The reason they give is, that the profusion of ornament which the Gothic order requires cannot be compressed into a small area. It must have vast spaces, massive pillars, huge vaults in the ceiling, immense windows, prolonged distances in nave and transept. Everything about it must be congruous with the grand and the magnificent. Therefore a Gothic cathedral in miniature is a contradiction. So it is often with the expression of thought in language.

Excessive beauty of style not an elegant style.

IV.—MEANS OF ACQUIRING DELICACY OF THOUGHT.

The foundation of elegance in delicacy of thought suggests, further, that we must find the fundamental means of cultivating this quality in the cultivation of refinement of perception. *Refinement in our habits of thinking, the habit of dwelling upon the beautiful in literature, distinguishing varieties of beauty, studying illustrations of beauty in external nature, observing analogies between the beautiful in nature and art and the beautiful in language, genial criticism of the best poetry, studious enjoyment of the best imagery in prose, attention to minutiæ of style in which elegance of construction chiefly appears:* in short, any and every exercise of mind which brings into chastened play that sensibility to the beautiful which every mind possesses, will refine our taste, and make our perceptions of beauty truthful and prompt.

Refinement of perception to be cultivated for delicacy in thought.

This leads us to observe, that all writers and speakers may possess it. It is a growth of that of which the germ exists in every mind. No man can escape it who aims persistently at anything like concinnity of culture. That is a fiction which some youthful writers entertain, that their minds are not fitted to the cultivation of those qualities which beauty in style represents. Clear writers they may become, forcible writers, precise writers, prolific writers perhaps, but not elegant writers. "The graces of rhetoric," says such an one, "are not for me." He narrows his culture, and contracts the range of his power in public speech immensely, who subjects himself to any such restriction. The elements which refined taste imparts to oral speech are no more "the graces of rhetoric" than those which energy imparts are the forces of rhetoric. They are graces of mind, innate in every mind, susceptible of growth in every mental life, inevitable to any mind which is disciplined by prolonged and symmetrical culture.

All may have this delicacy of thought.

ANALYSIS.

ELEGANCE OF STYLE.

I. Definition.
    A. An Ultimate Conception.
    B. A Partial Analysis.

II. Delicacy an Element of Elegance of Style.
    1. Smallness of Object Essential to Beauty.
    2. Delicacy the Feminine Quality in Thought.

III. Prejudice against an Elegant Style.
    1. Prejudice Intensified by Our Temperament.
    2. Prejudice often Aggravated by Literary Affectations.
    3. Answers to this Prejudice.
        (a) Perfected Forms of Nature.
        (b) Perfected Forms of Human Character.
        (c) Elegance not Simply Ornament.
        (d) Excessive Beauty of Form not an Elegant Style.

IV. Means of Acquiring Delicacy of Thought.
    1. By Cultivating Refinement of Perception.
    2. By Believing it a Possible Attainment for Everyone.

CHAPTER XX

ELEGANCE OF STYLE (CONTINUED)

The dependence of elegance of style on delicacy gives rise also to a second demand—that of delicacy of expression in the utterance of thought. Beauty in thought is more difficult of expression than energy in thought: it requires a more sensitive discrimination of the significance of language.

I.—Offences Against Elegance of Style in Choice and Arrangement of Words.

An elegant style, therefore, demands a more choice selection and arrangement of words. This obvious principle has also significant corollaries.

It suggests, in the first place, a large class of offences against elegance of style. They are that class which results, not from unfitness of thought, but from inelegant language. The choice of a vocabulary may disclose these defects. Words have their aristocracy. Some have a noble birth; a magnificent history lies behind them; they were born amidst the swelling and the bursting into life of great ideas. On the contrary, there are words which have plebeian associations. Some are difficult of enunciation; and, by a secret sympathy, the mind attaches to them the distortion, perhaps the pain, of the vocal organs in their utterance. A single uncouth word may be to style what an uncontrollable grimace is to the countenance. Neither is a thing of beauty. Words

Uncouth words.

not inelegant in themselves become so through pedestrian associations which colloquial usage affixes to them. Our Yankee favorite "guess" is a perfectly good word, pure English, of good stock, and long standing in the language. A better word, in itself considered, we have not in English use. But because it is a colloquial favorite, used by everybody, on every variety of subject and occasion, and often in a degraded sense, as in the compound "guess-work," it has become vulgar in the sense of "common;" so that in many connections in which the real meaning of it would be entirely pertinent, the word would be inelegant. "Conjecture," or some equivalent, must take its place.

"Guess."

Wordsworth's poetry, again, is not wholly defensible from the charge of using in poetic measure an inelegant vocabulary. He believed in the poetry of common things, common thoughts, common people, and their common affairs. It was the aim of his life to lift up into the atmosphere of romance things lowly and obscure. But, in his attempt to effect that revolution, he did lean to an extreme. Even his regal imagination could not dignify such lines as these, viz.:—

The vocabulary of Wordsworth's poetry.

> "A household tub, like one of those
> Which women use to wash their clothes."

But an objector inquires, and perhaps with half-suppressed indignation, "Is it not good English? and, if so, must we drop it because it is not elegant?" The answer is, yes to both queries. It is good English, yet not good poetry. If the idea is to be expressed at all in poetry—and it is not to be denied that it may be so expressed as to escape criticism—it must be by such a choice of language as shall conceal the steam and the soap of a washtub under some euphemism which

Good English but not good poetry.

shall be to the idea what the rainbow, which is sometimes seen over a washtub, is to that very necessary but homely article of household use. When beauty is to be expressed, we must have a choice vocabulary. If Thomas Hood could, by "The Song of the Shirt," throw a poetic halo over a very humble article of his daily toilet, why may not his equal do the same service for the weekly laundry? But not by the extreme literalism of Wordsworth's vocabulary.

II.—Offences against Elegance of Style in Construction.

Constructions, also, are exposed to peril of inelegance. Certain varieties of them impress us, first and last and always, with their want of ease ; and, no case, no beauty. It is as difficult to define them as to create them, yet illustration by examples would tax your patience beyond endurance. Few things are so unutterably dull as specimens of faulty construction in discourse, unless they are of the comic sort; and those would not be to the present purpose. Perhaps the following hints will be sufficient to recall them to you in your reading.

One is the *bungling* construction of *dependent clauses*. These are huddled together, and seem to tumble over each other. Mellifluous utterance of them is impracticable. They are the despair of the elocutionist. They seem as if the sole ambition of the writer had been to be able to say, as De Quincey said of the German sentence, "They are all there." Another is the *military* sentence. The materials march out as if on drill. They drop into rank too knowingly to be lively. Excess of order is never beautiful, because never life-like. Another is the *misplaced* or *excessive inversion of* structure. The thoughts appear to move like a crab ; are dragged forth—the first last, and the last first, and all looking the wrong

Dependent clauses.

way—after the manner of the stolen oxen backing into the cave of Cacus. Another is the *dislocated* structure. Connectives are either absent, or misplaced, or meaningless. The style jolts, like an uneasy vehicle on corduroy roads.

These constructions may be sufficiently perspicuous. They are often consistent with a good degree of energy. Cromwell's speeches are full of them. Yet he made himself understood, and so well understood that the English Parliament did not care to ask him what he meant a second time. But such constructions are not elegant. There is no comeliness in them. It would be a hard task to set Cromwell's speeches to the measure of a chant, or even to make an Italian, with vocal organs trained to the most euphonious language in the world, rehearse them at all.

Cromwell.

III.—Offences Against Elegance of Style in Imagery.

1. A similar defect betrays itself in *inelegance of imagery*. Imagery is painting in words: any blemish impairs its beauty. Therefore coarse imagery cannot express beauty in thought. Imagery the picture of which disgusts the mind's eye degrades the thought it represents. This is sometimes the designed effect. Macaulay designs it when he says, "after the Restoration, peerages were sold at Whitehall scarcely less openly than asparagus at Covent Garden, or herrings at Billingsgate." The image of an English coronet side by side with a bunch of asparagus and a red herring paints the degradation of the peerage as no literal description could. But Jeremy Taylor wrought the same effect, though undesignedly, when he compared the sufferings of Christ to "an umbrella," because "men used them to shelter unholy living."

Inelegance of imagery.

Macaulay.

2. For the same reason, *commonplace* in imagery cannot express, and still less can it impress, the beautiful in thought. A metaphor elegantly impressive when it was new may degrade an idea now because of its excessive use. Imagery wears out, as the gloss of silk does. The metaphor of the pebble, which creates ever-widening rings when dropped into the water, is an example. Few figures of speech bear criticism better than this. When it was original, it can scarcely have had its superior for beauty or suggestiveness. But does the memory of man go back to the time when it was original? It is exhausted : it needs to be allowed to slumber in oblivion. It should be disused till a future age shall re-invent it. So powerful is originality in pictured speech, that it will often ennoble a commonplace thought. A conception which we had ceased to feel the force of because of our monotonous familiarity with it, an original figure will often uplift, somewhat as death hallows in our memory a commonplace character.

<small>Commonplace imagery.</small>

3. Again : *unfinished* imagery cannot express beauty in thought. A metaphor unsustained, and therefore incomplete, conveys no impression of elegance. Yet, on the other hand, *finical* imagery is equally powerless. To be overwrought changes imagery to finery. The impression is that of pettiness, not of beauty. What is the defect in the message of the martyr Ridley to his fellow-sufferer Hooper as they were going to the stake? —" We have been two in white : let us be one in red ! " It speaks something for the nerve of a man, that he can crack his joke within sight of the pile which will soon shrivel his tongue to a cinder. But what can we say for the good taste of a man who can so treat such a death? We might expect it from a hunter in the backwoods, in view of Indian torture, but not from a bishop of the Church of England.

<small>Unfinished imagery.</small>

4. Further: *mongrel* imagery does not express beauty. Above all things else, beauty is self-consistent. Incongruity is death to it. At an international exhibition of the industrial arts in Vienna, was seen the figure of a kneeling Samuel, of the size of life, moulded of castile-soap. Why was it not "a thing of beauty"? Yet is Bishop Heber more successful in his attempt to improve the magnificent imagery of Milton? Milton sees in poetic vision "the gates of heaven on golden hinges turning." Why is it that Heber fails, when he attempts to save himself from plagiarism by representing the gates of heaven as "rolling back on their starry hinges"?

<small>Mongrel imagery.</small>

IV.—Elegance an Aid to Other Qualities of Style.

Before leaving this class of offences against elegance in style, it is worthy of remark, that, by avoiding them, a certain degree of beauty may be infused into other qualities of style. The polish of a steel blade contributes to the keenness of its edge; so elegance may enhance perspicuity, or precision, or energy of language. True, in such a combination, elegance is subordinate. The style is not constructed for it; the blade is not made for the polish: but, as a tributary, it serves the purposes of other qualities of style. An air of elegance may be imparted to the most forcible style by the choice of a select vocabulary, by finish of construction, and by a delicate congruity of imagery. Energy is not always convulsive. What was the defect of the style of an eminent preacher in Maine, who, speaking of men's rejection of Christ, said that "they treated him as they would a rotten apple"? It surely was not obscurity; it was not weakness: it was a want of that sensitive taste which ought to breathe its delicate sense of fitness into the plainest phraseology and the roughest imagery.

<small>Elegance and energy.</small>

In the works of nature, it is remarkable how often force and beauty are ranged side by side. In their impression on the beholder, they often intermingle. Flowers skirt the bases of volcanoes; rainbows grace the retiring thunder-storms. In the Falls of Niagara, the predominance of beauty or of sublimity depends on the mood of the spectator, both are so affluent in their display. Charles Dickens expressed the experience of the majority of thoughtful travellers in looking upon them, when he said, after giving utterance to his overpowering sense of their sublimity, that the final and permanent impression of them, which would live in his memory, was that of their beauty. Would not this be almost the sole impression made by them upon the mind of a deaf man, to whom they would present a picture only, not modified by the sound of mighty waters? *Falls of Niagara.*

Similar combinations of energy and elegance are found in human character. The choicest characters always contain them. The world's perfect ideal of a man is that of a *gentle-man*. Coleridge remarked, that he had never met with a truly great man who had not a large infusion of feminine qualities. One is impressed by the truth of the sentiment in reading the memoir of Daniel Webster. The ideal which history gives us of a military character is one in which gentleness adorns the heroic graces. The Christian ideal of manly force is that of executive power wreathed with passive virtues. That which we call the "force of truth" is often the more forceful for being tempered and adorned with the feminine qualities of thought, and therefore with the elegant graces of expression. They are best expressed by a select vocabulary, by finished constructions, and by congruous imagery. *Force and beauty in human character.*

The views here presented of the value of a refined taste to the style of public speech need to be balanced by a notice of the fact that luxuriousness of taste results in languor of style. This is the chief peril of a studied beauty in the forms of language. Composition is an art. Elegant composition is a fine art. But it is liable to this abuse: a fastidious taste attenuates thought. The style which grows out of it tends to elaborate feebleness through its expression of morbid sensibilities.

The chief peril of a studied beauty.

National literatures, so far as we can trace the stages of their decline, die first at this point of effeminate taste. Softening of the national brain begins in the organ of ideality. Violent death never comes upon a great literature in its adult strength. Barbarian irruptions, usurpations in government, and the conflagration of libraries, have come upon nations after literary decline has begun to show itself. The fatal and often the first clear sign that a nation deserves and is doomed to receive such visitations appears in the breaking-out of a diseased luxuriousness of taste in its literature, after a period of high culture.

The decline of national literatures.

ANALYSIS.

ELEGANCE OF STYLE (CONTINUED).

I. **Offences against Elegance of Style in Choice and Arrangement of Words.**
   1. Uncouth Words.
   2. Words Made Inelegant from Vulgar Usage.

II. **Offences Against Elegance of Style in Constructions.**
   1. Dependent Clauses.
      (a) In Disorder.
      (b) In too Rigid Order.
      (c) In too Inverted Order.

III. **Offences against Elegance of Style in Imagery.**
   1. Inelegant Imagery.

    2. Commonplace Imagery.
    3. Unfinished Imagery.
    4. Mongrel Imagery.

IV. Elegance an Aid to other Qualities of Style.
    1. Elegance and Energy.
        (a) Force and Beauty in Nature.
        (b) Force and Beauty in Human Character.
    2. Chief Peril of a Studied Beauty.
        (a) Decline of National Literatures.

CHAPTER XXI

ELEGANCE OF STYLE (CONCLUDED)

The analysis of beauty in a previous chapter leads us to consider elegance of style as dependent, in the second place, on the element of *vividness*.

I.—Vividness an Element of Elegance of Style.

Is vagueness of impression ever desirable in the expression of thought by language? Yes, it is sometimes a necessity, but never where beauty of impression is the chief aim of the discourse. Always a greater or less degree of vividness enters into our sense of the beautiful. *Vividness essential to beauty.* Why is a diamond the most beautiful of gems? Dealers in precious stones say that the popular taste for it never wavers. It is always salable, and is the standard by which the value of other gems is estimated. Yet the diamond has no beauty but its brilliancy. The human eye is the most vital organ in producing the impression of beauty in a human countenance, because it is the most vivid object in the countenance. Poets describe the sun as the "golden eye" of the heavens. The eye suggests life: it *is* life. All varieties of beauty in the eye possess this quality. The languid eye with drooping eyelash, if it expresses beauty, is never dull. It may represent life in repose, but still, life: no beauty of countenance fascinates if it is blurred by a dull eye. A corresponding principle appertains to thought as expressed in language. Vividness, in degree less or greater, is essential to all expression of beauty in human speech.

Perhaps a sufficiently definite qualification of the vividness which beauty demands is to say, that it must be such as shall consist with that delicacy of impression which we have seen to be an equal element of beauty in discourse. *Vividness and delicacy.* In the most overpowering beauty we shall find something which tempers vividness with refinement. In a tropical flower of high-wrought coloring we shall find refinement of texture, or gracefulness of outline, or delicacy in the shading of colors, or prismatic reflection of tints in the sunlight: otherwise we do not call it beautiful, but gaudy. The same combination of principles holds good in style. Vividness of thought in high degree, yet such degree as shall consist with delicate impression on the whole, is the requisite of beauty. The bearing of these principles upon elegance of style will be seen in several inferences.

II.—The Demands of Vividness.

1. We infer the obvious truth that elegance demands *distinctness of thought.* To some minds, whose conception of force is adequate to a strong style, the whole idea of beauty is hazy. It comes to *Distinctness of thought.* their consciousness through an uncultivated instinct. Hence it is, that juvenile attempts at the beautiful in language often result in crowded symbols which suggest only general ideas, and these diffusely, perhaps tautologically. Similes and metaphors, and rotund words, and rythmical constructions, are heaped into a page without stint, not because a definite beauty of conception is so refracted and multiplied to the mind's eye as to demand such a variety of elegant forms, but because a misty notion of that beauty is in the writer's mind, and he hastens to give it shape by the patches of finery which he has on hand. It is one of the thousand deformities of style in which form alone is made

to do the work of thought. The hollowness of it rings in the ear of a discerning critic. The only adequate corrective of such a defect is nothing more nor less than intenser thinking. The writer is not yet master of his work. He has not discovered the original of the image which has charmed him in his dream. He does not know whether it is an angel, or a woman, or a mermaid.

2. From the necessity of vividness to beauty in speech, we infer further the necessity of *sensitiveness of feeling* to those varieties of eloquence in which the beautiful predominates. As energy in style demands force of feeling, elegance demands sensitiveness of feeling. Both are founded on the same principle. The thing expressed must find its kindred in the emotive condition of the writer. No man can write vividly who does not write with feeling of some kind. But there is a vast difference between the feeling of one who is tormented by a truth, and that of one who broods over a truth affectionately, or carries on a mental play with it.

<small>Sensitiveness of feeling.</small>

Are there not some writers who impress you chiefly with a sense of the hardness of their natures? Their discourses may be solid, packed with thought, loaded with latent force; yet they seem to grind like a millstone. The defect in such writers is in their emotive nature. They have no play of sensibility, no wavelets of feeling, none of the tell-tale of a mobile countenance. Their style betrays all this on the principle of Buffon, that the style of a man is the man himself.

<small>Impression made by some writers.</small>

Men of this mould are seldom or never great orators. They may be great as men of affairs, wise on committees, forceful in executive miscellanies; but they have too much wisdom, and too little of emotive spontaneousness, to be great orators. Men noted for their reticence are not often mighty in eloquence. Certain powers which enter into all eloquence are reticent in them there. Close reasoners they may be in argumentative discourse, but for the want of mobile sensibilities, which express themselves in pictorial forms of speech, they are doomed to be uninteresting, and therefore their argument cannot get a hearing. Delicate and winsome discourse is not possible to such men in their present state of culture.

3. From the necessity of vividness as an element of beauty, we infer further, as a general fact, the necessity of *simplicity of language* to an elegant style. No other quality than beauty makes such an imperative demand for transparency. Simplicity of language. One of the most invariable concomitants of beauty in language is the absence of all appearance of effort. It is the production of a mind at ease Why are the biblical narratives such perfect specimens of elegance in historic style? The fact is often observed, that the evangelists, in their reminiscences of our Lord, never employ a commendatory epithet in description of his person. Contrast, in this respect, St. John with Homer. St. John and Homer. Beauty is the offspring of leisure. The writer seems not to go in search of, or to struggle for, anything: he takes and gives what comes to him.

But the necessity of simplicity to elegant expression is a general principle: it has exceptions. Profusion and intricacy of beauty in thought have their correlatives in style. The usual canons of criticism respecting simplicity must be accepted with qualifications. A cultivated taste recoils so sensitively from an affected style, that it often expresses its demand for a simple diction in hyperbole.

4. From the dependence of beauty on vividness of style, we infer, yet again, the importance of an *easy command of imagery* to an elegant style. The origin of alphabetic writing suggests the necessity of imagery to vivid speech. An easy command of imagery. The first form of written language known to history was the hieroglyph. So

the vividness of written language at present depends very much upon the relics of the hieroglyphic element which still remains in every language, and upon the imitations of it originated by authors in the form of more elaborate imagery. Write in pictures, and you cannot fail to write vividly. Imagery is essential to vivid expression, specially because the vividness of beauty must be felt intuitively, not derived by reflective process. It must reach the mind, as vision does, by a process which gives no sense of duration.

III.—Variety an Element of Elegance of Style.

The third element named in our analysis of beauty leads us to consider elegance of style as *dependent on variety*.

Hogarth's theory of the "line of beauty" depended largely upon this element of variety. In what does the beauty of a curve consist? You can discern in it nothing definable, other than variety and proportion. A straight line may have proportion, but it is monotonous. The curve adds variety, and this results in the elementary figure which artists declare to be inherent in all beauty of form. A serpentine path, the careering of a bird in the air, Connecticut River as seen from Mount Holyoke, the Rhine as seen from the Castle of Godesberg—these, as examples of figure and motion, are all emblems of beauty to which the rudest nature responds. The rainbow, the shifting of clouds at sunset, the plumage of a peacock, a mobile countenance—these, as specimens of color, are emblems of beauty; yet not one of them would excite our sense of the beautiful without its variety. Music also, as an example of beauty in sound, cannot exist without variety. A drum has none except in time; and how much beauty does a drum suggest?

Variety essential to beauty in general.

The same principle governs style. Monotony, even of that which is in itself an excellence, destroys the beauty of it. One critic defines the whole art of composing as the art of varying thought skilfully. Cutlers tell us, that the keenest razor will lose its temper, or whatever that is which gives it the susceptibility of taking an edge, if it is never allowed a period of disuse. No sharpening process will perfect it for use till it has for a while been at rest. Hair-dressers observe the phenomenon, and describe it by saying that razors get tired, as the hand does which wields them. So is it with the rarest and keenest excellence in style: sameness blunts it, in spite of the ingenuity expended upon repairs.

Variety essential to beauty of style.

IV.—MEANS OF ACQUIRING VARIETY.

1. How can variety of style be most readily acquired as a habit of the pen? The answer is, first, in sympathy with what has been already said, that variety of style must have its foundation in *versatility of thought*. Thought in a versatile mind may compel variety in its utterance. On the contrary, thought in a commonplace mind may be so monotonous that no art can create variety in its expression. Utterance must be what the mind is which thinks it.

Versatility of thought.

May it not have been one cause of the beauty of the Greek language and literature, that they grew up among a people who were passionately fond of the drama? "They left," says one critic, "for the world's admiration, theatres, while the Romans left amphitheatres." The love of the drama permeated the very structure of the Greek tongue, as did the Greek taste.

2. The elegance of a discourse as a unique structure is promoted by *variety in the method of discussion, by variety of divisions in form and substance, by variety in recapitulations of argument, by variety in applications*. Any prolonged discourse requires variation in the keynote of

the thought. Argument unmixed with illustration, poetic aspects of truth in unbroken succession, declamation un-mingled with didactic remark, are too wearisome to please the sense of beauty. Thought in the most brilliant pictures, unrelieved by passages of repose, satiates the sense of beauty. A traveller in Europe soon grows weary, and therefore undiscerning, in exploring rapidly a choice gallery of art. Its profusion of beauty becomes monotonous, and therefore antagonistic to its own meaning. Mind sympathizes with the weariness of the eye. Similar is the effect of that style of discourse of which a gallery of pictures is the emblem.

Frequent change of means in presenting a subject.

3. That variety which elegance requires demands, also, a *varied vocabulary and construction.* In this respect the most essential requisite is a thorough command of the synonyms of the language, and the history of its literature. Good taste revolts from the constant yet needless recurrence of the same word or the same collocation of words. Inelegances of construction are easily corrected if attention is given to them: they are the fruit of heedless composing. The following are the chief of them; viz., *monotony in the length of sentences, in the manner of beginning and ending sentences, in the connections of the emphatic and dependent clauses of sentences, in transitions, in the use of affirmative, negative, interrogative, and antithetic structures, in the use of personal and impersonal pronouns, in the use of the direct and the inverted orders of sentences, in the use of some favorite peculiarity of construction not easily definable by criticism.*

A varied vocabulary and construction.

One form of favorite mechanism in construction is that in which a regular succession occurs, like the swing of a pendulum. In other instances in which one feels the sense of monotony, but cannot at once detect the cause, it is found, on a closer scrutiny, that the sentences have more than two variations, but they occur in one invariable order, with the sameness of a treadmill. Dr. Johnson's style sometimes falls into this monotone in mechanism. Hazlitt criticises it, saying that to read or hear such passages from Johnson's writings is as bad as being at sea in a calm, in which one feels the everlasting monotony of the ground-swell. Charles Dickens sometimes falls under the tyranny of his ear in composing; and then his style assumes an arbitrary succession of a few constructions, in which thought is subordinated to euphony of expression. A roll and a swell and a return, in the *boom* of the style, if we may speak so incongruously, destroy the sense of everything but the sound. One is tempted to chant the passage. *Hazlitt's criticism of Dr. Johnson's style.*

4. Furthermore: that variety which beauty of style requires involves *variety of illustration*. This suggestion opens a boundless field of criticism. We can traverse it but very rapidly, noting only the most essential principles. Generally, repetition of the same illustration in similar connections should be avoided. If the illustration be a bad one, or an indifferent one, it does not deserve repetition: if it be a good one, repetition betrays the author's estimate of it as such, and has the look of vanity. In either case, an elegant taste is offended. Write rather as if you were unconscious of the quality of your style, and as if your mind were rich in its abundance of illustrative stores. *Variety of illustration.*

Some speakers plod in commonplaces by confining themselves, for illustrations, to the most common objects and phenomena of nature—such as the sun, the moon, the stars, rivers, mountains, forests, storms, clouds. Others limit their range of choice to principles in science; others, to the mechanic arts; a few, to the fine arts; a larger number, to civil government; many, to historical allusions, to mythology, to literary fiction, to military art and history. *Imagery of different writers.*

Cultivate a liberal acquaintance with the mechanic arts, the natural sciences, history, biography, the liberal professions, the trades, the fine arts, mythology, fiction, civil and social life. Be at home wherever you can lead the interest of your hearers for new analogies.

Again : for variety's sake, illustrations should not be restricted to any one rhetorical form. Do not commonly resort to the boldest of figures, nor always to the mildest. Illustration should rarely predominate over declarative or argumentative discussion ; yet it should not be limited to pictorial words. Elegance requires diversity in proportion, as in rhetorical form. The extent to which a prolific and inventive mind can execute illustrative variety is seen in the fact, that in sixty-four volumes of the works of Paul Richter, one of the most imaginative of German prose-writers, it is said that only two or three illustrations are repeated.

5. The variety which an elegant taste requires is assisted by *variety of delivery.* By this is meant, not only that a versatile delivery is the natural expression of a versatile style, but that it is a powerful auxiliary to the forming of such a style.

<small>Variety of delivery.</small>

A very broad theme is this of *the reciprocal effect of style and elocution.* A monotonous elocution insensibly yet inevitably gives character to the style of one who speaks much in public. A drowsy, drawling, nasal delivery, if such be a speaker's habit, will brood over and suffocate his writing. A brisk, energetic, versatile delivery is an inspiration to the pen. Unconsciously, we form our sentences, choose our collocations of words, adjust the length of our periods, select our rhetorical forms, and even manipulate our vocabulary, as we feel intuitively that we shall utter them in the act of delivery. *You will detect before long, if you care to do so, this silent infusion of the genius of your elocution into your written style.*

<small>Reciprocal effect of style and delivery.</small>

You may first observe it in the proportion of long to short sentences; but no feature of style escapes affinity with delivery. Other things being equal, your style will become what your manner is. Each will grow into fitness to the other.

Therefore variety in delivery will promote variety in style. A flexible voice, various intonation, gesture, and position, will aid the growth of a varied command of oral expression. Horne Tooke even goes so far as to say that *no man can write a good style in prose who is not a good conversationalist.* Mr. Hazlitt adds, "No style is worth a farthing which will not bear comparison with spirited colloquy."

It is true that instances occur which seem to contradict this view. Rapid speakers sometimes write for the press in a crawling style. This is said to have been true of Fox, the English statesman. Drawling speakers also sometimes write vivaciously. But such writers do not write *much* for the purpose of oral delivery. They do not write enough to give their delivery a chance to permeate their style. They either speak extemporaneously, and therefore do not write well for the platform or they do not speak at all, and therefore do not write well for oral utterance. Elocution and written style do not come in contact frequently enough to create the reciprocal sympathy of which mention has been made. *A seeming contradiction.*

An amusing account is given by Lord Macaulay of a criticism by Sheridan upon the style and manner of Fox and Lord Stormont in the British Parliament. Sheridan had returned one morning from the meeting of Parliament, and a friend asked him for the news of the day. He replied that he had enjoyed a laugh over the speeches of those two men. He said that Lord Stormont began by declaring in a slow, solemn, nasal monotone, that "when—he—considered—the enormity—and the—unconstitutional—tendency—of the measures—just—proposed, he was—hurried—away in a—torrent—of passion— *Fox and Lord Stormont.*

and a—whirlwind—of im-pet-u-os-i-ty." Fox he described as rising with a spring to his feet, and beginning with the rapidity of lightning, thus: " Mr. Speaker, such is the *magnitude* such the *importance* such the vital *interest* of the question that I cannot but *implore* I cannot but *adjure* the House to come to it with the utmost *calmness* the utmost *coolness* the utmost *deliberation*."

<small>An analysis of the case of Lord Stormont.</small> This surely does not look much like reciprocal sympathy between manner and style. But scrutinize it carefully, and you will find even in this rare extreme, that such a sympathy is struggling to unite them. What is the fact with Lord Stormont's case? Is it his drawling manner which gives him time to say in what a tempestuous passion he is. He is uttering what he knows to be untrue: a man in a genuine passion does not stop to tell of it. Such a blunder is in perfect keeping with the monotonous, crawling elocution. Note, also, the florid, figurative style in which he speaks of the torrent and the whirlwind, and the carefulness with which he supplies all necessary connectives. These are both exactly the mistakes which one is likely to make who affects the utterance of passion which has no existence. His style and his professed sentiments are inconsistent, but his style and manner are in conspiracy to betray the falseness of the sentiment.

<small>An analysis of the case of Fox.</small> What is the case rhetorically with Fox? Precisely the same. He is, in fact, anxious and impatient: his style and manner combine to reveal this, though the sentiment exhorts the House to be just the reverse. Observe his pithy, literal vocabulary. He does not know whether he is in a whirlwind or not. Lord Stormont did know. Note Fox's compact syntax, indicating his nervous haste by the absence of connectives: " Such is the importance such the magnitude such the vital interest," etc. The style gallops furiously to its goal. Lord Stor-

mont ambled along, sporting with torrents and whirlwinds by the way. Few examples can illustrate a more active affinity between style and manner. Both are more truthfully significant than the sentiment is, of the real state of the writer's mind. Let us not contemn, then, the graces and forces of delivery as mere externals. Some of the subtle influences which give character to discourse have their origin there.

ANALYSIS.

ELEGANCE OF STYLE (CONCLUDED).

I. **Vividness an Element of Elegance of Style.**
  1. Vividness Essential to Beauty.
  2. Vividness Compatible with Delicacy.

II. **The Demands of Vividness.**
  1. Distinctness of Thought.
  2. Sensitiveness of Feeling.
  3. Simplicity of Language.
  4. An Easy Command of Imagery.

III. **Variety an Element of Elegance of Style.**
  1. In general, Variety Essential to Beauty.
  2. In particular, Variety Essential to Beauty of Style.

IV. **Means of Acquiring Variety.**
  1. By Versatility of Thought.
  2. By Frequent Change of Means in Presenting a Subject.
  3. By a Varied Vocabulary and Construction.
  4. By Varied Illustrations.
      (a) 1st Rule. Have no Favorite Illustrations.
      (b) 2d Rule. Have no Favorite Rhetorical Form of Illustration.
  5. By Variety of Delivery.
      A. Reciprocal Influence of Style and Delivery.
      B. Seeming Contradiction of this Reciprocal Influence.
         (a) Fox and Lord Stormont, as Speakers in the House of Parliament.
         (b) The Characteristics of these Speakers Analyzed.

CHAPTER XXII

NATURALNESS OF STYLE

I.—Relation of Naturalness to all Other Qualities of Style.

THE philosophical idea of the "fitness of things" is, in some relations of it, an ultimate idea. We cannot carry analysis beyond it. For some of our convictions we can give no reason other than this—that a thing is, or is not, becoming. It does, or does not, fit into the nature and demands of other things. Style has a quality which expresses this relation of thought as clothed in language. It suggests the interlocking of cogwheels in machinery.

Fitness of things an ultimate idea.

More specifically, naturalness is *that quality by which style expresses the fitness of language to thought, of both thought and language to the speaker, and of thought, language, and speaker to the hearer.* In any complete example of it, it is thus complicated. It extends to all the fundamental elements out of which style grows. It stands related to them as proportion does to architecture. We respond to it, not by saying, "That is forcible, this is beautiful, the other is clear;" but we say, "It is becoming, it fits, the cogs interlock: therefore the movement is without jar or needless friction." Such a quality must obviously depend for its recognition entirely upon the intuitions of good taste. Primarily we do not reason about it: we feel it or we feel the absence of it. Being, as it is, the resultant of qualities

Naturalness and other qualities of style.

of style already discussed, the discussion of it as distinct from those must necessarily involve some repetition.

II.—CHARACTERISTICS OF NATURALNESS.

In what forms chiefly does naturalness of style become perceptible to good taste?

1. In answer, be it first observed, that good taste approves naturalness of style in a *certain fitness of expression to the subject of discourse.* Style has a certain temper, like that of steel. It pervades every particle. This may or may not be becoming; and the question whether it is so, or not, depends often on the simple relations of style to subject. Why is not a volatile style suited to a discourse on immortality? Why is a ponderous style unsuited to a comic song? To ask these questions is to answer them. The jests of the French revolutionists under the knife of the guillotine shock us, and the seriousness of a parody pleases us, for the same reason—the unfitness of things to things. "The Marriage-Ring," the title of one of Jeremy Taylor's sermons, suggests immediately the elegance of style which ought to characterize its treatment. The forty-seventh proposition of Euclid suggests the necessary absence of the qualities of style which "The Marriage-Ring" demands. Do not the opposite subjects "Heaven" and "Hell" compel us, by stress of subject only, to associate with them certain opposites in the style of their discussion? Ruskin contends for the same distinction as fundamental to good painting. He says, "Greatness of style consists first in the habitual choice of *subjects* which involve profound passions. The habitual choice of sacred subjects constitutes a painter, so far forth, one of the highest order."

Fitness of expression to subject of discourse.

Subjects which suggest their treatment.

2. Naturalness of style becomes perceptible to good taste

also, in a *certain fitness of thought and expression to the relations of hearers to the subject.* A painting attributed to Michael Angelo, in one of the galleries of Italy, represents the Virgin Mary standing erect and calm at the foot of the cross, without a tear or other trace of sorrow on her countenance. Artists defend the painting by the theory that the mother of our Lord was supposed to be divinely instructed in the meaning of the crucifixion and the mystery of atonement, and that inspired exaltation overpowered her maternal sorrow. But critics say, in reply, that this theory of the painter was true only to him. The painting does not explain it to the perplexed spectator. Spectators cannot be supposed to originate it. They must look at the artist's work from their position, not from his. A Protestant observer especially, who sees in the Virgin mother only a woman, not superior, perhaps not equal, to some others of her sex, cannot be supposed to divine the secret of the painter's theology.

<small>Fitness of thought and expression to the relations of hearers to the subject.</small>

<small>Michael Angelo's Virgin Mary.</small>

This may serve to illustrate one of the limitations which good taste imposes upon the style of discourse—that it should be adjusted to the relations of the audience to the subject in hand. It must express truth to their range and quality of conception: otherwise, it is an unnatural style, as much so as if it expressed a falsehood. Indeed, unnaturalness in this form may amount to falseness of impression. Refraction of truth may be equivalent to untruth. When no untruth is uttered, the impression of truth may be a failure, through the speaker's failure to appreciate the prepossessions, or prejudices, or ignorance of his hearers.

3. Further: naturalness of style becomes perceptible to good taste in a certain *fitness of discourse to the relations of the speaker to his subject.* The principle here in view may be best illustrated by a few examples of its violation. It is violated, for instance, by the *dogmatic style.* Not often by

a glaring conscious usurpation of authority, but by an indefinite undertone of discourse, a speaker may give to it a magisterial sound. He dictates when he ought only to instruct. He assumes what he ought to prove. Sometimes the evil consists not so much in what is said as in how it is said. *Fitness of discourse to the relations of the speaker to his subject.* A certain gait in the style betrays a swagger or a lordliness of stride which awakens resistance. Franklin, in criticising one of the appeals of the American Colonies to the king for a redress of grievances, advised a more manly style. Said he, "Firmness carries weight : a *strut* never does." When we detect the "strut" in discourse, we are instinctively aroused to cavil and to criticise.

III.—CHARACTERISTICS OF UNNATURALNESS.

1. Over against the form of unnaturalness just observed, is another, which may be termed the *apologetic style.* The tone of discourse in this case is apologetic, not for the subject, but for the speaker. *The apologetic style.* By explicit or implied confessions of incompetence, by deprecations of criticism, by the want of positive opinions, by the intimation of doubts, by a style which marks the want of mastery, a speaker may betray a want of confidence in his own ability, and therefore in his own right, to speak on the subject in hand. In the public speech, ability and authority are proportioned to each other. Might makes right. If, therefore, standing in the place of an instructor, the speaker shrinks from the prerogatives and responsibilities of an instructor, his style will disclose this. He will not rise to the level of his theme, and handle it as one who knows. A downcast air is given to his discussion which tempts a cold-blooded hearer to ask him by what authority he assumes to speak at all. Style is susceptible of a quality corresponding to the blush of a diffident man.

It deserves note, that audiences are not flattered by this apologetic treatment. They may give to it their pity, but not their respect. They bear with less impatience the dogmatic diction. Men love to be addressed confidently, respectfully indeed, but fearlessly. We would rather be browbeaten than to be fawned upon. We feel more respect for impudence than we do for imbecility. We respect a pugilist more than a coward.

<small>The audience and the apologetic style.</small>

2. One other form of this kind of unnatural discourse may be termed the *apathetic style*. The best description which can be given of some speakers is that they are apathetic as opposed to sympathetic. They manifest no sense of personal subjection to the truths the declare. They seem to feel no sense of the power of truth, and therefore no sympathy with hearers of quickened sensibilities. They speak it as a being from a superior world might speak.

<small>The apathetic style.</small>

The verdict of an audience upon such discourse is the most severe retribution that can fall on the head of a living man. They say to the speaker, "You have no heart. Your very fidelity in speech is grounded on your want of sympathy with us in feeling."

In opposition to all these forms of discourse a natural style requires a just, temperate, manly appreciation, on the speaker's part, of his own personal relations to the truth he utters. If he has this in living force, it will make itself felt in his discourse. He will not express it by conscious effort and in chosen words: it will express itself. His style will breathe it forth, like the exhalation of a spice-plant.

IV.—ADAPTATION OF NATURALNESS TO ORAL DISCOURSE.

Naturalness of style, again, becomes perceptible to good taste in a certain fitness of expression *to oral discourse*. The oral style of continuous discourse is distinct from that of the press on the one hand, and from that of conversation on the other. Precisely what it is which constitutes the peculiarity of the oral style, criticism cannot easily define. But in any striking example of it we detect several features.

1. One is *the predominance of concrete over abstract words in its vocabulary.* Oral discourse is essentially pictorial in its nature. It abounds in words which are images, in words which are things. It is opposed to that style which throws the whole burden of speech upon the literal truthfulness of abstract phraseology. It denies the necessity of this in the discussion of any subjects which are proper themes of oral discourse. It is specially hostile to that predilection for abstract phrase which leads a speaker, and more frequently a writer, to fear obvious expression. *Predominance of concrete expression.*

An eminent German philosopher is said to have rewritten some pages of his manuscript in the revision of it for the press, because, upon reading them to a company of friends, he found them intelligible at a single hearing. He recast those pages into a more recondite diction, on the ground, that, if his meaning were so obvious as to be understood by a hearer, the class of readers whom he aimed to reach would not deem his work worthy of their notice. Does not this deserve to be ranked with those affectations which have been elsewhere denominated the *cant* of literature? The style of nature in oral speech is very simple in its aims. It repudiates all forms of affectation. It betrays no fear of being understood. It shows no reluctance to being childlike in its love for pictures. The more that a style spoken to the ear can have of the resources which make thought visible to the eye, the more potently does it achieve the objects of oral utterance.

Affectation of the German philosopher.

2. Again: the oral style *inclines to a large excess of simplicity over involution in the construction of sentences.*

<small>Simplicity in construction of sentences.</small>

We are all sensible of the difference, in this respect, between the style of the press and the style of speech, when we compare our own styles constructed by the two methods. The very same materials, in the two methods of expression, we throw into totally different constructions. We extemporize in shorter sentences than we use in printed discourse, in more simply framed sentences, with less of inversion and introversion, and suspension of the sense. The difference is so great, that it affects the organs of speech. These are commonly less wearied by extemporaneous speech than by the delivery of a written address. Physicians well understand this. For the relief of bronchitis they often advise preachers to abandon their manuscripts in the pulpit.

3. One other feature in the style natural to oral discourse is *the dramatic quality, which makes the hearer active in the discussion of a subject.*

<small>The dramatic quality of oral discourse.</small>

This partakes of the nature of colloquy in effect, though not colloquy in form. You have doubtless witnessed, perhaps experienced, the power of this feature of style upon an audience. Did you never feel in listening to a speech as if the speaker were questioning you, and you were involuntarily responding? Did you never seem to be yourself the questioner, and he the respondent? Did you never carry on a silent dispute with a speaker through a whole discourse which commanded in you the interest of dissent.

These effects of powerful discourse in genuine oral style may be often witnessed, and sometimes evinced by visible signs.

<small>Whitefield and the sailor.</small>

The sailor, who in listening to Whitefield's description of a wreck forgot himself, and in response to the preacher's impassioned cry, " What more can he do ? " answered, " For God's sake take to the life-boat!" illustrated that which we have probably all of us felt, in less degree, when speakers have made us parties in their discussion, and thrown upon us the responsibility of its application. The illusions of the stage never gave to Garrick and Kean such advantage for moving an audience to the responsive mood as some speakers have found in their mastery of a dramatic diction. In this variety of their success, we pronounce such speakers *natural* orators. It is only, that, in obeying the natural intuitions of an orator, they practise as well the canons of criticism and the laws of good taste in adjusting style to the object of oral speech.

V.—Means of Acquiring Naturalness of Style.

The views we have considered respecting the cognizance of naturalness of style by good taste suggest further the inquiry, By what means may a natural style be most effectually acquired? These may, for the most part, be named with brief remark, because they are not recondite, and they are found chiefly in certain things which lie back of the study of style as such. They are not greatly involved in the *minutiæ* of criticism.

1. You will anticipate me in mentioning as the first of these means of gaining naturalness of style *the habit of mastering subjects of discourse.* Let the word "habit" be emphasized in this statement. Style depends more upon the permanent *state* of a writer's mind than upon any expedients of discipline, or moods of composition. It has always its foundation in a speaker's character. What the man is, his style will be. Naturalness especially is a fruit and a sign of a certain state of mental discipline and a certain habit of mental action, which will not permit a man to write or speak upon a subject which is not well mastered. We do not walk naturally

The habit of mastering subjects of discourse.

in utter darkness. Neither do we speak naturally of that of which the chief thing we are thoroughly conscious of is our ignorance, or our bungling knowledge. Mastery is needed to create ease of movement. Style must have the movement of conquest, not of struggle. Says Ruskin, "Without absolute grasp of the whole subject, there is no good painting." Partial conception is no conception.

2. Another tributary to this quality of style is *self-forgetfulness in the act of composing*. Unnaturalness in almost any form of it may spring from a want of composure. A speaker may be master of his theme, yet not master of himself, and therefore not at ease about himself. In such a mood he speaks nervously. A constant strain is manifest in his style. He speaks as if he were constantly thinking of his style. Its movement is like that of one walking on tiptoe. The remedy is the habit of self-forgetfulness in composing, whether with pen or tongue. That state and habit of mind which led Isocrates to spend fifteen years in adjusting the sentences of his Panegyric could not fail to drill all nature out of it. One might as well hope to acquire natural vision by twisting and straining for fifteen years to get a sight of one's own eyeballs.

<small>Self-forgetfulness in the act of composing.</small>

3. A natural style is assisted by an *absorbing interest in the aim of a discourse*. Note briefly a distinction between interest in the details of a discourse and interest in its aim. An example of one of these will best illustrate both. In a speech delivered in the American Congress by the elder Josiah Quincy, on the repeal of the embargo laid upon our commerce with Great Britain before the war of 1812, we find the following passage, viz.:

<small>An absorbing interest in the aim of a discourse.</small>

"An embargo liberty was never cradled in Massachusetts. Our liberty was not so much a mountain- as a sea-nymph. She was free as air. She could swim, or she could run.

The ocean was her cradle. Our fathers met her as she came like a goddess of beauty from the waves. They caught her as she was sporting on the beach. They courted her as she was spreading her nets upon the rocks." In this strain the orator proceeds. Mark now the quality of this style as related to the professed aim of the whole speech. What was that aim? The ships of the merchants of Boston and Salem and Newburyport and New London and New York were rotting in their harbors. The aim of the legislation advocated by Mr. Quincy was to remove the embargo, and send those ships to sea. Was his mind intent on that in the passage here quoted? Did this passage assist that aim, or could it naturally do so? Not at all. The paragraph is vivacious; its metaphors are novel; its diction is compact and clear; it is a specimen of what passed in those days for fine oratory. But it was quite too fine for the sober and rather rough work which the orator had before him. His interest just then, all the enthusiasm of his mind in the business, was expended on the embellishment of his style. He was thinking of the beauty of it as a work of art. He was speaking to Harvard College and its environs, not to the Southern Congressmen whom it was his business to win over to the commercial interests of New England. If his own fortune had been embarked in one of those rotting ships, and he was intent with his whole soul on saving it by a vote of the Congress, he would have found something to say more to the purpose than courting a sea-nymph on the rocks.

This illustrates the importance to natural discourse of an absorbing interest in the *aim* of it as distinct from the development and embellishment of its details. *Keep always the practical object of the discourse in sight; keep it close at hand; let the shadow of it cover the whole structure from beginning to end.* This unity of aim is itself nature. It will often give to an author the most essential element of power, when many other elements are wanting. Again we involuntarily disclose the secret of its power when we call it *natural* eloquence.

4. One additional means of acquiring a natural style remains to be noticed: it is *practice in composition*. Did you ever observe that a young man's chirography, originally stiff, awkward, angular, bearing every mark of juvenility, becomes often, in the process of time, flowing and business-like, through mere practice in rapid writing? Though it may not gain the kind of finish which belongs to the engraving of the copy-book, yet you pronounce it superior to that, because it is a *natural* hand. It expresses somewhat of the individuality of the writer.

<small>Practice in composition.</small>

Similar to this is the indefinable elegance which style may receive from large practice in composing. In the history of the fine arts, the most illustrious painters are those who have painted most abundantly. Ruskin says, "Of two touches as nearly as possible alike in other respects, the quickest will invariably be the best." Of perfect execution, velocity is an invariable quality. This is, in part, the explanation of the fact that large practice in composing tends to create a perfect style: it is because much composing necessarily involves rapid composing. It does not follow that the most voluminous writers will necessarily be the most perfect writers. But it does follow that practice in this, as in other arts, will re-act upon natural genius, and develop it in natural work.

Other things being equal, the most prolific writer will be the most natural writer. The man who writes the largest quantity with critical care will write most naturally. In many instances in which other requisites to a natural style exist, writers fail in this quality for no reason other than that they have not written enough to write naturally. They have not become acquainted with nature. Composing was a drudgery,

<small>The prolific writer the natural writer.</small>

and they allowed it to remain such by avoiding it when it was not compulsory.

Izaak Walton wrote for the love of writing. Charles Lamb wrote all his works for recreation in the intervals of leisure from his clerkly toil in the East India House. Probably not a page that he ever wrote was a drudgery to him. Walter Scott, till his brain gave way, composed always in a glee of enthusiasm. His daily contributions to the press he *captured* with the ardor of a sportsman. He often hesitated between the two — whether to sit down at his desk, or to go out among the hills with his dog and gun; for he enjoyed both his pen and his gun with equal zest. He gained this pleasurable ease in composition by long and constant practice. He used to involve himself in literary engagements purposely, that they might crowd him. He said that he "never wrote so well, or felt so well, as when the press was thundering at his heels with the demand for more copy."

Izaak Walton.
Charles Lamb.
Walter Scott.

The same phenomenon is seen in the history of Shakespeare's authorship. Scarcely any other feature in his professional life is so marvellous as the amount of his work and its rapidity. His working life was compressed into about twenty-three years. During that time he gave to the English stage an average of two dramas a year. This, for such productions as his, and continued through a series of years, was a miracle of intellectual fertility. From the age of thirty years to that of fifty-three, Shakespeare's mind must have lived in a state of habitual production.

Shakespeare.

This prolific state, so far from degrading the quality of production, elevates and enriches it. As the force of a cannon-ball is augmented by its velocity, so the mental power of composition is reduplicated by rapidity of creation, if regulated by good taste. This mental condition, in which composition becomes a delight, a necessity, a demand of nature upon a full mind, is a habit which you cannot acquire but by large practice. Thinking will never give it to you. Study of rhetorical treatises will never create it. General reading will never do it. Criticism of the works of others or of your own is powerless of itself to meet the necessity. You must write and speak, speak and write, till pen and tongue move spontaneously and joyously.

ANALYSIS.

NATURALNESS OF STYLE.

I. Relation of Naturalness to all Other Qualities of Style.

II. Characteristics of Naturalness.
   1. Expression fitted to the Subject of Discourse.
   2. Thought and Expression fitted to the Relations of Hearers to the Subject.
   3. Discourse fitted to the Relations of the Speaker to his Subject.

III. Characteristics of Unnaturalness.
   1. An Apologetic Style.
   2. An Apathetic Style.

IV. Adaptation of Naturalness to Oral Discourse.
   1. Predominance of Concrete Expression.
   2. Simplicity of Construction of Sentences.
   3. The Dramatic Quality in Oral Discourse.

V. Means of Acquiring Naturalness of Style.
   1. By the *Habit* of Mastering Subjects of Discourse.
   2. By Self-forgetfulness in the Act of Composing.
   3. By an Absorbing Interest in the Aim of a Discourse.
   4. By Practice in Composition.

PART II

PRACTICAL EXERCISES

IN THE

FUNDAMENTAL QUALITIES OF ENGLISH STYLE

PRACTICAL EXERCISES

IN THE

FUNDAMENTAL QUALITIES OF ENGLISH STYLE

In this Part of the text-book, exercises, illustrating every important suggestion and direction of the Chapters on Purity, Precision, Perspicuity, and Energy in the First Part, are provided as a help to the practical mastery of these qualities of English style. Some of the exercises, without any assigned preparation, can be used in the class-room for immediate illustration of the subject of the hour. Others can be prepared by the text-book alone. The larger number and most valuable part of the exercises, however, is arranged, as is said in the preface, to lead the student to something like independent study in his work in English. This supposes a daily examination of the dictionaries—Webster and Worcester especially, because the most accessible to the larger number of students—and a frequent examination of other books of reference. In this way the student is expected to form his judgments, for which he is to give good reasons when tested by other members of his class and by his teacher.

It is hoped that not only with the study of Precision, but with each lesson assigned in the text-book throughout the course, the student will be required to prepare at least a number of synonyms by reference to the dictionaries. The value of this work as an aid to Precision and Energy of Style, has been elsewhere suggested. But provided the class is not able to do much work outside of the text-book, the exercise in synonyms, or something of a kindred nature, should be required that the student may be helped to form the habit of consulting the dictionaries and other books of recognized authority on matters of speech.

EXERCISES IN PURITY OF STYLE.*

CHAPTERS II., III., IV., V., AND VI.

OBSOLETE AND OBSOLESCENT WORDS.

THE student will apply the test which James Russell Lowell gives, page 20, to see whether or not the following words, marked *obsolete* or *obsolescent* in Webster's International Dictionary, are permissible archaisms:

Abscond, to	(used transitively).
Addict, to	(to make suitable).
Admire, to	(to wonder at).
Advantage, to	(to avail one's self of).
Buckle, to	(to yield, give way).
Collide, to	(used transitively).
Commodity	(a quantity of goods).
Concealment	(a secret).
Conceited	(fanciful).
Delineature	(delineation).
Disremember, to	(to forget).
Discord, to	(to disagree).
Down, to	(to bring down).
Divers	(diverse).
Drave	(imperfect of drive).
Eat (ĕt)	(ate).
Ecstasy	(madness).
Example, to	(to instance).
Exploit, to	(to achieve).
Famoused	(renowned).
Fartherance	(furtherance).
Farthermore	(furthermore).

* For Exercises in Purity of Style, without reference to dictionaries and other books, see pages 229-247.

Figured	(figurative).
Forbiddance	(prohibition).
Great-hearted	(high-spirited).
Habited	(accustomed).
Imbursement	(act of imbursing).
Incidently	(incidentally).
Indefensive	(defenseless).
Inexpected	(unexpected).
Justiceable	(belonging to a court of justice).
Kind	(natural instinct).
Leany	(lean).
Lowlily	(humbly).
Lug, to	(to move slowly).
Mid	(middle).
Misdeem, to	(to misjudge).
Mockish	(mock).
Musculosity	(muscularity).
Naught	(vile).
Neighbor, to	(used intransitively).
Outerly	(utterly).
Overmore	(moreover).
Overmost	(above all others).
Prenticeship	(apprenticeship).
Profanate, to	(to profane).
Rejournment	(adjournment).
Requitement	(requital).
Restiff	(restive).
Southren	(Southern).
Suspensely	(in suspense).
Thereto	(besides).
Unactive	(inactive).
Unvaluable	(invaluable).

Contractions and Abbreviations.

Examine the following list, and point out which of the words or phrases are vulgarisms, and which in certain forms of composition and speech have the countenance of reputable writers and speakers.

Daily	for	daily paper.
Editorial	"	editorial article.
Elective	"	elective study,
Electric	"	electric car.
Freight	"	freight car.
Governments	"	government securities.
Obituary	"	obituary article.
Optional	"	optional course of study.
Postal	"	postal card.
Day before yesterday	"	the day before yesterday.
Democracy	"	democratic party.
Honorable	"	the Honorable.
Photo	"	photograph.
Prof.	"	Professor.
Reverend	"	the Reverend.
Sensation	"	a noteworthy event.
Cotemporary		(contemporary).
Captain, to		(to be the captain).
Clerk, to		(to work as a clerk).
Electrocute, to		(to put to death by electricity).
Lotion, to		(to apply a lotion).
Referee, to		(to be the referee).
Suicide, to		(to commit suicide).
Umpire, to		(to be the umpire).

E'en, e'er, ere, o'er, of't, 'gan, 'neath, ne'er, 'twixt, ain't, don't, doesn't, exams, gents, gym, hain't, ma'am, pants, wa'rn't.

Expansion of Old Words.

Apply to these examples of expansion of old words the test which was applied to contractions and abbreviations.

Agriculturalist	for	agriculturist.
Casuality	"	casualty.
Confliction	"	conflict.

Clarionet	for	clarinet.
Deputize, to	"	to depute.
Dentrifrice	"	dentifrice.
Downwards	"	downward.
Effectuate, to	"	to effect.
Experimentalize, to	"	to experiment.
Forehanded	"	forehand.
Forwards	"	forward.
Grieviance	"	grievance.
Illy	"	ill.
Issuance	"	issue.
Jeopardize, to	"	to jeopard.
Leniency	"	lenity.
Towards	"	toward.
Unbeknown	"	unknown.
Underhanded	"	underhand.
Upwards	"	upward.
Admit of, to	"	to admit.
Ascend up, to	"	to ascend.
Crushed out	"	crushed.
End up, to	"	to end.
Fall down, to	"	to fall.
Open up, to	"	to open.
Remember of, to	"	to remember.
Rise up, to	"	to rise.
Sink down, to	"	to sink.
Smell of, to	"	to smell.

New Words.

Professor Earle in his "English Prose" gives, with other words, the following list, which has been issued as he says "mostly in the time of the last generation."

Test each of these words by applying the six principles given in Chapter IV. and decide whether or not the word is to be accepted as good English. Answer also Professor Whitney's three questions: "is the word called for? is it accordant with the analogies of the language? is it offered or backed by good authority?"

Appointee	Walter Bagehot.
Artistry	P. G. Hamerton.
Ashamedness	S. Wilberforce.
Belieffulness	Arthur Hugh Clough, 1853.
Carnalization	Frances Power Cobbe.
Criticaster	James Payn.
Dampen, to	Mark Twain.
Dispeace	*The London Times*, 1878.
Expertise	*The London Times*, 1876.
Fad	
Featureliness	Walter Bagehot.
Finality	*The Guardian*, 1851.
Intellectualist	James Baldwin Brown.
International	
Jural	Sir H. S. Maine.
Kaleidoscopic	*The Spectator*, 1874.
Knowingness	George Eliot.
Lovingness	Alexander Ewing.
Loveable	*The London Times*, 1885.
Mannerist	*The Saturday Review*, 1874.
Millionaire	*The Spectator*, 1873.
Neolithic	Sir John Lubbock.
Northness	Dr. I. I. Hayes.
Objective	The opposite of subjective. S. T. Coleridge.
Open-mindedness	*The Daily News*, 1876.
Optimism	*The Spectator*, 1874.
Palmary	F. C. Cook.
Pedantocracy	Professor Bain.
Prigdom	Walter Besant.
Quietude	*The London Times*, 1877.
Racial	*Nineteenth Century*, 1878.
Rascaldom	J. A. Froude.
Rationalistic	H. Parker, 1885.
Realism	A. C. Swinburne, 1888.
Ritualist	E. B. Pusey, 1874.

Sacerdotalism	Earl Russell.
Sanitation	1877.
Saxon-dom	Carlyle.
Scientist	*Blackwood's Magazine*, 1874.
Scoundreldom	J. A. Froude.
Seamy	*The London Times*, 1884.
Seascape	*Macmillan's Magazine*, 1876.
Settledness	James Bryce, 1877.
Solidarity	George P. Marsh, 1860.
Storiologist	*The Academy*, 1886.
Transliteration	F. W. Farrar.
Unknowable	*The Church Quarterly Review*, 1875.
Unyieldingness	T. A. Trollope.
Uphillward	F. W. Farrar.
Vaticanism	*The Hour*, 1875.

Apply the same principles to the following words which Webster's International Dictionary marks *recent:*

Eliminate, to	(to obtain by separating, to deduce).
Entrain, to	(to put aboard, or to go aboard).
Exploit, to	(to utilize, or to make the means of illegitimate gain).
Humanitarian	(a philanthropist).
Outsider	(a person not belonging to the party mentioned).

By reference to standard dictionaries see whether or not the critics are right who call these words *recent:*

Acquests,	Immigrant.
Evolute,	Proclivity.
	Productivity.

AMERICANISMS.

The following words, which Webster's International Dictionary gives as *Americanisms*, are to be examined that it may be seen whether they are of American or of English birth, and, if of American birth, whether or not they are a provincial necessity, and, therefore, good English words.

Some of these words the student will do well to examine by reference not only to other standard dictionaries, but also to De Vere's "Americanisms," Bartlett's "Dictionary of Americanisms," and the Glossary of James Russell Lowell's "Biglow Papers."

Appreciate	(to raise in value).
Arctic	(a warm overshoe).
Barge	(a large omnibus).
Blatherskite	(a blusterer).
Boggle, to	(to make a botch of).
Book-store	(a bookseller's shop, Eng.).
Bunk	(a wooden bed).
Bureau	(a chest of drawers for clothes).
Caption	(a heading).
Carry	(a portage).
Cinch	(a strong saddle-girth).
Claim, a or the	(the thing claimed).
Clerk	(an assistant in a shop or store).
Coast, to	(to slide down hill).
Comforter	(a woollen tippet).
Conduct, to	(to behave).
Conductor	(a person having charge of a public conveyance).
Cook-book	(a cookery book).
Corn-dodger	(a cake made of the meal of Indian corn and baked under the embers).
Dicker, to	(to barter).
Dime	(the tenth of a dollar).
Domestics	(cotton goods of home manufacture).
Dump, to	(to unload by tilting the cart).
Eagle	(a gold coin).

Emptyings	(yeast).
Firkin	(a small wooden vessel).
Forehanded	(in easy circumstances).
Gums	(overshoes).
Help	(a domestic servant).
Hoosier	(a nickname of an inhabitant of Indiana).
Inaugural	(an address).
Inflationist	(a person who favors a very large issue of paper money).
Jayhawker	(a guerilla).
Kuklux	(a secret political organization in the South after the civil war).
Lobby, to	(to influence the votes of members of a legislative body).
Lobbyist	(a member of the lobby).
Local	(a train accommodating a certain district).
Location	(that which is located).
Logy	(heavy in motion or thought).
Northerner	(an inhabitant of the Northern States).
Praise meeting	(a religious service of song).
Raider	(a person who engages in a raid).
Renewedly	(once more).
Rily	(roily).
Rooster	(a cock).
Scrimp	(a miser).
Settle, to	(to establish in the pastoral office).
Set-back	(a counter current).
Sidewalk	(a foot pavement).
Slip	(a pew in a church).
Southerner	(an inhabitant of the Southern States).
Veteranize	(to re-enlist for service as a soldier).

American and English Usage of Words.

The following words which American usage largely substitutes for words in use in England, the student is to examine for approval or criticism by reference to the dictionaries, and to Richard Grant White's "Words and their Uses," and De Vere's "Americanisms."

Baggage	for	luggage.
Bring	"	fetch.
Backward and Forward	"	forward and forth.
Crackers	"	biscuit.
Elevator	"	lift.
Fleshy	"	stout.
Loan, to	"	to lend.
Mail, to	"	to post.
Pitcher	"	jug.
Preserves	"	sweets.
Railroad	"	railway.
Raise, to (corn, wheat, etc.)	"	to grow.
Sick	"	ill.
Stage	"	coach.
Store	"	shop.
Street railroad	"	tramway.
Stylish	"	smart.

Words Condemned by Verbal Critics.

These words deserve especial attention. As many of them are used by reputable writers and speakers, the student will learn by the careful consideration of these words something more important than which of them offends purity of style. He will come to know as in no other way, at this period in his rhetorical training, the relative force of usage and of the laws of the language. In the examination of these words he should, therefore, consult, besides the dictionary, such works as Gould's "Good English," Alford's "The Queen's English," Moon's "The Dean's English," Hodgson's "Errors in the use of English," Earle's "English Prose," and especially White's "Words and their Uses," "Everyday English," and Fitzedward Hall's "Modern English."

It will be a profitable exercise to make the propriety of the use of some of these words or forms—as *reliable, standpoint, is being done*, etc.—the subject of a written discussion, in which members of the class shall, according to choice, present the affirmative and the negative side of the question.

Above	(as an adverb).
Advocate	(as a verb).
Allow, to	(to accede to an opinion).
Alternatives	(referring to more than one).
Antiquarian	(for antiquary).
Anyhow	(for in any manner).
Assemblyman	(for member of assembly).
Authoress	(for author).
Certain, certainly	(with more or most).
Champion	(as a verb).
Commence	(for begin).
Complete, completely	(with more or most).
Congressman	(for member of Congress).
Defalcate, to	(to embezzle).
Divine	(a clergyman).
Dress	(gown).
Execute, to	(to put to death a human being).
Experience	(as a verb).
Extempore	(as an adjective).
First-rate	(of the highest excellence).
Folks	(folk).
Graduates	(is graduated).
Gratuitous	(without reason, unfounded).

Ice cream	(iced cream).
Ice water	(iced water).
Infallible	(inevitable).
Is being done	(is doing).
Juxtapose, to	(for to place in juxtaposition).
Less	(used for number instead of fewer).
Mistaken be, to	(to mistake).
Now	(used as an adjective).
Noways	(nowise).
Official	(officer).
Partially	(partly).
Poetess	(for poet).
Present, to	(to introduce).
Progress	(as a verb).
Reliable	(for trustworthy).
Remit	(to send money in payment).
Restive	(for restless).
Spending time	(passing time).
Standpoint	(for point of view).
Then	(used as an adjective).

COLLOQUIAL WORDS, CANT, AND SLANG.

The following words, marked *colloquial* in Webster's International Dictionary, are to be examined so that the student may see which are permissible in informal oral discourse, and which are always to be avoided as vulgarisms as are the words marked *Cant* or *Slang*.

COLLOQUIAL WORDS.

Aggravate, to	(to irritate).
Bosh	(empty talk).
Bounce, to	(to eject violently).
Brassy	(impudent).
Breeches	(trousers).
Buzz, to	(to talk incessantly).

Coach, to	(to train by special instruction).
Chuck, to	(to pitch).
Clip	(a blow with the hand).
Cotton, to	(to make friends with).
Cracked	(crack-brained).
Cute	(sharp, acute).
Dangerous	(in a condition of danger).
Den	(a snug retreat).
Disgruntle, to	(to anger).
Doctor, to	(to repair).
Downs	(a state of depression).
Drummer	(a commercial traveller).
Engineer	(to manage).
Feminine	(a woman).
Fib, to	(to speak falsely).
Fight	(pugnacity).
Figure, to	(to scheme).
Fishy	(improbable).
Fizzle	(a failure).
Fry	(a state of excitement).
Gallowses	(a pair of braces).
Getter-up	(a person who contrives anything).
Gush	(effusive speech).
Gusher	(a person who gushes).
Happen in, to	(to happen to come in).
Headachy	(afflicted with headache).
Heft	(weight).
Hunk	(a large piece).
Kelter	(proper condition).
Kinky	(crotchety).
Know-all	(a wiseacre).
Laze, to	(to waste time in sloth).
Locate, to	(to settle).
Lot	(a great deal).
Miff, to	(to offend slightly).
Moonshiny	(moonlight).
Muffish	(awkward).
Nag, to	(to tease in a small way).

Natty	(spruce).
Notion	(an inclination).
Offish	(shy).
Outside	(to the extreme limit).
Patter, to	(to chatter).
Peeper	(the eye).
Pokerish	(adapted to cause fear).
Pull	(the act of rowing).
Railroading	(managing a railway).
Rattle, to	(to disconcert).
Rattle, to	(to talk idly).
Reckon, to	(to think).
Right along	(continuously).
Right away, or right off	(at once).
Roomer	(lodger).
Rubbers	(overshoes).
Rugged	(vigorous).
Run	(a trip).
Run, to	(to manage).
Scamp, to	(to do work imperfectly).
Scare	(a fright).
Scoot, to	(to go hastily away).
Seedy	(shabby looking).
Set back	(a repulse).
Set out	(a display).
Settle	(to pay).
Shaky	(easily shaken).
Shaver	(a boy).
Ship, to	(to get rid of).
Shoppy	(pertaining to shops).
Sight	(a great number).
Slam-bang	(with a slamming noise).
Sleeper	(a sleeping car).
Snake, to	(to drag or pull).
Spin, to	(to move swiftly).
Startlish	(skittish).
Stem-winder	(a stem-winding watch).
Stop, to	(to stay).
Tantrum	(a fit of ill-humor).

Teeny	(tiny).
Teetotal	(total).
Ten-strike	(a decisive act).
Thick	(intimate).
Thumping	(heavy).
Tip	(a fee).
Upcountry	(inland).
Vim	(energy).
Weazeny	(shrivelled).
Wire, to	(to telegraph).
Yank, to	(to jerk).
Younker	(a young person).

CANT AND SLANG.

Boodle	(bribe money).
Boss, to	(to act the boss).
Candidating	(the preaching of a clergyman as a candidate).
Doctor, to	(to adulterate).
Enthuse, to	(to make enthusiastic).
Glim	(light).
Greek	(a knave).
Kid	(a young child).
Mossback	(an old partisan).
Mugwump	(an Independent).
Pipelaying	(making political combinations).
Plug	(a worthless horse).
Pull	(an advantage).
Rummy	(strange).
Rope in, to	(to decoy).
Run into the ground, to	(to overdo).
Resurrect, to	(to disinter or reanimate).
Retiracy	(retirement).
Scalawag	(a scapegrace).
Shag-rag	(the ragged part of the community).
Shine	(a fancy).

Sockdolager	(that which ends a matter).
Sorehead	(a person disaffected by failure of some kind).
Splurge	(a great display).
Sport	(a sportsman).
Swell	(a showy person).
Swell	(having characteristics of rank and importance).

Errors in the Use of Prepositions.

The following examples of the wrong use of prepositions are given that the student may have occasion to consult the valuable catalogue of verbs and the prepositions to be used with them, in the Preface to Worcester's Unabridged Dictionary:

1. He is accused with a grave offence.
2. It is not agreeable for him to meet his old acquaintances.
3. He is angry with his ill-treatment.
4. I connect this line to that.
5. The wives of the soldiers were frightened with the announcement.
6. He is too greedy for popularity.
7. He is destined for high service.
8. May I ask from you a favor?
9. He is yoked to goodness itself.
10. It is made with good material.
11. I hope that it is consonant with your wishes.
12. He has a dislike for his captain.
13. The child's antipathy for the man is strange.
14. There is need for more help.
15. He sympathizes now for his rival.
16. He bargained about the property for a long time.
17. The decision is acceptable with most of the heirs.
18. It is something peculiar with this stream.
19. What larger incentive for his best efforts could the man have?
20. Is this disagreeable for you.

21. He truly repents for his evil influence.
22. The instruction is not adapted for such pupils.
23. He is possessed with a large estate.
24. He is a witness for the truth.
25. This I know will be a cure for the difficulty.
26. The child will die from the disease.
27. Is he emulous for honors?
28. The more a man gives for this cause the larger will be his ultimate reward.
29. He made an apology of what he had done.
30. One element of the school did not assimilate with the other.
31. He is descended of a good family.
32. She is careless with her valuables.
33. He concedes with my proposition.
34. The man grappled at him.
35. He is overwhelmed in trouble.
36. They mingle in good society.
37. He does not confide with me.

Miscellaneous Errors.

In the following examples, the student will name the error in the use of the italicized word or phrase as a *Barbarism*, a *Solecism*, or an *Impropriety*, and substitute for it the proper word or phrase. These examples will be useful as a means to a general review of earlier studies in English. With a large number of common errors in the use of words, the examples include the mistakes in elementary grammar which experience in examining students for admission to college, not to speak of what is often heard later in their extemporaneous and sometimes even in their prepared work, has shown to need faithful attention until correct habits of speech are formed.

1. He has tried to *resurrect* popular feeling, but the people do not *enthuse*.
2. In discussing this matter he *plead* that the change had succeeded elsewhere.

3. I *would* have liked to *have asked* him about his brother.
4. *You* speaking of it, reminds me of the occurrence.
5. It grows *everywheres* here.
6. His manner was *some* improved after a few weeks in the school.
7. I maintain, *firstly*, that it is the safest course for the party.
8. It is with *those* sort of plants that he succeeds.
9. *Thusly*, it follows from what has been said.
10. The decision was more *unanimous* than was expected.
11. He was treated *illy* by the other workmen.
12. His statement is now *proven* to be false.
13. Whichever way he *lead* I followed.
14. I knew of *him* succeeding once.
15. The *seldom* use of it.
16. He is not *as* tall as his brother.
17. I hoped to get *quite a* number of names.
18. *Among* this class you will find some good students.
19. The *catcher's* accident.
20. *It's* success is sure.
21. He is like a beast of prey *who* destroys without mercy.
22. A high spirited girl *like* her mother was.
23. I do not remember *of* saying that he was there.
24. The severity of all these diseases *depend* on their early treatment.
25. I *promise* you that we could not have arranged a better trip for the same time.
26. After the failure of all other subjects to interest, this nauseating scandal was brought *on the carpet*.
27. This philanthropic tendency has interfered with his daily *avocation*.
28. A *capacious* hole made the boat useless.
29. Exercise physical, mental and moral *are* essential to the best development.
30. *Our country's* great territory.
31. Is this *your's?*
32. I have *constantly* met him going to town.
33. At the same time I *were* speaking to you.
34. Are you confident that he *shall* succeed?
35. He *drunk* the water with feverish thirst.

36. The tornado *decimated* the orchard leaving scarcely a tree upright.

37. It is a report that should be wholly *discounted*.

38. *Judson's* the butcher.

39. A *female* has often governed England.

40. What was the *future* career of Aaron Burr, we know.

41. I have a *limited* acquaintance.

42. For a *lengthened* period in the latter part of his life he was a helpless invalid.

43. He *partook* of his dinner alone.

44. *Prolific* hailstones have visited us this season.

45. Since competition began in that line of furniture such articles can be bought at a *limited* price.

46. That is the student *who* I gave the book to.

47. Why did you *adopt* that route?

48. I was told of *him* winning the case.

49. Hardly had that disease left me *than* this attacked me.

50. He is now quite *well*, but hopes to be *entirely* well before he returns.

51. My confidence in him is so *implicit* that I shall make no inquiries.

52. He had *rode* twenty miles to meet me at the train.

53. *Will* I see you in the winter?

54. Every one of the taxpayers who built this hall *have* reason to complain.

55. The *balance* of the audience remained until the end of the entertainment.

56. I *expect* it was an expensive experiment.

57. He handed me a *couple* of books.

58. Neither of these authors *were* men who had to earn their living.

59. I did not know that it was *her's*.

60. With his wealth he *may* do it easily.

61. I *will* be expected there to-morrow.

62. Your *postal* came in time for me to get this *electric*.

63. He expects a *raise* in his salary next year.

64. It was he who came between you and *I*, and made this ill-feeling.

65. *Male* and *female* teachers have been engaged.

66. It is one of many storms that *has* been peculiar to this season.
67. Our *country's* great territory.
68. It was *myself* who told you.
69. I knew him when he was a *collegiate*.
70. I do not like this *party*, he seems conceited.
71. When the kettle was *hanged* over the newly made fire.
72. The boy held firmly to a *banister* of the staircase.
73. They *had a right* to compel him to give back the money.
74. "It is *me*," I answered.
75. He denied that he had *done* it.
76. I pitied him *laying* so helpless before me.
77. I left an order at *Johnson's* the tailor.
78. His benevolent *actions* last winter everyone remembers.
79. He was not able to take part in the *observation* of the anniversary.
80. The ropedancers were seen by a great *audience*.
81. *Mother-in-laws* are the inspiration of much cheap wit.
82. He *enters* the house, saw his victim alone, and brutally killed him.
83. He *laid* down for a little rest.
84. A long *cortége* followed him to the grave.
85. She looks *beautifully* to-night.
86. *Deo volente*, I will come Wednesday.
87. Where *was* you when he arrived?
88. The *never-to-be-forgotten* description of the death of Helen Pendennis.
89. He *wired* him to get ready for a *boom* in building lots near the river.
90. The *curricula* of our college is too large for our faculty.
91. His strength of will and habits of application *makes* him successful in whatever he attempts.
92. A young man *don't* go to the top in this business because he has friends to *boost* him.
93. They were *cotemporary*.
94. The *democracy* has this year in New York State a larger vote than the republican party.
95. *Gents* can get *pants* and *kids* at a very low price while we are reducing our stock.

96. Field day will not be changed unless the *whole* of the students favor the change.
97. This he suffered for *conscience's* sake.
98. The exercise in *gym* is not long.
99. The dropping of a few *shovelsful* of earth, and it will all be over.
100. The news from the strike *are* conflicting.
101. It *hadn't ought* to be such a burden to you.
102. He *set* there for more than hour.
103. Before we agree to this let us ask *cui bono?*
104. The appointment is to be given to *whosoever* the record of the season shows to be the best man.
105. *Ere* we do this let us ponder *o'er* the matter.
106. I *inaugurated* the term with a letter home.
107. My friend and *myself* will join you at Antwerp.
108. Will you try *and* learn it?
109. I met a *quantity* of friends while in Europe.
110. The enthusiasm has *overflown*, and we see the bad result in a sentimental freshet.
111. Was it *her* or *him* who told you?
112. A lady stood in the *bow window*.
113. Before the guilty man was hung he *plead* earnestly for a week's respite.
114. It is difficult to *perfectly* translate this passage.
115. He *waiteth* for the morn but it *cometh* not.
116. *Who* are you calling.
117. One should be ready to do *his* duty whatever the cost.
118. Book after book added *themselves* to the useless pile.
119. Tell me *who* he injured.
120. Each of these facts *are* strong arguments.
121. I am sure that you *shall* do this after what has been said.
122. Will you call on this gentleman *whom* I have told you is to visit me?
123. You are *real* kind to help me out of this difficulty.
124. Charles has such a craze for baseball that his friends call him a *crank*.
125. *Directly* he saw me at the window he came to my room.
126. He does not live in this *section*.
127. The *balance* of the vacation went quickly.
128. Have you decided whether or *no* you will remain?

EXERCISES IN PURITY OF STYLE

129. He will tell you which of the two roads is the *least* difficult.
130. He *flew* from the burning building only in time to save his life.
131. I have *every* confidence in him.
132. He is *quite* a football player as well as *quite* a musician.
133. He cannot speak *any*.
134. She *donates* this year a large sum to the hospital.
135. He *loaned* the young man a sum sufficient to pay his expenses at college.
136. It was an *abortive* bonfire.
137. Whenever such a man talks to me he *aggravates* me.
138. I have travelled *all over* the state.
139. *At length* the meeting ended and we left the hall.
140. She thinks that she has now a sure *preventative*.
141. His business has *ameliorated*.
142. He has worked *above* his powers.
143. If you were *posted* you would not say that.
144. The prevalence of baseball and football in our schools and colleges *have* not been without their moral as well as physical advantage.
145. Several *officials* were seen on the grounds.
146. He is one of those men who *hopes* to be famous some time.
147. Did you *anticipate* my arrival to-day?
148. She has beauty and wealth, and *likewise* goodness.
149. Take two *spoonsful* every hour.
150. My guide and *myself* were in doubt.
151. Why *don't* it come?
152. The new manager is a *success*.

Exercises Without Reference to Dictionaries and Other Books.

The following notes on violations of Purity are by Professor Phelps. These notes, with the exercises for correction which come immediately after them, will provide means, without further reference, for applying many of the principles of the chapters on Purity.

1. ADMIRE is improperly used in the sense of "desire;" as in the expression "I should admire to go." In the seventeenth century it

was used to express wonder alone. Jeremy Taylor wrote, "In man there is nothing admirable but his ignorance and his weakness;" that is, nothing surprising. Modern usage has added, in its use of the word, to the idea of wonder, that of approval.

2. ALTERNATIVE is often used, in improper construction, in the phrase "which of two alternatives." In strict definition, an alternative is a choice between two things. We say, "This was the alternative," and then specify two things between which the choice must be made. Two alternatives imply four objects of selection. Dr. Chalmers employs the word correctly when he says, "My purpose might have been expressed in the following short alternative: that, if I got my arrangements in the parish of St. John's, I would not take the professorship; but, if I did not get them, I would think of it." Here are two hypotheses making one alternative.

3. ANON is now obsolescent. In the phrase "ever and anon" we sometimes hear it, but even there the word is retiring behind the cover of poetic license.

4. AS is improperly used for "that." "I do not know as I shall go" was once good English: now "as" thus employed is a vulgarism.

5. AWFUL in the sense of "disagreeable" is an impropriety. It is a provincialism of New England. Lambert, in his "American Travels," says, "The country-people of New England speak of everything that creates surprise as being awful: they say an 'awful wind,' 'an awful hole,' 'an awful mouth.'" Robert Hall, by a singular lapse from his usually pure dialect, employs the word in the same sense. Two travellers at Rome once criticised Michael Angelo's statue of Moses. "Is it not awful?" said one. "Yes," answered the other: "it is sublime."—"No, no!" rejoined the other: "I meant awfully ugly." The second speaker used the word in its legitimate sense of "inspiring awe." Dr. Barrow speaks of God as an "awful Being." Dr. Watts describes the joys of heaven as involving "awful mirth." This is another sense of the word, that of being "filled with awe," once in good use, but now obsolete.

6. BASE used in the sense of "found:" "He based his argument on testimony." This use, till a very recent period, was condemned by critics; but it has made its way into the language. Dr. Whately employs it, and he rarely uses a word not good English.

7. BELITTLE.—We need this word: we have no exact equivalent.

Some dictionaries admit it. But at present it is not supported by the best usage. Mr. Bartlett, the author of the most valuable work we have on Americanisms, says that Thomas Jefferson is the only author of distinction who has employed it. He is not sufficient literary authority for the creation of a word. This word is one of a large class of compounds of the word "be" which tempt a loose writer. The fact deserves notice, that more than a hundred of these compounds found in one of our standard dictionaries are not good English.

8. CALCULATE for THINK is a provincialism of New England. Its proper meaning is to "reckon." By a singular coincidence, this latter word is also used as a provincialism at the West and at the South for the idea for which "calculate" is employed in New England.

9. CAN BUT *vs.* CAN NOT BUT.—Which? Shall we say, "I can not but think," or "I can but think"? The best usage prefers the former.

10. CHRISTIANIZATION.—We have no such word in classic use, though the dictionaries contain it. The participle "Christianizing" is employed in a substantive sense. Good taste avoids, if possible, words of six syllables. Saxon idiom chooses brevity.

11. CHRISTLESS is to be found in dictionaries, but not in the best authors. It is a barbarism of the pulpit.

12. COMMUNITY should not be used without the article, to express the idea of "population." The article is often omitted when the word expresses the abstract idea, as in the phrase "community of goods." But to indicate the people of a city we should say "the community."

13. CONDITIONED, in the sense of "dependent upon." American dictionaries recognize this; but in the best usage, the word is still restricted to its old meaning; that is, "stipulated."

14. CONDUCT is often improperly used without the reflexive pronoun; as in the phrase "he conducts well." It should be "he conducts himself well."

15. COMPOUND WORDS.—The following memoranda deserve notice:

(1) The presumption is always against the purity of compounds of great length. The license, in this respect, in which the German mind luxuriates, the English language does not tolerate. The Saxon taste,

which inclines always to brevity, keeps multitudes of words of this structure at bay. Individual authors coin them, but the national mind rejects them.

(2) The study of the German language and literature should be conducted with precaution against the use of compounds. German taste manufactures them without restriction. The German language admits them without violence to its structure and its history. Not so the English language. Yet our language suffers from the use of German importations by students of German literature who are not classic in their rhetorical tastes.

(3) Therefore, whenever a compound word betrays a foreign origin, it should be regarded with suspicion. Some such words have doubtless become good English, but multitudes of other such have not.

(4) Compounds which from their signification are likely to be of clannish or technical origin should be suspected. Such words should be presumed to be barbarisms till their right to a place in the language is proved by investigation.

(5) Compounds which by reason of their construction are odd, or difficult of enunciation, are presumptively not good English. Dr. Orville Dewey coins the word "rich-man-ness" to express pride of purse. The oddity of the word should be enough to condemn it. Scholarly taste never can have coined such a word. A member of the American Congress once said that he was not a good speaker, and that he was obliged to hold on to his desk and steady himself, if he attempted to use the word "eleemosynary." Many of the compound words which are lying around loose upon the outskirts of our language, if tried by the same test, would fail of admission.

(6) Compounds which evidently descend to low or comic style are presumptively not pure English. A writer in our current literature coins the word "go-ahead-a-tive-ness." One need not pause to investigate usage to know that such an abortion as this has no place in classic English. An interesting phase in the history of such compounds is witnessed in the history of the Greek literature. In its earliest periods, when the language was in its infancy, as in Homer and Hesiod, compound words abounded. When the language reached its maturity, in the works of the later poets and philosophers, but few such words were used, or recognized by classic authority. They are not favorites with Plato. At that period the large majority of long compounds are found in the comic writers alone. Aristophanes

abounds with them. He is reported to have once coined a word of seventy-seven syllables. They were used as an expedient for expressing low or ludicrous ideas.

A striking similarity to this is seen in the use of such words in our own language. They multiply in number as we descend from serious and dignified productions to the comic and the vulgar. Their spawn is in the swampy low grounds of our literature.

(7) Yet it must be admitted, that, in our language, compounds of two syllables are very numerous. It is an old Saxon usage to coin new words by linking two old ones. Such compounds as "dog-star," "day-labor," "state-rights," are perfectly good, and, scores like them. Why some, and not others, are admitted by the national taste, it is often impossible to say. A cultivated taste and a delicate ear must gradually form one's style till extensive reading has given to it a classic character. Years of unbridled license in the use of compounds can only corrupt one's style hopelessly.

16. DECLENSION is improperly used to signify the act of declining. It is a good word to express the state of decline, or the process of decline. But we cannot say, "He sent in his declension of the office." Webster's Dictionary admits the word in this sense, but it is not found in the works of the first class of English authors. We need a word to express the act in question : we have none but the participle "declining." Somebody was in distress for the right word who reported that a certain officer had sent in his "decleniency." "Declinature" may yet make its way into reputable use.

17. DEED used as a verb is a technicality of law, not good English elsewhere.

18. DEITY should not be used without the article except to express the abstract quality of divinity. It is not the proper synonym of "God."

19. DESK for PULPIT, in the phrase "sacred desk," is an Americanism.

20. DEPUTIZE is one of the numerous coinages of verbs by the Greek termination *ize*. The right word is "depute."

21. DONATE is one of the counterfeit coins of verbs from substantives never used by writers of critical taste. The substantives "donation" and "donative" are good words.

22. DON'T.—The contraction is noticeable as being often used colloquially for "doesn't." To say, even conversationally, "he don't," is not grammatical, unless the subjunctive mood is employed.

23. DOXOLOGIZE.—It is astonishing that so scholarly a critic as Dr. Worcester should have admitted this word into his dictionary on the obsolete authority of the early editions of an English dictionary from which it was afterwards excluded.

24. DROUTH for DROUGHT.—A relic of Anglo-Saxon orthography. Used by Lord Bacon, now a vulgarism.

25. EFFECTUATE.—We have no such word in classic use, though dictionaries contain it.

26. ENERGIZE is improperly used to signify exerting energy: its true meaning is to impart energy.

27. ENGLAND for BRITAIN.—The error here is not that of calling the three countries by the name of one ; that is politically correct, and sustained by usage. The error is the anachronism of designating the three kingdoms by the single name of England before their union. The most scholarly usage would not authorize us to say that " Cæsar invaded England ;" he invaded Britain. So Gaul was conquered by the Romans, not France.

28. EVANGELIZATION is one of the long-winded words which more classic use has curtailed to the participial noun " evangelizing."

29. EVENTUATE is a barbarism, like " effectuate," the origin of which is unknown.

30. EXHUMATE.—Somebody has coined this verb from the good English noun " exhumation." The true verb is " exhume."

31. EXPECT for THINK is a vulgarism, probably suggested by the similar use of the word " suspect " as the synonym of " think." Both are provincial vulgarisms of New England.

32. EXTREME should not be used as if it were the positive form of the adjective : it is the superlative. Good usage, therefore, does not authorize the phrases " more extreme," " most extreme."

33. FALL for AUTUMN is not objectionable colloquially ; but, in public discourse, " autumn " is in better taste. It is to be regretted that we have not retained uniformity of Anglo-Saxon titles for the four seasons. We need the word " harvest " in place of autumn, the old Saxon " hearfest." In the rural districts of England one often hears the seasons indicated by the titles spring, summer, harvest, winter.

34. FELLOWSHIP is improperly used as a verb. This use of it is generally condemned as an Americanism. But it was thus used by

Sir Thomas Mallory, in the "History of King Arthur," and published by the celebrated printer Caxton, in 1485. This error is therefore of English origin; but it has fallen out of good use there, and is probably one of the words retained in this country by the early emigrants from Great Britain. Many words and significations of this class are now supposed to be Americanisms which are really old English, now obsolete in the mother-country, but not so here.

35. FIRSTLY for FIRST.—"Secondly," "thirdly," etc., are correct; but "first" is itself an adverbial form. Charles Dickens generally uses "firstly." De Quincey also employs it.

36. FIX, in the sense of "to put in order," is incorrect. It is an Americanism which has no authority in scholarly usage. The proper meaning of the word is "to make firm."

37. FIXITY for FIXEDNESS is a barbarism. It is probably imported from the French *fixité*. To illustrate the distress for a barbaric style which literary men sometimes manifest, the error of Robert Boyle, the Irish philosopher, deserves notice, in coining the word "fixidity."

38. GIFT improperly used as a verb is sometimes heard. We have the participial form "gifted," and probably the verbal use of "gift" has been coined from that.

39. GOSPEL.—Improperly employed as an adjective in a host of compounds; such as, "gospel-light," "gospel-privileges," "gospel-truth," "gospel-preaching," "gospel-sinners," etc. Not one of these is in classic use.

40. HAPPIFY is a barbarism. Even "dictionaries unabridged" do not contain it.

41. HEAVEN is improperly used as the synonym of "God." Milton speaks of "the permission of all-ruling Heaven." It must be conceded that old English usage authorizes this, but any impersonal title of God should be generally avoided.

42. HEAVENLY-MINDEDNESS is one of the cant words for which we are indebted to the Puritan pulpit. "A heavenly mind" expresses the idea perfectly. "Heavenly minded" carries the compound to its extreme.

43. HOPE is improperly used for "hope for." Dr. Channing, who is not often guilty of unscholarly English, says, "We may hope the blessing of God."

44. HOW is often improperly employed interrogatively for some

such query as, "What did you say, sir?" This is a colloquial vulgarism of New England. Thus used, the word has no meaning to which it can be grammatically applied. A man not accustomed to the dialect of cultivated society, if he has not understood the remark of a friend says, "How?" meaning that he desires a repetition of the remark. Polite usage, in such a case, prescribes the formula, "I beg your pardon," or "Excuse me, sir." These have a meaning pertinent to the case. "How?" signifies nothing. Such colloquial errors would not deserve a place here, were it not that the indulgence of them in conversational habit inevitably creates similar violations of good taste in written style. Dr. Oliver Wendell Holmes remarks, that the two signs of ignorance of cultured society are, that a man eats with his knife, and says, "Haow?"

45. ILLY for ILL was in good use in Jeremy Taylor's time, but is now obsolete.

46. IMPLICIT in the sense of "undoubting," as in the phrase "implicit trust," is recognized by the dictionaries, but not by the most scholarly authors. Its proper meaning is the opposite of "explicit." "Did he assent to the contract? Not explicitly, but implicitly;" that is, by implication. Etymology still rules the signification of both these words. "Involved" and "evolved" express the contrast of ideas.

Yet it must be conceded that the word, in the sense here condemned, is making its way into good use. Only the more scrupulous authors now reject it. De Quincey makes a concession to it, when he says, that, in all his reading, he had found only two authors, Coleridge and Wordsworth, who uniformly employ it in its old etymological meaning. If only two writers within a large range of literature are faithful to its ancient use, it must be far on towards establishment in the language.

47. INAUGURATE in the sense of "introduce" is an impropriety. The proper sense is "to invest with office." It always refers to some official solemnity. The derivation of it from the old Roman *augur* indicates this; the augurs being the officers who invested the emperors with office by religious ceremonies. Yet so scholarly an authority as *The North American Review* says that a certain ship "was only a copy of a model inaugurated by Mr. Collins." Grant White, commenting upon this, suggests that the writer should have added, that "the President of the United States was invented on the 4th of March."

48. INCIDENT is improperly confounded with "liable." Says a living writer "The work was incident to decay." He should have turned it end for end. Decay may be incident to a work: the work is liable to decay.

49. INTEND.—A very common impropriety is the use of this word as the synonym of "mean." To intend is to purpose, to will. Dean Trench commits this error in his "Study of Words."

50. IRRELIGIONIST is another of the barbarous coinages of recent years.

51. JEOPARDIZE is an Americanism, coined with the Greek form of termination. The English word is "jeopard."

52. LAY and LIE.—The preterites of these two verbs are often confounded. Scholarly thoughtfulness is requisite to enable even an educated man always to avoid the error. Says a graduate of Harvard College, "He laid down." He should have said, either " He lay down," or " He laid himself down."

53. LENGTHY for LONG is very common in this country, and is used by some English reviews, and commended by some authorities. But "lengthy" certainly contains an idea which "long" does not contain. It includes the idea of tediousness, and therefore it is not wholly useless. It is employed by Coleridge and Lord Byron.

54. LIEVE for LIEF.—The latter is the English word. Shakespeare is classic in saying, "I had as lief the town-crier spoke my lines." The meaning is "willingly." Spenser, in the "Faerie Queene," employs "lief" as an adjective. That use is obsolete. The word is an old Saxon adverb.

55. LONG used as a noun is a very frequent error in the style of Alison the historian. "He was gone for long," says Alison, meaning, "for a long time."

56. MEAN for MEANS.—Till recently the Scottish writers favored the singular form; the English, the plural. Since the time of Addison, English and American use has adopted the plural. It is now used with either the plural or the singular pronoun.

57. METHINKS for I THINK was an old Anglo-Saxon form, but it has become obsolete except in poetry. Yet there are two remarkable authorities for it. One is Edward Everett in his celebrated vision of "The Mayflower:" "Methinks I see it now!" The other is Hawthorne. Both are good authorities; but it is improbable that either would use it if living now.

58. MIGHTY for VERY should not find a place here if it were not used by graduates of colleges. "Mighty small," "mighty weak," etc., are among those improprieties which creep into one's written style if indulged in colloquially. It was in reputable use in England two hundred years ago.

59. MILITATE WITH should be "militate against." We say, "Conflicts with," obeying the etymology of the verb; but the other phrase has no such defence.

60. MISSIONATE, in the sense of "to act as a missionary."—It occurs in *The Missionary Herald*, and is occasionally heard in sermons. We have no such word in the language.

61. MOOT, improperly employed in the phrase "moot-point."— The word is a technicality of schools of law, in which imaginary courts are held for the disciplinary exercises of students. It has no classic authority.

62. NEWS.—Is it singular, or plural? Illiterate usage asks, "What are the news?" Milton says, "Ill news rides fast."

63. NICE in the sense of "agreeable" is an Americanism. We speak improperly of a "nice day," a "nice fortune." A common vulgarism in metropolitan society is to designate certain persons as "nice people," meaning that they are agreeable people. The correct meaning of the word is "fastidious." A nice critic is a critic of fastidious taste.

64. NO.—The phrase "whether or no" in pure English should be "whether or not."

65. NOTIFY.—Should we "notify" a meeting, or "notify" an audience of a meeting? The English and American usages differ. The English adopt the first; and the American, the second. The English follow the original Latin etymology, deriving the word from *notifico*. The Americans follow the secondary derivation of the word, from the French *notifier*. The English form is the better of the two; that is, it is in closer affinity with the structure of the language. To "notify," by the analogy of other words of similar termination, should signify, "to make a thing known." Therefore we should notify the meeting, not the audience.

66. OBLIGATE for OBLIGE.—Richardson's Dictionary says that this word "is the more common among the common people." Smart's Dictionary says that it "is never heard among those who conform to the usage of the upper classes." The "British Critic"

says, "It is a low, colloquial inaccuracy." Dr. Worcester says, "It is much used in the United States." Webster admits it without objection. The history of the word is indicated in this succession of authorities. Doubtless it was formerly a barbarism, but has been growing toward, if not into, good use. Some critics contend that the derivation of it from the unexceptionable word "obligation" should settle the question. But a speaker in the American Congress once declared, "Mr. Speaker, I hurl the *allegation* back with scorn upon the head of the *allegator*." Did the correctness of one word here follow as a necessity from the accuracy of the other? English usage has no law for coining as a thing of course one word from another closely resembling it. Every word stands on its own merits; yet not always on its merits, but on the sheer will, even the caprice, of the national mind.

67. ONTO is a vulgarism. The two prepositions "on" and "to" may occur consecutively, but the combination is often used where the second preposition is useless. "He fell onto the rocks." "Upon" would be the better form.

68. OPEN UP is a phrase recognized as idiomatic English by lexicographers, but meaningless in its structure, and not used by the best authors. Why "up," rather than "down" or "out"? A good general rule in composition is to check one's pen in the writing of any phrase which seems to be redundant, or without obvious sense.

69. OUGHT.—It should not be, but it is, necessary to caution even graduates of American colleges against the use of vulgar inflections of this word; such as, "hadn't ought," etc.

70. PLEAD, used as a preterite form for "pleaded," is a corruption of long standing in the language; is found in Spenser's "Faerie Queene," but is almost universally avoided by scholars.

71. PLENTY, used as an adjective for "plentiful."—Dr. Webster is almost alone among lexicographers in admitting this. Shakespeare, however, employs it: "If reasons were plenty as blackberries, I would give no man a reason on compulsion." But good use is generally averse to it at present.

72. PREDICATE in the sense of "found" is an Americanism, confined chiefly to the usage of the bar, as when an advocate says, "I predicate my client's claims upon admitted facts;" meaning, "I found," etc. This is entirely opposed to the classic English use. "Predicate" means "to assert," nothing else.

73. PROFANITY and PROFANENESS.—Which? Usage is not uniform. The latter form is in closer analogy than the former with the structure of the English language. Professor Park says, that, if one says "profanity," one *may be* supported by good usage, but that, if one says "profaneness," one is *sure* to be thus supported; that is, the first of these forms is of doubtful authority.

74. PROFESSOR, used as the synonym of "communicant" in the church, is an impropriety limited to the dialect of the pulpit and to that of those who take their habits of speech from it. It is never used by secular authors of any rank.

75. PROGRESS, employed as a verb intransitive, should be marked as doubtful. Dr. Worcester says that the majority of authors of the first class avoid it. Critics commonly condemn it as an Americanism, but it is not such. It is found in the elder English authors, and probably was in good repute two centuries ago. Shakespeare, in King Lear, says, "Let me wipe off this honorable dew, that silverly doth progress on thy cheeks." The pronunciation of the word in Shakespeare's time probably accented the first syllable. If so, the word was one of those forms in which the verb and the noun are distinguished by difference of accent; as in the words "*con*duct" and "con*duct*."

76. QUITE in the sense of "very" is not good English; as in the expression "quite recently," or "the discourse was quite long." The true meaning of "quite" is "entirely."

77. RAISE is improperly employed in two American provincialisms, one used in the Southern States, and the other in the Northern. Southern usage says, "He was raised in Alabama;" "raise" being used in the sense of "to bring up." Northern usage says, "They raised a committee;" "raise" being used in the sense of "to appoint." Classic English admits neither.

78. RATHER, in the phrase "I had rather," should be preceded by "would" instead of "had." "Rather" expresses a preference. "Had rather" is probably a corruption of the phrase "had better," which is a pure English idiom. The translators of the Old Testament into English committed the error in making the Psalmist say, "I had rather be a doorkeeper in the house of my God."

79. RELUCT and RELUCTATE are both barbarisms, though some dictionaries admit them on the authority of authors of inferior rank.

80. REMORSE should not be employed to express only the sense of

sin. Remember always, in the use of this word, its etymological meaning, "*remordeo*," "to bite back." This idea the word has never lost. Remorse is retaliatory, not salutary. It tends to no good. Shakespeare says, "Nero will be tainted with remorse." Penitence and hope should accompany a sense of sin, then remorse ceases. The sense of sin then becomes remedial, as distinct from retributive. It is doubtful whether John Randolph, when on his death-bed he could not speak, but wrote on a card the word "remorse," meant anything more than that he felt himself to be a great sinner.

81. REMOVE, in the phrase "an infinite remove," is erroneous. Usage limits the use of the word in such connections to a small distance. Addison says, "A freeholder is but one remove from a legislator."

82. RETROSPECT used as a verb.—It is admitted by some lexicographers, but rarely acknowledged by good writers.

83. SANG, SPAKE, SPRANG, have, for the most part, yielded to the more modern forms, "sung," "spoke," "sprung." These double forms originally expressed different numbers of the tense. "Sang" was the singular; and "sung" the plural. The disappearance of this distinction leaves no occasion for the retention of both forms, and the old singular forms are obsolescent.

84. SAVE for EXCEPT is obsolete, except in poetry and in biblical quotation.

85. SCRIPTURALITY is not used by authors of the first class. Yet we have no one word to take its place.

86. SELFSAME is obsolescent, and was never in classic use. "Same" expresses the whole idea.

87. SHALL and WILL are improperly interchanged. In Ireland, "will" is frequently employed for "shall;" and in Scotland the reverse is common. In the Southern and some of the Western States of this country, the Irish error is frequent. "I will need the means of going," says a native of Virginia. The structure of our language tempts one to this error. In declension we are taught to say, "I will, you shall, he shall;" but we reverse the forms, and say, "I shall, you will, he will." It is out of this irregularity of declension, probably, that the error has arisen.

Worcester's Unabridged Dictionary and Webster's International Dictionary should be consulted for further consideration of *shall* and *will*.

88. SHEW for SHEWED, and pronounced as if it were "shue," is a singular corruption, often heard in the city of Boston among some who call themselves people of culture. "He shew me how to do it."

89. SHORTCOMINGS is authorized by the dictionaries, but when you are tempted to use it, remember that "Cummings" is a not uncommon family name in New England, and that those who bear it *differ in stature*. De Quincey condemns the word as a Scotticism. He says that it is "horridly tabernacular," that "no gentleman would touch it without gloves."

90. SIDEHILL should give place to the more classic form "hillside."

91. SOME is improperly used for "somewhat." "Is the patient better?"—"Some better." "Does it rain?"—"Yes, some."

92. SOLEMNIZE, in the sense of "to make solemn."—"Solemnize our minds" is often heard in extemporaneous prayer. This and the word "shortcomings" are the potent arguments for a Liturgy. "Solemnize," however, is not a barbarism: it is a good and ancient English word. It means "to celebrate a religious ceremony." We properly speak of "solemnizing" a marriage. In Shakespeare's time, even the word "solemn" was employed in similar connections, but without any necessary idea of seriousness. It was employed in reference to any important ceremony. Macbeth, on the occasion of his coronation, says, "To-night we hold a solemn supper;" that is, "a festival of inauguration." From such a history the word "solemnize" has grown.

93. SOUL.—This word has in Webster's Dictionary no less than thirty-five compounds, of which not more than three can be said to be in classic use. All the rest are a burden of barbarism upon the force of the language.

94. SPIRITUAL-MINDEDNESS.—"A spiritual mind" expresses the whole idea, and is a form which would not repel a scholarly taste.

95. STATION *vs.* DEPOT.—Which? By authority of usage, both; but by that of good taste, "station" is the purer English. It is English in its structure, and is generally used in England. "Depot" is of French origin; and, in the American use of it, it is diverted from its French signification, which is "a depository for freight." If we follow the French, why not do so in pronunciation of the word? Our language would be improved by the adoption of

both words, retaining severally the English and the French significations. Let passengers be deposited at a "station," and freight at a "depot."

96. STRICKEN for STRUCK is an impropriety, except in the usage of legislative bodies. A clause is spoken of as "stricken" from a legislative bill. In other connections the word is the synonym of "afflicted."

97. SUNDOWN should give way to the more classic form "sunset." Even the common people of England prefer the latter form.

98. SYSTEMIZE.—One of the few cases in which usage has triumphed over the Saxon love of brevity in the growth of our language is, that we must say, not "systemize," but "systematize."

99. TALENT *vs.* TALENTS.—Which? Both, but not as synonyms. "Talent" should not be employed collectively. We may not say, "a man of talent," but "of talents."

100. TEMPER for ANGER.—The proper English sense of the word "temper" is just the opposite of anger. It contains the same idea which is in its derivative "temperate." It means moderation or self-possession. Pope writes, "teach me . . . to fall with dignity, with *temper* rise."

101. THANKS! for the phrase *I thank you*, is an exclamation in colloquial use, of recent origin. It is criticised by a respectable class of conservators of good English. Yet it is a curious fact that the innovation is practised chiefly by those who profess to be men and women of culture. Rarely do we hear it from the lips of the common people. It is an affectation originated by somebody who mistook eccentricity for smartness. It is, however, one of those affectations of urban society which the sturdy good sense of the people will reject. Already protests against it begin to be heard. It is said that one of the most eminent groups of literary men in this country has agreed to avoid it in the interest of Saxon purity of colloquial English. Tennyson, if report speaks truly, reproved it in one of his own guests by responding to it, "Thanks, yes, or Thanks, no?—which is it?"

It is a safe general rule, never to adopt the colloquial novelties which the society of cities originates, on such authority alone. Metropolitan taste, as such, nowhere represents either the most accomplished scholarship or the soundest good sense in the use of language. If the backwoods and the low grounds of society corrupt the language in their speech, the ruling classes of great cities do the same, with less excuse for their error. The impure English originated by them would make a small dictionary by itself. The multitude of the great middle classes in the social scale, as a rule, speak purer English than either extreme.

102. THEN should not be used adjectively. Edmund Burke, who does not often fall into errors of style, speaks of himself as being "unknown to the then ministry." Had he said "the then existing ministry," he would have used good English.

103. THIS or THAT for THUS.—"This much," "that much," are modern corruptions. They have no hold upon good authority.

104. TRANSPIRE.—What is its meaning? To "happen," or to "become known"? The latter surely: it has no other signification in good English use, the dictionaries to the contrary notwithstanding. This is one of the cases in which the liberty allowed by lexicographers degenerates into license. The idea of this word is very accurately given by the phrase "to leak out." "Transpire" and "perspire" are etymologically nearly identical. They both imply the passing out of something imperceptibly. Usage, therefore, has taken the word "transpire" to express the coming of a secret thing to publicity. If you associate these two words in your minds, the one may assist you to remember the true meaning of the other. A New York journal spoke of the Mexican War as "transpiring in 1847." Grant White, commenting on the style, observes, that, considering the latitude in which the war occurred, the writer might as properly have said that "the war perspired in 1847."

105. UGLY, in the sense of "ill-natured," is, for the most part, found only in this country. The English sense of the word is "disagreeable in personal appearance." In pure English we speak of an ugly countenance, not of an ugly disposition.

106. UNBEKNOWN is a vulgarism. We have no such word in the language.

107. UN.—Let this prefix be noted for the sake of observing that one of our standard dictionaries admits nearly three hundred words of compound structure of which this is the initial syllable; yet scarcely more than one-half of these are probably extant in the writings of eminent English authors, unless they are employed, as so many compounds were in the Greek literature, for comic purposes.

108. UNWISDOM and UNREASON are examples of compounds, not

good English. The style of some writers and speakers seems to be constructed on the theory that any word which is pure English may give birth to its opposite by prefixing the negative prefix " un."

109. VARIATE is corrupt English for " vary." In New England may be sometimes heard in prayer the petition, " Do thou variate thy mercies," etc.

110. WAS for WERE.—Many cultivated men and women have not learned the simple law of grammar which forbids the phrase " You was," and the interrogative, " Was you ? "

111. WERE for WAS is a still more inexcusable corruption, because it is commonly an affectation. People whose aspirations after the name of culture exceed their acquisitions, often have a hazy idea that something is wrong in certain uses of the word " was," and that " were " is at any rate more literary. Therefore one says " When I were in New York ; " and another responds, " I were in Europe then." Probably the error has grown out of a confusion of the indicative with the subjunctive mood. Because it is often wrong to say, " If I was," some adopt " I were " for the indicative, when they strain to be very accurate. When they think nothing about their style, they probably talk good English, and say, " I was."

By the directions of the older grammarians we were required to say, " if I were, if he were," etc., wherever the subjunctive was used ; that is, the " past tense " of the subjunctive was not recognized. Usage broke over that rule long before the grammarians saw the necessity for doing so.

112. WHOLE for ALL is a very frequent corruption in the writing of Alison the historian. He speaks of " the whole citizens of the State." How many fragments of citizens were there ? Alison's History is a splendid thesaurus of illustrations of bad English.

Apply the criticisms of Professor Phelps to the following sentences.

1. I should admire to be present when the prizes are awarded.
2. I calculate that you are right.
3. The body was exhumated.
4. We hope his recovery.
5. Methinks, I am again in the midst of strife.
6. He was born in Ireland but raised in this country.
7. We are to progress only as we improve in character.

8. Full of temper he struck him a fatal blow.
9. I will be with you anon, and tell you about this strange event.
10. Did he conduct properly?
11. It is a most extreme application of the law.
12. How? I did not hear what you said.
13. He is a mighty good scholar.
14. Four monitors were raised on the basis of scholarship.
15. His shortcomings are as many now as formerly.
16. This much may be said in favor of the motion.
17. The position should have a man of talent.
18. The go-ahead-a-tive-ness of the man you will admire.
19. In the fall there are two holidays.
20. He has inaugurated a new play in the game.
21. This plan militated with all my other plans.
22. He said that he had rather go home.
23. The accident came from coasting on the side hill.
24. He was very ugly because of the opposition, and did not become good-natured for a long time.
25. It has been awful weather for a month.
26. Has his declension of the call been received.
27. Ought we to fellowship men so heretical?
28. All such enterprises are incident to great losses.
29. He has given himself to missionating.
30. I greatly reluctate to accept this responsibility.
31. In one way he is some better, in another he is some worse.
32. Was this unbeknown to you?
33. This was unbeknown to me.
34. I will deputize him to act for me.
35. After he announced his firstly, I anticipated his secondly and thirdly.
36. He has become an irreligionist.
37. The news are bad to-day.
38. He is a long remove from his brother in ability and scholarship.
39. It is a soul-inspiring scene.
40. Why will they follow a man of so much unreason and unwisdom?
41. England in the first century of the Christian era gave little promise of its future greatness.

42. When my room is fixed I shall be glad to have you see it.
43. So valuable a life ought not to be jeopardized in such a cause.
44. He is obligated to do it.
45. As I retrospect I feel a depression of spirits.
46. The loss of spiritual-mindedness is soon recognized in change of conduct.
47. To variate our methods is to give new life to our work.
48. It will eventuate in time.
49. I am satisfied with its fixity.
50. He would as lieve be a private as an officer.
51. The observation of this law will be strictly enforced.
52. His rugged health did not come wholly from inheritance.
53. Our train is now at the depôt.
54. Was you there? I were, but I did not see you.
55. We cannot have our pay except we work for it.
56. We ought to give them the gospel-light.
57. Is he away for long?
58. The tree blew over and fell onto me.
59. While his bearing was not good, he spake well.
60. Mr. B. was stricken down with paralysis.
61. The whole of the pupils did not attend the lecture.
62. It must happify him to have such a welcome.
63. I love peaches.
64. He has opened up a suggestive field of thought.
65. I should not do this save for friendship.
66. To accomplish more you must systemize more.
67. A walk along the hill at sundown is always enjoyable.
68. His heavenly-mindedness is recognized in whatever he says or does.
69. I like simplicity and purity.
70. He knew that he hadn't ought to do it.
71. The selfsame thought came to me.
72. He has a magnificent arm.
73. Fruit is so plenty that it is very cheap.
74. It is the use of the right mean to the end that gives success.
75. I predicate this statement on facts which are known to me.
76. His book is full of interesting memories of his eventful life.
77. It was quite early when we started.

EXERCISES IN PRECISION OF STYLE *

CHAPTERS VII., VIII., IX. AND X.

EXAMPLES FOR CORRECTION OR CRITICISM.

ERRORS IN THE USE OF THE WORD "IT."

1. It is a country whose laws are made, its government is administered, its chief officers are appointed, and its revenues are disbursed by a foreign state.

2.† Next to thinking clearly it is useful to speak clearly and whatever your position in life may hereafter be it cannot be such as not to be improved by this, so that it is worth while making almost any effort to acquire it, if it is not a natural gift: it being an undoubted fact that the effort to acquire it must be successful, to some extent at least, if it be moderately persevered in.

3. He died in the island of which he was a native, and had lived in it all his life.

4. To come within easy distance of Rome and not to see it — I could never forgive myself for it.

5.† The best way in the world for a man to seem to be anything is really to be what he would seem to be. Besides that, it is many times as troublesome to make good the pretence of a good quality as to have it; and if a man have it not, it is ten to one but he is discovered to want it, and then all his pains and labors to seem to have it are lost.

ERRORS IN COMPARISON.

6. No general ever had so much devotion shown him as Napoleon.

7. I know of no book that is so valuable for the student as a good dictionary.

8. This system of heating is the most economical of all other systems.

* For Exercises in Precision of Style, without reference to dictionaries and other books, see pages 265-274.

† To correct 2 and 5 it will be necessary to divide and to recast the sentences.

9. President Cleveland has done more than any member of his party to accomplish tariff reform.

10. The success which now came was greater than he had gained in the whole of his eventful life.

11. The winds at this point are the strongest that are met at any other part of the ascent.

12. I know of nothing so easily learned as history when it is properly taught.

13. He was the very man of all others in our party who seemed most unlikely to fail.

14. In comparing Shakespeare and Milton, we may say that Shakespeare was the greatest dramatic poet and Milton the greatest epic poet.

15. This king was the only one of his predecessors who had from first to last a peaceful reign.

16. To William Ewart Gladstone who has just withdrawn from public life England owes more than to any living man.

17. The task was the most difficult that I ever attempted before.

18. The task was more difficult than I had ever attempted.

19. He showed the same spirit in this last act as in every act of his life.

20. No wonder that we were so moved by the sight, for in the whole world there is no scene that can equal it in sublimity.

ERRORS IN THE USE OF TENSES.

21. I shall have great pleasure in accepting your invitation.

22. I intended to have spoken to you about the matter.

23. He was proved to be sentenced for a serious offence before this arraignment.

24. I thought when I came to have visited all my friends.

25. It was my purpose to have insisted on your staying with me.

26. I shall be happy to accept your invitation.

ERRORS IN THE USE OF VERBS FROM ELLIPSIS.

27. Is it reasonable to expect that to happen which never has?

28. But you will endure it as you have so many other trials.

29. Lincoln and Garfield knew what it was to be born in poverty as almost all our great men have.

30. We often think that what is, always has, and always will be.

31. I never have, and never will do for personal advancement what my conscience condemns.

32. Missing the prize as others have he like others opposes the competitive system.

ERRORS IN THE USE OF THE SUBJUNCTIVE MOOD.

33. If the horse was mine I would sell it.

34. Let a few more dry summers follow in succession, and there would be some movement to protect the forests.

35. If the landlord were ready to pay the expense, why should the tenant object?

36. If ever a man's devotion to the interests of the people deserve recognition, it is the service of our mayor.

37. Were he willing to do for himself my help shall not be withheld.

38. If the house were unpromising without, it proved to be comfortable within.

MISCELLANEOUS ERRORS IN MOOD.

39. Can I ask you for another favor?
40. You can go now, as I promised you.
41. May I run faster than he, do you think?
42. Can I cross these grounds, or do you object?
43. May I cross these grounds, or is there no road open?
44. If he was here he would put matters right.
45. When the weather be favorable, when the roads are good, such a trip is always enjoyable.
46. It ought to make a man miserable, if he have ruined his friend.
47. Life would lose its interest for most men so soon as Mr. Bellamy's scheme shall be put in operation.
48. If his brother were willing to let him have the property, why should he refuse it?
49. Were it as you say, and we were to blame, would there be an excuse for such cruel treatment.
50. Let a few more games be lost and the spirit of the college would be no longer enthusiastic.

ERRORS IN THE USE OF CONNECTIVES.

51. Do not come except you find it convenient.
52. An upright, earnest man like his father was before him.
53. The Chinese, he said, would never become good American citizens, and that they did not wish to remain in this country.
54. Directly the game began, the shouting became so loud as to be deafening.
55. There is no other friendship so helpful than that of an older, wiser person.
56. It is as high or higher than this mountain.
57. What man has labored more earnestly or so ceaselessly for the cause as he?
58. I prefer not to have your help without you wish to give it.
59. Fatal injuries seldom or ever occur in the game.
60. I had scarcely reached the platform than I was called on for a speech.
61. Hardly had that disease left me than this attacked me.
62. I have at present no means to help you than that of my recommendation.
63. This example is of all others the most convincing.
64. This musician has done more for his art than any musician of this age.
65. I have a watch and which I highly value because it was my grandfather's.
66. We are in a time of financial depression and in which many changes of fortune are seen.
67. Such is the spirit of the man, and which may be seen in his writings, as it has been manifested in his life.

ERRORS IN THE USE OF SYNONYMS AND OF WORDS SIMILAR IN ORTHOGRAPHY.

68. His grateful *acceptation* of the gift pleased the congregation.
69. She gained *accession* to the home by bribing an old servant.
70. She showed her oriental tastes in her *barbarous* ornaments.
71. His *actions* of late have been much criticised.
72. He *captivated* the book after a struggle.

73. Thackeray has represented Colonel Newcome as a *childish* character.
74. He is a *ceremonial* man.
75. He held a *deathly* weapon.
76. He was *distinctively* heard.
77. Some favored his *continuity* in the office.
78. He is a man of such *equitable* temper that he is rarely moved to anger.
79. I *depreciate* this bad feeling and hope that it is only temporary.
80. It is a kind of amusement that weakens character and makes it *feminine*.
81. The *last* letter from him came yesterday.
82. He has prepared a *monogram* of several pages.
83. As he has *politic* ambitions he will not offend the party.
84. When she paid for the goods she asked for a *recipe*.
85. He did not act from *principal* which ought to be the *principle* motive.
86. Her *rendition* of the poem was warmly applauded.
87. I *suspect* that he will come on the evening train.
88. The new friendship was a *stimulation* to better work.
89. My *visitant* proved to be a book-agent.
90. The author is still *extant*.
91. The *enormousness* of the crime calls for the severest punishment.
92. An *antiquated* castle.
93. Although poor he is a man of large *beneficence*.
94. The *argument* established positively the prisoner's guilt.
95. His *avocation* had demanded all his time and strength for many years.
96. He showed *greediness* of learning and *avidity* of wealth.
97. His *character* has been injured by these false reports of his habits.
98. *Compare* them and see in what they differ.
99. The house is *complete* but not *perfect*.
100. His *arrant* tendencies have made him a great traveller.
101. He could not *confute* all the personal accusations.
102. Ought *corporeal* punishment to be allowed in our schools?
103. What did the merchant say is the *cost* of the article?

104. The sentence for his *sin* is imprisonment for life.
105. The *decay* of the empire.
106. The statue is *defaced* by the loss of an arm.
107. His love of circumlocution and detail makes him a *diffuse* writer.
108. This peasant girl has the *elegance* of a princess.
109. Much of his *evidence* did not seem to have any connection with the case.
110. She *exceeds* her sister in music.
111. We must check the *luxuriance* of the foliage or it will shut out the view.
112. You will *succeed* him in the procession.
113. The *blaze* of the candle was unsteady.
114. This despot *governed* for many years.
115. I saw his *imminent* danger and warned him in time for his escape.
116. His fierce temper is *inherent*.
117. He will *learn* his brother how to swim.
118. His uncles were all *notorious* preachers.
119. As he could not write he gave me a *verbal* report.
120. Send him a *verbal* answer by the messenger.
121. As this is to be a *verbal* exercise, you will not need materials for writing.
122. The *common* course of nature.
123. The appearance of things was *plausible*.
124. His speech had a *specious* tone but it did not deceive.
125. Is it true that whatever is *possible* is *practicable*?
126. Because it is right he *should* do it.
127. This fine *product* of art.
128. He is a *prudential* man.
129. It is a charming *rustic* scene.
130. My *safety* is such that I am without even apprehension of danger.
131. In our *accidental* business every day, I had an opportunity to judge the man.
132. The painter of these signs is a worthy *artist*.
133. He has for many years been addicted to the *crime* of intemperance.
134. Galileo *discovered* the telescope.

135. Newton *invented* the law of gravitation.
136. This was the *decided* battle which closed the campaign.
137. The physician exposes himself as he comes in contact with persons having *infectious* diseases.
138. He thinks that he deceives us with his *ambiguous* statements.
139. The *emigrants* who arrived this week were all in good condition.
140. He has my high *estimation* for his moral worth.
141. I *guess* I'll see the game this afternoon.
142. He *fractured* a blood-vessel.
143. He has an *odium* toward me.
144. Men are *subject* to mistakes in political matters.
145. I enjoyed his *ridiculous* speech and laughed at it heartily.
146. He has an easy *native* manner.
147. The *sewerage* for a year has been sold to a contractor.
148. They gave the Chautauqua *salutation*.
149. The *robber* who stole my coat from the hall has been detected.
150. A *voluntary* burst of enthusiasm.
151. This *union* of feeling promises well.
152. A *tall* building.
153. He is *qualified* by natural gifts for the position.
154. He swallowed the *venom*.
155. An *officious* man questioned me about my personal matters and my private affairs.
156. His *depravation* is sad for one so young.
157. These two great men were *coeval*.
158. His *adhesion* to his high purpose is admirable.
159. The meaning is so *apparent* as to require no study.
160. His appetite for drink is *imperative*.
161. His manner is *noxious*.
162. No matter how unpopular he is his *vanity* sustains him.
163. Good men ought to have *sympathy* with this criminal.

BLUNDERS IN CONSTRUCTION.

The following examples are taken from Hodgson's "Errors in the Use of English."

164. "One of the combatants was unhurt, and the other sustained a wound in the arm of no importance."

165. "A piano for sale by a lady about to cross the Channel in an oak case with carved legs."

166. "The Moor seizing a bolster, full of rage and jealousy, smothers her."

167. "The Board of Education has resolved to erect a building large enough to accommodate 500 students three stories high."

168. "A clever magistrate would see whether a witness was deliberately lying a great deal better than a stupid jury."

169. "Sir Morton Peto spoke of the notion that the national debt might be repudiated with absolute contempt."

170. "They followed the advance of the courageous party, step by step, through telescopes."

Synonyms to be Prepared from Worcester's Unabridged Dictionary.

The synonyms in these lists from Worcester's Unabridged Dictionary and Webster's International Dictionary are the words between which there is most often failure to discriminate with precision. It is expected that the preparation of these synonyms for oral or written examination will be an important part of the study of rhetoric. If so, the gain will be not simply in precision; for let pains be taken to express the differences between the words in pointed, antithetic clauses or sentences as far as possible, and the exercise will be also a valuable training in energy of style. In fact, there is no other exercise in words more profitable as a means of logical and rhetorical training than the study of synonyms. It is, therefore, suggested that the student carefully prepare a number of synonyms from the dictionaries, or from the works of Soule, Smith, or Crabb, for each exercise.

Abstinence	and	temperance.
Acquire	"	obtain.
Adjacent	"	adjoining.
Alarm	"	apprehension.
All	"	every.

Alone	and	only.
Alter	"	change.
Amuse	"	divert.
Answer	"	reply.
Argument	"	proof.
Argumentation	"	reasoning.
Authentic	"	genuine.
Avocation	"	vocation.
Avidity	"	greediness.
Behavior	"	conduct.
Benevolence	"	beneficence.
Brothers	"	brethren.
Candid	"	frank.
Careful	"	cautious.
Cause	"	reason.
Celebrate	"	commemorate.
Celebration	"	celebrity.
Certain	"	sure.
Chance	"	accident.
Character	"	reputation.
Cheerfulness	"	mirth.
Circumstance	"	fact.
Clearness	"	perspicuity.
Coast	"	shore.
Coerced	"	restrained.
Commission	"	authorize.
Compare	"	contrast.
Complete	"	perfect.
Compunction	"	remorse.
Confute	"	refute.
Conquer	"	subdue.
Contemplate	"	meditate.
Contemptible	"	despicable.
Continual	"	perpetual.
Continuation	"	continuance.
Conviction	"	persuasion.
Corporal	"	corporeal.
Cost	"	price.
Countenance	"	face.

Courage	and	fortitude.
Crime	"	sin.
Criminal	"	guilty.
Criterion	"	standard.
Darkness	"	obscurity.
Decay	"	decline.
Deceive	"	impose.
Deception	"	deceit.
Dedicate	"	consecrate.
Deed	"	act.
Defection	"	revolt.
Defective	"	deficient.
Definition	"	explanation.
Delivered	"	saved.
Deny	"	refuse.
Desperate	"	hopeless.
Diffuse	"	prolix.
Disclaim	"	disowned.
Dismiss	"	discharge.
Dispense	"	distribute.
Disregard	"	slight.
Distinction	"	difference.
Distinguish	"	discriminate.
Divide	"	separate.
Doctrine	"	dogma.
Doubt	"	hesitation.
Duty	"	obligation.
Earth	"	world.
Eat	"	feed.
Edifice	"	structure.
Effect	"	consequence.
Elegance	"	grace.
Elocution	"	eloquence.
Emphasis	"	stress.
Enemy	"	foe.
Enough	"	sufficient.
Epithet	"	adjective.
Ethnography	"	ethnology.
Evidence	"	testimony.

Example	and	pattern.
Exceed	"	excel.
Excellence	"	superiority.
Excite	"	incite.
Exist	"	live.
Expedient	"	resource.
Expostulate	"	remonstrate.
Exuberant	"	luxuriant.
Famous	"	celebrated.
Fatigue	"	weariness.
Feign	"	pretend.
Firm	"	fixed.
Flame	"	blaze.
Flourish	"	thrive.
Follow	"	succeed.
Foretell	"	predict.
Formal	"	ceremonious.
Foundation	"	basis.
General	"	universal.
Genteel	"	polite.
Gift	"	present.
Glory	"	honor.
Good	"	benefit.
Govern	"	rule.
Happiness	"	felicity.
Help	"	assist.
Heretic	"	dissenter.
Hinder	"	prevent.
Human	"	humane.
Ideal	"	idea.
Imminent	"	impending.
Impediment	"	obstruction.
Impervious	"	impassable.
Incapable	"	incompetent.
Inconsistent	"	incompatible.
Increase	"	addition.
Inherent	"	innate.
Insinuate	"	ingratiate.
Intercede	"	interpose.

Invidious	and	envious.
Knowledge	"	science.
Lack	"	need.
Learn	"	teach.
Literature	"	learning.
Little	"	small.
Malicious	"	malevolent.
Nautical	"	naval.
Novel	"	new.
Notorious	"	noted.
Opposite	"	contrary.
Oral	"	verbal.
Ordinary	"	common.
Orthodox	"	evangelical.
Ought	"	should.
Particular	"	peculiar.
Penetrate	"	pierce.
Perceive	"	see.
Plausible	"	specious.
Polite	"	civil.
Possible	"	practicable.
Poverty	"	pauperism.
Prayer	"	petition.
Principle	"	motive.
Priority	"	precedence.
Production	"	product.
Proposition	"	proposal.
Prudent	"	prudential.
Refuse	"	decline.
Relation	"	relative.
Respect	"	regard.
Restrain	"	restrict.
Rural	"	rustic.
Safety	"	security.
Science	"	art.
Seem	"	appear.
Sensation	"	perception.
Sensible	"	sensitive.
Site	"	situation.

Shade	and	shadow.
Social	"	sociable.
Slander	"	calumny.
Special	"	particular.
Strength	"	force.
Thankfulness	"	gratitude.
Thoughtful	"	considerate.
Timeserver	"	temporizer.
Tolerate	"	permit.
Unavoidable	"	inevitable.
Variation	"	variety.
Visitor	"	guest.
Wakeful	"	watchful.
Whiten	"	blanch.
Wisdom	"	prudence.
Wit	"	humor.

Synonyms to be Prepared from Webster's International Dictionary.

Abdicate	and	reign.
Ability	"	capacity.
Absolve	"	acquit.
Absurd	"	preposterous.
Abuse	"	invective.
Accidental	"	incidental.
Accomplish	"	achieve.
Accordingly	"	consequently.
Acquaintance	"	intimacy.
Admonition	"	reproof.
Advantage	"	benefit.
Allegiance	"	loyalty.
Also	"	likewise.
Amazed	"	astonished.
Animosity	"	enmity.
Announce	"	publish.
Antagonist	"	opponent.
Anticipate	"	expect.
Argue	"	debate.

Artist	and	artisan.
Bashfulness	"	shyness.
Be	"	exist.
Beg	"	ask.
But	"	however.
Cabal	"	faction.
Care	"	anxiety.
Choose	"	prefer.
Commit	"	consign.
Contagious	"	infectious.
Contemptuous	"	contemptible.
Contest	"	conflict.
Convene	"	convoke.
Courage	"	bravery.
Crime	"	vice.
Decorum	"	dignity.
Decrease	"	diminish.
Deference	"	respect.
Depravity	"	depravation.
Differ with	"	differ from.
Directly	"	immediately.
Discover	"	invent.
Disability	"	inability.
Education	"	instruction.
Efface	"	deface.
Effect	"	consequence.
Egoism	"	egotism.
Emigrant	"	immigrant.
Emulation	"	rivalry.
Equivocal	"	ambiguous.
Evade	"	prevaricate.
Faculty	"	expertness.
Factitious	"	unnatural.
Fanciful	"	fantastical.
Fallacy	"	sophistry.
Fine	"	beautiful.
Final	"	ultimate.
Forbid	"	prohibit.
Fracture	"	rupture.

Gaze	and	stare.
Gratify	"	indulge.
Guess	"	think.
Hatred	"	odium.
Haughtiness	"	disdain.
Help	"	aid.
Hint	"	suggestion.
Humility	"	diffidence.
Idiom	"	dialect.
Idle	"	indolent.
Ignorance.	"	illiterate.
Impertinent	"	officious.
Inconsistent	"	incongruous.
Intrude	"	obtrude.
Kingly	"	regal.
Kill	"	murder.
Laconic	"	concise.
Labyrinth	"	maze.
Lasting	"	durable.
Liable	"	subject.
Liberty	"	freedom.
Liberal	"	generous.
Lifeless	"	inanimate.
Ludicrous	"	ridiculous.
Marvelous	"	wonderful.
Massacre	"	carnage.
Mercantile	"	commercial.
Mercenary	"	venal.
Method	"	manner.
Midst	"	middle.
Natural	"	native.
Negligence	"	neglect.
Normal	"	abnormal.
Pertinacity	"	obstinacy.
Pitiable	"	piteous.
Pique	"	grudge.
Pleasant	"	agreeable.
Poison	"	venom.
Portion	"	part.

Precarious	and	uncertain.
Pretense	"	pretext.
Privilege	"	prerogative.
Project	"	design.
Preternatural	"	supernatural.
Qualified	"	competent.
Quit	"	leave.
Reformation	"	reform.
Repentance	"	contrition.
Resolution	"	decision.
Sabbath	"	Sunday.
Salutation	"	salute.
Sentimental	"	romantic.
Serf	"	slave.
Sewerage	"	sewage.
Sneer	"	scoff.
Spontaneous	"	voluntary.
Subsidy	"	tribute.
Taciturn	"	silent.
Talkative	"	garrulous.
Tall	"	high.
Tease	"	vex.
Temerity	"	rashness.
Term	"	word.
Thief	"	robber.
Thither	"	there.
Unison	"	unity.
Utility	"	usefulness.
Whither	"	where.

Words Confounded.

Words that are often confounded with each other or that are otherwise misapplied by resemblance of form or sound, or by the prevailing indiscriminate use of abstract and concrete words from the same root, are—

Acceptation *	and	acceptance.
Accession	"	access.

* The student will learn by reference to any standard dictionary why each word should not be used for the opposite word.

Advancement	and	advance.
Advertise	"	advise.
Admissible	"	permissible.
Approbation	"	approval.
Arrant	"	errant.
Around	"	round.
Barbaric	"	barbarous.
Captivate	"	capture.
Ceremonious	"	ceremonial.
Childish	"	childlike.
Completion	"	completeness.
Conscience	"	consciousness.
Construe	"	construct.
Deadly	"	deathly.
Definite	"	definitive.
Depreciate	"	deprecate.
Disclose	"	discover.
Disposition	"	disposal.
Distinctly	"	distinctively.
Distraction	"	abstraction.
Effeminate	"	feminine.
Enormousness	"	enormity.
Equable	"	equitable.
Exceptionable	"	exceptional.
Extant	"	existing.
Genii	"	geniuses.
Import	"	importance.
Individual	"	individuality.
Incredulous	"	incredible.
Intention	"	intent.
Latest	"	last.
Limitation	"	limit.
Masculine	"	manly.
Merit	"	demerit.
Meretricious	"	meritorious.
Monogram	"	monograph.
Nationality	"	nation.
Novice	"	novitiate.
Needful	"	needy.

Pitiable	and	pitiful.
Politic	"	political.
Principal	"	principle.
Predication	"	prediction.
Recipe	"	receipt.
Relation	"	relative.
Rendition	"	rendering.
Resort	"	resource.
State	"	estate.
Stationary	"	stationery.
Stimulation	"	stimulus.
Suspect	"	expect.
Unusual	"	uncommon.
Vacuity	"	vacancy.
Visitor	"	visitant.
Womanish	"	womanly.
Yellow	"	yellowness.

Exercises without Reference to Dictionaries and Other Books.

The following notes on words which are often improperly used for each other, are by Professor Phelps. If circumstances do not permit the use of dictionaries and other works on synonyms, this list will be found unusually large and varied for a text-book on rhetoric.

1. ABILITY and CAPACITY are not exact synonyms. The one expresses active power; the other, receptive power. But the plural "abilities" includes both ideas.

2. ADHERENCE and ADHESION were once interchangeable. Now the one is restricted to things mental and spiritual; the other, to things material. We speak properly of adherence to a principle, and of the adhesion of iron.

3. ALONE is improperly used in the sense of "only;" as in the phrase "the alone God." This word was originally written "all-one." Later usage, it is to be regretted, has abandoned the ancient form, and so lost from the word the ancient idea of unity.

4. AMONG and BETWEEN are not interchangeable. "Between" is

the right word when only two are concerned; "among," when more than two.

5. ANCIENT and ANTIQUATED are not synonyms. An antiquated thing is ancient; an ancient thing may not be antiquated. An ancient institution may, for that reason, be the more worthy of respect; an antiquated institution has outlived respect.

6. APPARENT is in some connections improperly used as the synonym of "obvious." To say that an occurrence is apparent does not necessarily mean that it is real, but may mean the reverse. We speak of an apparent contradiction, which we do not admit to be a real one. The phrase "heir-apparent" suggests the contingency that the heir may not come to the throne.

7. APPREHEND and COMPREHEND are improperly interchanged. To apprehend a truth is to perceive it, to have some intelligible notion of it: to comprehend a truth is to understand it in all its compass. We may represent the mysteries of religion as apprehensible by the human mind, but not as comprehensible. To apprehend them is sufficient ground for faith: to comprehend them would be an act of reason.

8. APPREHENSIVE is improperly employed in the sense of "understanding." "Apprehend" and "understand" are synonyms: "apprehensive" and "understanding" are not. The element of fear enters into the meaning of "apprehensive." We say, "I am apprehensive that it is too late." It is rarely used now in its etymological sense except as a technicality in philosophy.

9. AVERSE FROM *vs.* AVERSE TO.—Which is right? Usage is divided. Some cling to the first phrase on etymological grounds. Others contend that the second phrase has vanquished etymology, and is authorized by usage. Noah Webster and Dr. Todd, the editor of Johnson's Dictionary, contend for "averse to:" Dr. Witherspoon and Sir James Mackintosh prefer "averse from." In the present balance of authorities, either form is allowable; but it can hardly be doubted that the etymological form will be displaced, and "averse to" will hold ascendency in the language. It is a curious phenomenon, that, when an etymological form has begun to yield its place, it rarely becomes firmly fixed again. The drift of usage is to its exclusion. It is like a loosened tooth.

10. BESIDE and BESIDES are not synonyms, yet are very frequently so used by writers. "Beside" means "by the side of:" "besides" means "in addition to."

11. BETRAYAL *vs.* BETRAYMENT.—Which? Dr. Whately uses the first; Thomas Jefferson, the second. Both are condemned by some critics. But we surely must have one of them. "Betrayal" is the more frequently used, but "betrayment" has the more regular English construction. At present either is allowable, but usage inclines to the first.

12. CHASTITY and CHASTENESS are not synonyms. Dean Swift is eminent for chasteness of style, but not for chastity of thought. As applied to authorship, "chasteness" means rhetorical purity. "Chastity" means moral purity. A pure woman has chastity; a pure style has chasteness; and both are chaste. Yet De Quincey improperly speaks of "chastity of style."

13. CHRISTEN for BAPTIZE cannot be condemned as bad English so long as the English Church retains it. But it does not at all express the true idea of baptism. In perfect English, "to christen" is to Christianize. A heathen nation is christened when converted to Christianity. An old writer says, "The most part of England was christened in the reign of King Ethelred." From this use, the word was transferred to the rite of baptism; that, in the sense of baptismal regeneration, being synonymous and the doctrine of the Book of Common Prayer. In Shakespeare's drama "Henry the Eighth," the king is informed of the birth of his daughter Elizabeth, and asks Cranmer to baptize her, saying, "I long to have this young one made a Christian."

14. CONCEPT and CONCEPTION have a history. "Concept" was once good English as the synonym of "conception." Then it fell into disuse, and now is revived again by Sir William Hamilton and others, but not as the synonym of "conception," but to signify the idea conceived. But in any sense "concept" must be as yet regarded as a technicality of psychological science.

15. COEVAL and CONTEMPORANEOUS involve a nice distinction, for which etymology furnishes no reason, but which usage authorizes. "Coeval" is applied to institutions; "contemporaneous" to individuals. Authors are contemporaneous, not coeval.

16. CONFORM WITH *vs.* CONFORM TO.—Which? This is one of the cases in which etymology has given way to usage. The Westminster Catechism obeys the usage of its own day and of ours in saying, "Sin is any want of conformity *unto* the law of God."

17. CONTINUAL and CONTINUOUS are not exact synonyms.

"Continual," commonly, not always, means "with constant recurrence." "Continuous" is the stronger word, and means, "without intermission." We should be correct in saying, "Continual interruptions prevent continuous study."

18. DECIDED *vs.* DECISIVE.—These are not synonyms. A decided fact is one which is beyond dispute; a decisive fact is one which puts an end to dispute. You may have a decided opinion, but it may not be decisive of a controversy. A decided victory may not be decisive of a campaign.

19. DELICIOUS *vs.* DELIGHTFUL.—The first should always be restricted to pleasures of sense. We should not speak of a delicious joy, or peace, or communion. Even the phrase "delicious music" implies the predominance of the sensuous element in the pleasures of song.

20. DELUSION *vs.* ILLUSION.—These are not exact synonyms, though the dictionaries interchange them. Coleridge writes, "That illusion, contradistinguished from delusion." Dr. Whately indicates the distinction tersely by recalling the etymology of the two words: *illudo*, "to make sport of;" *deludo*, "to lead astray." Illusion exists in the imagination only: delusion affects conduct in real life. The one is a mental error in a passive state; the other, a mental error in active working. The same error may be first an illusion, and then a delusion.

21. DEPRAVITY and DEPRAVATION are not interchangeable. Depravity expresses the state or the quality; depravation, the act or the process.

22. DICTION and STYLE are not exact synonyms. Style refers to thought and language; diction, to language only. Yet where exact definition is not necessary, these words may be interchanged.

23. DIFFER WITH *vs.* DIFFER FROM.—Which? Dr. Worcester and the last editors of Webster's Dictionary defend the first of these forms as being in good use in England, and gaining ground in this country. They give Lord Brougham and Mr. Canning as authorities. These are hardly conclusive authorities. In this country, observation will detect the phrase chiefly in the style of newspapers. If we admit it, we must admit the phrase "differ from" also; for of that there can be no doubt. "Differ with" we may note as doubtful.

24. DISBELIEF and UNBELIEF involve a distinction of great moment. "Unbelief" expresses less than "disbelief." It may

arise from ignorance or the want of evidence. "Disbelief" is more positive: it implies that evidence has been considered and rejected. The folly of an atheist consists in the fact that he affirms the negative of that of which no human mind can know a negative. Yet the distinction is of comparatively recent origin. When our English Bible was translated, the distinction was not clearly recognized in the language. Our Lord, therefore, is represented as denouncing the sin of unbelief, when the thing he did denounce was the more positive sin of rejecting evidence.

25. ENDOW and ENDUE have a nice distinction in good English use. "Endow" may be employed in reference to any qualities, mental, moral, or physical; "endue," to mental and moral qualities only. Solomon was endowed with wealth, and endued with wisdom.

26. ENTHUSIASM *vs.* FANATICISM.—Formerly both words were employed to signify defects, both being morbid excitements, differing only in degree. Recent usage has rescued the word "enthusiasm" from association with mental disease, and authorizes now its use to signify a healthy and normal excitement. Says a living author, "The Puritans were enthusiasts for religious liberty, not fanatics." Fifty years ago that distinction was unknown.

27. EPOCH and ERA should be distinguished. In loose usage they are interchanged, and the principles on which our dictionaries are compiled lead them to recognize this. Yet the distinction is valuable, and the language is improved in precision by retaining it. An era is a succession of time: an epoch is a point of time. An era commonly begins at an epoch. We live in the Christian era, in the Protestant era, in the era of liberty and letters. The date of the birth of Christ was an epoch: the period of the dawn of the Reformation was an epoch.

28. ETERNAL and EVERLASTING are critical words. Modern usage has developed a distinction which did not formerly exist. "Everlasting" means now "without end:" "eternal," without beginning or end. Once they were interchangeable. Now we should not designate the past eternity of God by the word "everlasting" except in biblical quotations, as in the phrase "from everlasting to everlasting." On the same principle of conformity to usage, we drop the word "eternal," and substitute "everlasting," in defining the doctrine of future punishment.

29. EXCEPT and UNLESS are confounded by heedless writers. "You cannot have it except you earn it" should be, "unless you earn it." The one is a preposition; the other, a conjunction. The improper use of "except" is a Southern provincialism.

30. FALSEHOOD for FALSENESS.—The thing for the quality of the thing is not precise. The lie is the falsehood: the untruthfulness of it is the falseness.

31. GENIUS *vs.* TALENTS.—What is the distinction? Criticism is uniform in admitting a distinction, not so in defining it. The words should be noted as by no means interchangeable. See the word "genius" in Webster's Unabridged Dictionary.

32. HABIT, CUSTOM, USAGE, are improperly confounded. "Habit" is commonly, in strict use, limited to the individual; "custom" implies the consent of numbers; and "usage" is a long-established custom. Thus Shakespeare says, "How use doth breed a habit in a *man!*" And Hooker writes, "Of things once received and confirmed by use, *long* usage is a law sufficient." It may not be that these are all the distinctions among these words established in the language, but they are true so far as they go.

33. HASTE and HURRY are not synonyms. The first does not imply confusion: the second does. A man may reasonably be in haste, never in a hurry. Napoleon, after a great defeat, when minutes of delay might bring the enemy upon his retreat, wrote a proposal for an armistice of a few hours; and when it was suggested, that, to save time, he should seal the document with a wafer, he said, "No: give me the sealing-wax and a candle. A man should never seem to be in a *hurry.*"

34. HEALTHY and HEALTHFUL.—A valuable distinction has grown up in recent years, which is not yet insisted upon by the lexicographers; but scholarly usage should recognize it. "Healthy" expresses the condition: "healthful" means "producing health."

35. IMAGINATION and FANCY.—See Wordsworth's Preface to his "Lyrical Ballads." That essay is a fine specimen of literary criticism, and a striking example of the power of a great author to evolve from a language a latent distinction which the national mind, as represented by its educated classes, has felt vaguely between words, which, because of their vagueness, have been for generations used loosely. Probably Wordsworth has fixed those two words, with their present meanings, in the language for ever. What is the

distinction? Both words express exercises of the mind's creative power; but "imagination" is the more profound, the more earnest, and the more logical. "Fancy" is the more superficial, the more playful, and often the more capricious. The national mind has for a long time felt this difference, and has expressed it in the words "imaginative" and "fanciful." It did not clearly recognize the same difference between "fancy" and "imagination" till Wordsworth disclosed it.

36. IMPERATIVE and IMPERIOUS are very far from being synonyms. One means "authoritative;" the other "domineering." God's law is imperative, never imperious. Imperiousness is always offensive. "This imperious man will work us all from princes into pages."—SHAKESPEARE. "His bold, contemptuous, and imperious spirit."—MACAULAY.

37. IN SPITE OF is not synonymous with "notwithstanding." It is a surly phrase. Is there no difference in rhetorical effect between saying, "in spite of your argument," and saying, "notwithstanding your argument"? Does not Shakespeare imply a threat, when he says, "I'll keep mine own in spite of all the world"?

38. LEARN for TEACH was once good English, signifying either to give or receive knowledge. The Book of Common Prayer so employs the word. At present it retains but one of these senses.

39. LIKE for LOVE.—We detect the difference between these words as soon as attention is called to it. Yet it is one of the frequent evidences of the want of colloquial culture, that they are employed interchangeably. A man should love the truth, not like it: he may like a leg of mutton, not love it.

40. MEMORIES for REMINISCENCES.—"Sunny Memories of Foreign Lands" is the title of a book by Mrs. Stowe. The attractiveness of the title is gained at the expense of pure English. We detect the error by putting the word into the singular. We do not speak of a single reminiscence as a memory. Why not, if the plurals of the two words are synonyms?

41. MOMENT and MINUTE are not synonyms. The "minute" is the sixtieth part of an hour: the "moment" is the shortest possible measure of time. Says St. Paul, "In a moment, in the twinkling of an eye." The eye does not require a minute for the act of twinkling.

42. MUTUAL and COMMON are confounded in the phrase "mu-

tual friend:" it should be a "common friend." In the plural, "mutual friends" would not be inaccurate, meaning that two persons are friends each to the other. "Common friend" means that a third person is a friend to two or more other persons. "Mutual" implies interchange.

43. OBSERVATION and OBSERVANCE.—Are they synonyms? No. The one means the act of "taking notice of:" the other means the act of "performing some duty." We should not say, "The observation of the sabbath," but "The observance," etc. Astronomers have recently taken observations of the transit of Venus. Faithful Christians practise the observance of the Lord's Day.

44. PATERNAL and FATHERLY.—Which? Both are good words; one Latin, the other Saxon. The Latin is the more stately, the Saxon the more cordial, in its associations. The Latin might be the more becoming in a diplomatic paper; the Saxon, vastly the more effective in a sermon.

45. PITIFUL, PITEOUS, and COMPASSIONATE.—Are these words synonyms? By the authority of dictionaries, and to some extent by usage, we may answer both Yes and No. That is to say, contradictory meanings are attached to them. Thus, "pitiful" is used to express "feeling pity, exciting pity," and "exciting contempt." The same is true of "piteous." Usage will uphold us in saying that God is a pitiful, that is, a compassionate being; and that a certain man is a pitiful, that is, a contemptible being. Usage sometimes gives a liberty which good taste condemns as license. As a general rule, we may meet all the necessities of speech by employing the word "compassionate" to express the idea of "exercising pity," "piteous" to express the idea of "exciting pity," and "pitiful" to express the idea of "exciting contempt." Thus, the good Samaritan was a compassionate man; the man who fell among thieves was in a piteous condition; the thieves were pitiful fellows.

46. PRIDE and VANITY.—It is a popular error that interchanges these words. The sin of pride is denounced when the connection indicates that the thing denounced is not that, but vanity; not the self-contained vice which despises other men, but the superficial vice which depends for its indulgence on the opinion of other men. The Scriptures are keen in their analysis of human nature, when they condemn pride as the most concentrated of mental vices and the

most corrosive to upright character. Satan is pride personified. We do not know that he was ever weak enough to be vain.

47. RATIONAL and REASONABLE are not interchangeable. "Rational" refers to the existence of reason; "reasonable," to its exercise. To say that an opinion is irrational is to say that it implies the loss or suspension of reason: to pronounce an opinion unreasonable is only to say that the arguments in support of it are not sufficient. One may hold unreasonable opinions which are not irrational: the deficiency may be in a perverted use of reason, not in the loss of it.

48. RIDE and DRIVE.—English usage makes a distinction between these words which is not commonly recognized in this country, but is a valuable one, and it augments the precision of the language. A "ride" is in the saddle: a "drive" is in a carriage.

49. RUGGED and HARDY are not synonyms. "Rugged" is "rough." We should not speak of "rugged health."

50. SECURITY and SAFETY are often interchanged, yet are not synonyms; and the distinction between them is one which it is desirable to retain. "Security" retains somewhat of its etymological meaning of "freedom from care."

51. SELF-LOVE and SELFISHNESS have a very marked distinction which ever since Bishop Butler's day has been established. He says, "Men would be much better than they are if they had more self-love." Self-love is a legitimate and unavoidable exercise of intelligent beings: selfishness is not such. The one is innocent; the other, a sin.

52. SENSUAL and SENSUOUS are liable to confusion. The former always involves moral wrong: the latter is only a philosophical term. All men are sensuous beings: only bad men are sensual beings.

53. SYMPATHY and PITY are not exact synonyms. "Sympathy" has never lost entirely its etymological sense of feeling *with* another. It is a finer exercise of benevolence than "pity." We may pity one whom we despise: we cannot sympathize with such a one.

54. THE.—This article is noted for the sake of observing the error of omitting it from a variety of words for which precision requires it. We have observed its omission from the word "community." Other words are subjected to the same decapitation. "Opposition," "ministry," "presbytery," "council," "congress," are examples. We say, "*The* Senate, *the* House of Representatives:" why not "*the* Congress" as well? This *was* the usage of the most scholarly men

among the statesmen of the first age of the republic. It is said to have been revived by President Arthur. The most unscholarly omission of the article, in which the error is open to the charge of irreverence, is in the use, without the article, of the titles of the divine Trinity in the formula of baptism and the closing ascription in prayer: " In the name of Father, Son, and Holy Ghost!" Is not the use of the article before each title more reverent? By the more deliberate utterance which it compels, the sentiment of reverence gains time to express itself. A hearer said that a certain preacher's rapid utterance of the trinitarian formula without the article reminded him of the title of a mercantile firm, like " Smith, Jones, & Robinson."

EXERCISES IN PERSPICUITY OF STYLE

CHAPTERS XI., XII., XIII., AND XIV.

FIGURATIVE LANGUAGE.

In examining figurative language, especially the metaphor, the student should apply the rule given by Dr. Blair. The rule is, in substance, that we are to test the propriety of the figure by forming from it a picture. If the parts are so incongruous as to make when put together " a monstrous image," as Dr. Blair says, the figure is bad. If the parts so agree as to present the subject " in one natural and consistent point of view," the figure is good.

According to this test, make a mental picture of each of the following examples, and name the good and the bad figures.

1. "How terrified should we have been had one of these lack-lustre eyes but rolled in its orb, or opened its leathern jaws."
2. "You with nice ear on tiptoe strains pervade."
3. "Speech is silver, silence is gold."
4. "A heroine as wild, fascinating, romantic, and extravagant as ever trod the stage of theatre or page of romance."
5. "Long aisles of oaks returned the silver sound,
   And amorous echoes talked along the ground."
6. "I'd be a butterfly; living a rover,
   Dying when fair things are fading away."
7. "Seemed washing his hands with invisible soap,
   In imperceptible water."
8. "We join ourselves to no party that does not carry the flag and keep step to the music of the Union."
9. "John Brown, God bless you! You have struck a noble blow; you have done a mighty work; God was with you; your

heart was in the right place. I send you across five hundred miles the pulse of a woman's gratitude."

10. "Arrest Simoom amid his waste of sand,
   The poisoned javelin balanced in his hand;
   Fierce on blue streams he rides the tainted air,
   Points his keen eye and waves his whistling hair;
   While, as he turns, the undulating soil,
   Rolls in red waves and billowy deserts boil."

11. "Sir, She (Bulgaria) was man enough to resist Russia."

12. "The voice of England which sounded so clearly at the last general election, would be lost sight of."

13. "The germ, the dawn of a new vein in literature lies there."

14. "When another commits a fault, it is a great dead tree bare and hideous; but when we do it, think of the reasons climbing around it like a thousand clinging vines, and turning it into a beautiful object."

15. "Every heart is like a theatre in one respect; there are certain effects produced, but you do not want every one to see all the ropes and pulleys."

16. "He speaks the voice of Boston, the home of Sam Adams, in this glorious hour."

17. "He launched the ship of state on seas white with the fervor of the Revolutionary love of liberty."

18. "The old vices that shipwrecked him all through his old life, leavens this production."

19. "From the throats of three hundred cannon poured a shower of balls which winnowed the English ranks."

20. "We will burn all our ships, and with every sail unfurled steer boldly out into the ocean of freedom."

21. "Do not dare to be so absorbed in your own life, so wrapped up in listening to the sound of your own hurrying wheels, that all this vast pathetic music made up of the mingled joy and sorrow of your fellow-men shall not make you rejoice to give yourself for them."

22. "The mountains to the Hebrew were always full of mystery and awe. They stood around the sunlit level of his daily life robed in deep clouds, the home of wandering winds, flowing down with waters, trembling as it seemed, with the awful footsteps of God."

23. "Opposite in the blue vault stood the moon like a silver shield raining her bright arrows on the sea."

24. "We congratulate ourselves on having torn off Cobbett's mask and revealed his cloven hoof."

25. "Throw open the flood-gates of democracy, and you pave the way for a general conflagration."

26. "Suffering, like work, strengthens the capacity for happiness. It sees on the steep paths which it makes you climb, sweet, smiling flowers which the profane have never known."

27. "We must put our soul less and less into books and speeches. Let us lay our hand to the clay, let us take the spade, the hammer, the goad, the whip, and in place of tracing characters on paper, let us grave them on living hearts. Instead of crying, 'Forward! Fire!' let us be ourselves the first to attack."

28. "The German army at Austerlitz had muscle enough; at Sedan brain enough."

29. "In the last analysis, it will be found that Cæsar was Rome's escape from communism; the rich were being plundered by the poor. They lifted up their voices in wild alarm, and the avenging eagles hastened across the Rubicon."

30. "From dome to dome, when flames infuriate climb,
  Sweep the long street, invest the tower sublime,

  . . . . . .

  While with vast strides and bristling hair aloof,
  Pale danger glides along the falling roof;

  . . . . . .

  Nymphs! you first taught the gelid wave to rise,
  Hurled in resplendent arches to the skies;
  In iron cells condensed the airy spring,
  And imp'd the torrent with unfailing wing;
  On the fierce flames the stream impetuous falls,
  And sudden darkness shrouds the shattered walls;
  Steam, smoke, and dust in blinded volume roll,
  And night and silence repossess the pole."

31. "Ideas rejected at the time often rankle, and bear fruit by and by."

32. "Out of the dark regions of philosophical problems, the poet suddenly lets swarms of song dive up carrying far-flashing pearls of thought in their beaks."

33. "The chariot of the revolution is rolling along, and gnashing its teeth as it rolls."

34. "Once Europe was peopled only here and there by men who beat at the door of nature, and upon the heads of one another with sharp flints."

35. "The soul's dark cottage, battered and decayed,
    Lets in new light thro' chinks that time has made."

36. "It is the theory that God made a little of this human clay into porcelain vases to hold the dizzy wine of exclusive power, but the most of it into common crockery for base uses."

37. "Yes, the long-awaited client had come at last. Scarred, scorned, and forsaken, that cowering and friendless client was wronged and degraded humanity."

38. "The spark that was kindled at Fort Sumter fell upon the North like the fire upon the autumnal prairies."

39. "The South had builded herself upon the rock of slavery. It lay in the very channels of civilization, like some Flood rock lying sullen off Hell Gate."

40. "Our treasure did not melt away in the fiery furnace of French tribulation and German triumph."

41. "The sad faces and joyous music formed an incongruous sight."

42. "The fruits of our present are to be the stepping-stones into our future."

43. "No Austria, no Prussia, one only Germany, such are the words that your Imperial Majesty has always in his eye."

44. "One effect of the Irish Union would be that the barren hills would become fertile valleys."

45. "When God means to make a great man He does not fling His hero like an aërolite out of the sky. He bids him grow like an oak out of the earth."

46. "Down the crack which some transgression makes in the fair face of a smooth and blooming life, we can see waiting for God's judgment-word, the fire before which that life shall be at last consumed with fervent heat."

47. "The will is the helmsman of the ship; when it wavers and is at a loss, fear shipwreck."

48. "Spires whose silent finger point to heaven."

49. "I am as a weed,
    Flung from the rock, on ocean's foam to sail,
    Where'er the surge may sweep, the tempest's breath prevail."

50. "A man passes for what he is worth. Concealment avails him nothing, boasting nothing. His vice glasses his eye, cuts lines of mean expression in his cheek, pinches his nose, sets the mark of the beast on the back of his head, and writes O fool! fool! on the forehead of a king."

Saxon-English Words Substituted for Words of Latin or Greek Origin.

The student will, by reference to any standard dictionary, give a Saxon-English substitute for each word in the following list :

(1) abundance, (2) accident, (3) accommodate, (4) alleviate, (5) anticipate, (6) anterior, (7) appropriate, (8) apprehend, (9) archaic, (10) alternate, (11) attract, (12) audacity, (13) benediction, (14) belligerent, (15) cachinnation, (16) calligraphy, (17) cinerary, (18) conflagration, (19) conflict, (20) conjecture, (21) consternation, (22) corpulent, (23) criminality, (24) decadence, (25) demolition, (26) demented, (27) desperate, (28) detriment, (29) development, (30) division, (31) disruption, (32) desolation, (33) domiciliary, (34) donation, (35) effulgent, (36) emaciated, (37) emancipated, (38) epidemical, (39) extensive, (40) extenuate, (41) fascinate, (42) flagellation, (43) formidable, (44) gradient, (45) gratitude, (46) gregarious, (47) habitude, (48) hirsute, (49) horizontal, (50) hostility, (51) inane, (52) increment, (53) indignation, (54) ingenuous, (55) infraction, (56) inhabit, (57) ingenuity, (58) inopportune, (59) intimidate, (60) invest, (61) irritate, (62) janitor, (63) jocularity, (64) labyrinth, (65) liberality, (66) licentious, (67) magnitude, (68) margin, (69) mendacious, (70) mercenary, (71) merit, (72) monotony, (73) moribund, (74) negotiation, (75) abjurgation, (76) obtuse, (77) operose, (78) parental, (79) parsimonious, (80) penetration, (81) perpetual, (82) population, (83) potation, (84) precipitate, (85) proceed, (86) propel, (87) prosecute, (88) radiance, (89) ramification, (90) remuneration, (91) respiration, (92) reticence, (93) saccharine, (94) salutation, (95) signification, (96) similitude, (97) select, (98) solicit, (99) stentorian, (100) strident, (101) sudorific, (102) sufficient, (103) superintendent, (104) temptation, (105) termination, (106) tortuous, (107) translucent, (108) tremulous, (109) turbid, (110) vacant, (111) vagary, (112) valedictory, (113) valetudinarian, (114) vegetation, (115) velocity, (116) vernal, (117) verisimilitude.

Generic Words and Specific Words.

By reference to Webster's International Dictionary, the differences in meaning between each generic word and each of the specific words opposite to it, are to be given.

GENERIC.	SPECIFIC.
Acquaintance	familiarity, intimacy.
Ask	request, beg, petition, solicit, entreat, implore, beseech, supplicate.
Attack	assail, assault, invade.
Choose	prefer, elect.
Cloister	monastery, abbey, priory.
Commit	intrust, consign.
Communicate	impart, reveal.
Company	group, concourse, meeting, convention, assembly.
Contemn	despise, scorn, disdain.
Contest	conflict, combat, encounter.
Danger	peril, hazard, risk, jeopardy.
Deceive	delude, mislead.
Disease	disorder, distemper, malady, affection.
Dislike	aversion, reluctance, repugnance, disgust, antipathy.
Effect	consequence, result.
Get	obtain, gain, earn, acquire.
Gratify	indulge, humor.
Greeting	salutation, salute.
Hate	abhor, detest, abominate, loathe.
Hide	conceal, disguise, dissemble, secrete.
Insanity	lunacy, madness, derangement, delirium, mania, monomania, dementia.
Language	speech, tongue, idiom, dialect.

GENERIC.	SPECIFIC.
Laughable	droll, comical.
Leave	quit, abandon, relinquish, forsake, depart from.
Memory	remembrance, recollection, reminiscence.
Overcome	conquer, vanquish, subdue, subjugate.
Renounce	adjure, recant.
Say	allude, remark, utter, pronounce, proclaim, assert.
Sign	emblem, symbol, type.
State	situation, condition.
Think	expect, believe, guess, anticipate.

The student is to give all the specific meanings which he can learn have been assigned to any of the following words, and also the specific words which can be substituted for each word in the list. Jevons's "Lessons in Logic," Chapters IV. and V., Whitney's "Study of Language," Lecture III., Trench's "Study of Words," as well as the dictionaries, will be found useful in this exercise.

Animal.	Law.
Board.	Metal.
Church.	Move, to.
Crime.	Post.
Flower.	Round.
Fish.	See, to.
Foot.	Smith.
Fowl.	Sound.
Government.	Stock.
Hear, to.	Strike, to.
Implement.	Take, to.
Insect.	Vehicle.

In the following list, the generic word in each group of words is to be selected, and the specific words of the group arranged in a series, each term of a more general meaning being placed before one of the next specific meaning.

1. Road, elevated steam railway, means of communication, steam railway, railway, New York's elevated steam railway.
2. Duruy's History of Modern Times, European History, book, printed book, history of modern Europe, history.
3. Purple, color, red.
4. Rectilineal figure, triangle, figure, isosceles triangle.
5. Man, Episcopalian, animal, Protestant, mammal, christian, biped, being.

Arrange the following group of clauses so as to give a description of the coming of spring in an oriental country. In this description the most general statement is, "The winter is past." To this statement is to be added in a series the other clauses, as each gives in order the next specific sign of the approach of spring.

The winter is past—and the vines with the tender grape perfume the air,—the rain is over and gone,—and the voice of the turtle is heard in our land,—the fig-tree putteth forth her green figs,—the flowers appear on the earth,—the time of the singing birds is come.

The student before leaving the subject of general and specific language, should study the speech of Mark Antony in Shakespeare's play of Julius Cæsar, Act III., Scene II. Beginning with Antony's first and most general reference to Cæsar, the student should follow the series of specific references, observing not only their careful gradation, but also the change in the feelings of the mob as the description of Cæsar's character and wrongs grows more and more particular.

Abstract Words and Concrete Words.

Give, as far as possible, the concrete expression corresponding to each of the following abstract words.

Action, animality, beauty, corporeity, equality, hardness, gratitude, individuality, intention, length, nationality, rationality, relation, reverence, shrubbiness, substantiality, usefulness.

Give the abstract word corresponding to each of the following concrete words.

Aged, author, bookish, ether, grateful, ink, mute, nation, natural, relatives, soap, speed, stone, stupid, timorous, wood, wool, vacuous, vain.

Examples for Correction or Criticism.

Errors in the Arrangement of Pronouns and Their Antecedents.

1. There are many things to be said against the state's controlling the sale of liquor with which we are all familiar.
2. He removed the cords from her hands with which she was bound.
3. He had to defend himself from a ceaseless opposition by an equally constant watchfulness that was unjust.
4. While he held this office he gave much time to feeble attempts at writing poetry which was not his.
5. He now lives in a larger house but he has not any yard which is built of brick.
6. This is an instance of a man fearing to show himself the admirer of a most amiable woman who had fought many battles.
7. It is not wise to provide for a rainy day by robbing all the other days which may never come.
8. The knight made a solemn vow to his king never to dishonor by word or deed his bright fame.

ERRORS IN THE USE OF THE SAME PRONOUN WITH DIFFERENT ANTECEDENTS.

9. The monkey picked up the book and laid it on the table, and then opened it and turned its leaves as it had seen its master do.

10. The workmen wished to follow their leaders, but were forced by the sufferings of their families and their fears that worse troubles might come to decide against their inclinations.

11. When men become envious of others they seem to think that in some way their gain is their loss.

12. Mr. A. met his friend and told him what was his plan; and further that if he would get for him the influence of his uncle, he should have a certain share of the profits.

ERRORS IN FAILURE TO EXPRESS DIRECTLY, IF IN ANY WAY, THE ANTECEDENT OF THE PRONOUN.

13. I was delighted at my success in riding my friend's bicycle, and promised myself to do it again.

14. It is our purpose to make the bridge strong whatever may be the opposition, for it is expected of us.

15. While as a man he had only contempt for such methods, as a politician he did not show it.

16. Such surroundings have a sad influence on his mind who knows that there is no escape from them.

17. He first bought a coat and then changed it for a silver watch, and afterward in another trade got for it some cigars.

18. The game to-day was as interesting as it usually is.

19. A few men of the team are doing well, but most of them are too indifferent.

20. He soon saw that the moral qualities of the young man were not to be judged by those of his diffident speech and awkward bearing.

21. These seemingly useless parts of the human body were not understood until the evolutionists explained them by those in the lower animals.

ERRORS IN THE CASE OF THE PRONOUN.

22. The man whom they thought was a clergyman, and who made the first speech, proved to be a layman.

23. When did we ever find an Anglo-Saxon, whether Englishman or American, who had any doubt of their right to rule the world.

24. These were the men whom he believed were able to carry out the project.

25. His decision remained unchanged, although numberless but not successful reasons to change them were given.

ERRORS IN THE NUMBER OF THE VERB WHEN A PRONOUN IS THE NOMINATIVE.

26. His lecture was one of the most suggestive and stimulating of the lectures that was given last season.

27. The course of the reformer at this critical time was one of the bravest that has been taken in like circumstances.

28. There is not one of his public acts which do not show honesty of purpose.

ERRORS FROM OMISSION OF RELATIVE PRONOUNS WHEN THE GOVERNMENT IS CHANGED.

29. It was at the lower end of the athletic field with which I am not familiar, and have not even visited.

30. He took his political views from an old leader with whom he was intimate, and succeeded in office.

31. It was a cause to which he had early given himself, and sacrificed everything.

32. The friend from whom he had received so much help, and so warmly admired and loved, had been taken from him.

33. The great end toward which we are always striving, and constantly beckons us on, seems to recede steadily from us as we think we are approaching it.

ERRORS IN THE ARRANGEMENT OF ADJECTIVES AND ADVERBS.

34. They were very much elated at their success as they nearly caught one hundred fish.

35. She only lived for her child.

36. He did this while he had all these men at his command alone.

37. He is considered generally intelligent.

38. Not only the father but all the family were taken prisoners.

39. What do you mean by saying that John was there when you just said, that James and John were not there?

40. It is probably thought that he will succeed.

41. She has a very small income, as she nearly lost all her property.

42. Where there are so many competitors one can only excel by specializing.

43. Whatever may be our other qualities, it is goodness alone that can satisfy the conscience.

44. He spoke to the young men who had been intoxicated most earnestly.

45. She reads the novels of George Meredith as they appear eagerly.

46. I only speak of what I have seen, not of what I have heard.

47. He won the game as he caught the ball which came from the second baseman's hand quickly.

48. He will only wear well fitting clothes.

49. He only pays for his breakfast.

50. She has been all over the house.

51. Not merely this book but all the books which he had collected were destroyed.

52. We never remember to have seen the river so high.

53. She simply said that she desired a comfortable home.

54. The boy solely writes about the games of the school.

55. I never remember to have spoken to this man.

56. He merely talks of books.

57. I scarcely ever remember to have known a warmer day.

58. The result is not agreeable to us only because it is what we asked for, but because it is what we need.

59. He is neither inclined to favor high protection nor absolute free trade.

60. She was neither qualified by early training nor by later associations to govern a country like Scotland.

61. His career is neither like that of his father nor that of any of his ancestors.

ERRORS IN THE ARRANGEMENT OF QUALIFYING CLAUSES.

62. The steamer was swiftly bearing him to seek his fortune where he did not know what might happen to him in another world.

63. He went to his evening service after he had led in family worship with a quick step.

64. Struggling for a career that was more than life to him his hope and faith kept strong to the end.

65. This man will not miss his reward ultimately, because he is unjustly kept from it now.

66. An old man was at the door cutting wood with a pipe in his mouth.

67. The boy evidently received my lecture on the wickedness of stealing fruit with a good spirit.

68. Being one of the best schools in the country, it was natural for the boys to pride themselves on its training.

69. Amazed at the anger of the man, every word that had passed between us was quickly reviewed to detect the cause.

70. While playing ball one Sunday a pious old man spoke to him.

71. He has said that the country is to prosper only by every man doing his duty in one of his ablest speeches.

72. When he struck me I knocked him down, but I do not think I hurt him for which I am sorry.

73. I learned what an inefficient woman I was later in life.

74. Sometimes disturbances arise, but they are usually checked before much harm is done by the policemen.

75. He has written a story about a remarkable courtship that is to appear next month.

76. Working for his daily support and yet developing his noble philanthropic plan, is it any wonder that there came in time complete prostration of body and spirit?

77. This is the spot about which I will tell you when we come to that part of the story where stood the house of the murderer.

78. There will be two new courses, if the number choosing them is sufficiently large, to cover the remaining parts of the subject.

79. He said that his travelling bag had been stolen while sleeping in the car.

80. Riding quickly to the other end of the line, the command of the officer came sharp and clear.

81. The preacher spoke of the evils of gambling without manuscript or note.

82. He is in the country when business permits fishing, reading and idling.

Errors in the Order of Thought in the Whole Structure of the Sentence.

Examples of these errors, with an explanation of the exercises and the directions how to use them, are taken from Abbott's "How to Write Clearly."

"The following exercises consist of extracts from Burnet, . . . , and Clarendon, modernized and altered with a view to remove obscurity and ambiguity. The modernized version will necessarily be inferior to the original in unity and style, and in some other respects. The charm of the author's individuality, and the pleasant ring of the old-fashioned English, are lost. It is highly necessary that the student should recognize this, and should bear in mind that the sole object is to show how the meaning in each case might have been more clearly expressed. . . . These exercises can be used in two ways. The pupil may either have his book open and be questioned on the reasons for each alteration, or, after studying the two versions, he may have the original version dictated to him, and then he may reproduce the parallel version, or something like it, on paper."

Burnet.

"The principal faults in Burnet's style are the use of heterogeneous sentences; the want of suspense; the ambiguous use of pronouns; the omission of connecting adverbs and conjunctions, and the excessive use of "and;" and an abruptness in passing from one topic to another. The correction of these faults necessarily lengthens the altered version."

83. ORIGINAL VERSION.

"And his maintaining the honor of the nation in all foreign countries gratified the *vanity which is very natural to Englishmen;* of which he was *so careful* that, though he was not a crowned head, yet his ambassadors had all the respects paid them which our *kings'* ambassadors ever had: he said the dignity of the crown was upon the account of the nation, *of which the king was only the representative head;* so, the nation being the same, he would have the same regards paid to his ministers."

PARALLEL VERSION.

"He also gratified the English feeling of self-respect by maintaining the honor of the nation in all foreign countries. So jealous was he on this point that, though he was not a crowned head, he yet secured for his ambassadors all the respect that had been paid to the ambassadors of our kings. The king, he said, received respect simply as the nation's representative head, and, since the nation was the same, the same respect should be paid to the nation's ministers."

LORD CLARENDON.

"The principal faults in this style are, long heterogeneous sentences, use of phrases for words, ambiguous use of pronouns, excessive separation of words grammatically connected together."

84. ORIGINAL VERSION.

"It will not be impertinent nor *unnatural to this present discourse,* to set down in this place the present temper and constitution of both Houses of Parliament, and of the court itself, and *it* may be the less wondered at, that so prodigious an alteration should be made in so short a

PARALLEL VERSION.

"And now, in order to explain as far as possible, how so prodigious an alteration could take place in so short a time, and how the royal power could fall so low as to be unable to support itself, its dignity, or its faithful servants, it will be of use to set down here, where it comes most naturally,

time, and the crown fallen so low, that it could neither support itself nor its own majesty, nor *those who would appear faithful to it.* some account of the present temper and composition not only of both Houses of Parliament, but also of the court itself."

ERRORS IN THE USE OF ELLIPSIS.

85. Every good man ought to battle against municipal corruption as earnestly as Dr. Parkhurst.

86. The captain in his indignation was not less determined to humiliate the rival team than the other members of the home eleven.

87. He did not more resemble his brother than his father his brother.

88. Rising from obscurity, and obtaining his position by force of genius and industry, the obstacles that disheartened other men had for him no intimidation.

89. We dislike to see drunkards as much as prohibitionists.

90. Look at my brother's sketch book, and tell me what you think of them.

91. The Secretary and Treasurer of the company.

92. I was so unfortunate as to have to ride for an hour with a rogue and fool.

93. When he said the pitcher and catcher of the nine, I wondered what he meant.

94. The feeling in the game is intense, and serious injuries have occurred.

95. Duty no less than pleasure will have my faithful performance.

96. If a pupil is fond of learning he needs no stimulus, and if the opposite is true no stimulus will be of any avail; but as he is either fond of learning or dislikes it, the effect of stimulus must be the one or the other so that stimulus should not be applied.

97. The ends of a divine and human ruler are no more the same than time and eternity are the same.

98. A captain on a White Star and Anchor Line Steamship are paid very different salaries.

99. He was disciplined for doing and for not doing what he ought not and what he ought.

100. A good heart and a good head feel and know what is the right thing to be done.

ERRORS IN THE INTRODUCTION OF IRRELEVANT MATTER INTO THE SENTENCE.

"To this succeeded that licentiousness which entered with the restoration, and from infecting our religion and morals, fell to corrupt our language; which last was not likely to be much improved by those, who at that time made up the court of King Charles the Second; either such as had followed him in his banishment, or had been altogether conversant in the dialect of these fanatic times; or young men who had been educated in the same country; so that the court, which used to be the standard of correctness and propriety of speech, was then, and I think has ever since continued, the worst school in England for that accomplishment; and will so remain, till better care be taken in the education of our nobility, that they may set out into the world with some foundation of literature, in order to qualify them for patterns of politeness."—*Swift*.

"It is asserted, as a general affection of human nature, that it is impossible to read a book with satisfaction until one has ascertained whether the author of it be tall or short, corpulent or thin; and, as to complexion, whether he be a 'black' man (which in the 'Spectator's' time, was the absurd expression for a swarthy man), or a fair man, or a sallow man, or perhaps a green man, which Southey affirmed to be the proper description of many stout artificers in Birmingham too much given to work in metallic fumes; on which account the name of Southey is an abomination to this day in certain furnaces of Warwickshire."—*De Quincey*.

"There are extant numberless books, wherein the wisest and most ingenious of men have laid open their hearts, and exposed their most secret cogitations unto us; in pursuing them we may sufficiently busy ourselves, and let our idle hours pass gratefully; we may meddle with ourselves, studying our own dispositions, examining our own principles and purposes, reflecting on our own thoughts, words, and actions, striving thoughtfully to understand ourselves; to do this we have an unquestionable right, and by it we shall obtain vast benefit."—*Barrow*.

"Sir, to borrow the words of one of your own poets, whose academic sojourn was in the building in which we are now assembled, (and in what language but that of Milton, can I hope to do justice to Bacon and Newton?) if their star should ever for a period go down, it must be to rise again with new splendor."

EXERCISES IN ENERGY OF STYLE

CHAPTERS XV., XVI., XVII. AND XVIII.

SHORT WORDS AND LONG WORDS.

In the following sentences substitute a short or simple word of like meaning for the word which is italicized.

1. Will you *accord* him this favor?
2. The young *scion* is a promising *juvenile*.
3. See that the *apartment* is *ventilated*.
4. Such *penurious* tendencies are not to be *extirpated*.
5. The trouble is a *membranaceous covering*.
6. This is to be his *domicile*.
7. Let there be an *interstice* between the two parts.
8. The *termination* of his career does not fulfil the promise of its *commencement*.
9. She does not speak even her *vernacular* with propriety.
10. You had better put an *impediment* on his rashness.
11. We shall have a *collation* before the ride.
12. To *effectuate* your purpose, get his influence.
13. Mr. C. *donated* the organ,
14. The school-room is *palatial*.
15. The new training field will *enhance* athletics.
16. He *manipulates* the mandolin well.
17. The architect will make good use of all the *potentialities* of the old building.
18. He is to *inaugurate* the new drill to-morrow.
19. The *cicerone* was an old woman who took her husband's place.
20. My companion seemed lost in his *cogitations*.
21. To *approximate* to such a standard, is better than to reach a lower one.
22. He has *precipitated* his return to this country.

23. The lecturer is a fine looking *personage* but not an interesting speaker.
24. This fact alone ought not to *invalidate* his argument.
25. Why does he take *cognizance* of mere trifles?
26. The *celerity* and the *dexterity* of his movements are remarkable.
27. The singer has a *captivating* manner.
28. His constant *sternutation* is very disagreeable.
29. How *insensate* is such conduct.
30. The *mendacity* of this report is shameful.
31. It is a fine *locality*.

Rewrite the following sentences using short words and a simple style.

1. Not even the sacred desk could be rescued from the devouring element.
2. He evinces too great diversification of purpose to succeed.
3. The thief will be apprehended as he has but an inconsiderable advantage of the officer who is in pursuit.
4. The concatenation of circumstances which surrounds him is not to be escaped.
5. I shall not animadvert on his conduct although it has eventuated in our being in this melancholy predicament.
6. So much ostentation is not becoming in the sanctuary.
7. He was engaged in making a series of excavations for his long proposed fence.
8. The enterprise which has this magnificent culmination was initiated on a diminutive scale.
9. He has recuperated sufficiently from the disease to partake of his customary food.
10. Before retiring he proceeded to the culinary department to give orders for his morning banquet.
11. Will you permit me to transmit this epistle by you?
12. He was impervious to the vituperations of individual indignation but felt most bitterly the opprobrium of the populace.
13. It was not his own predilection but fortuitous circumstances entirely beyond his jurisdiction that made him an instrument for the persecution of his persuasion.

14. She has been the recipient of many attentions, and the brilliancy of her achievements this season eclipses all the antecedent successes of her professional experience.

15. Public taste has suffered decadence, so that in the vicissitudes of a long artistic career, his former popularity is passing into obsolescence.

16. I extend to the individual an invitation to my apartments.

Words having Sound Significant of their Sense.

Give words which in their sound suggest sounds made by the wind, by insects, serpents, by falling water or falling timber, by the opening of gates on smooth or on harsh hinges, by the music of the flute, the violin, by the noise of the drum and of the trumpet. The following sentence from Edward Everett's description of the voyage of the Mayflower illustrates the power of words to convey meaning by their sound.

"The awful voice of the storm howls through the rigging: the laboring masts seem straining from their base: the dismal sound of the pumps is heard: the ship leaps, as it were, madly from billow to billow: the ocean breaks and settles with ingulfing floods over the floating deck, and beats with deadening, shivering weight, against the staggered vessel."

Some of the sentences in Henry Ward Beecher's "Loss of the Arctic" get their finest effect from the use of words similarly suggestive. From a like use of words comes largely the power of Victor Hugo's description of the struggle of the gun and the gunner, in "Ninety-three," and of the battle of Waterloo in "Les Misérables." Instances of the oratorical effect of such words may be found in the speeches of John Bright, as also in the speeches of Burke, and of other great orators. Examination will show that the words which produce this effect are as a rule Saxon-English, and, therefore, most often comparatively short words.

Number of Words.

EXAMPLES FOR CORRECTION OR CRITICISM IN TAUTOLOGY.

1. Then came a clangor and a harsh ringing sound that startled the waiting multitude.
2. In this secret and clandestine marriage began the troubles of her life.
3. He came out of this danger and peril a sadder but a wiser man.
4. The society is without outward sign, symbol, or emblem.
5. He surprised his victim by an inaudible and a noiseless approach.
6. With his purpose and strength of will, he can vanquish and overcome every inherited tendency to vice.
7. It stands on the border and outskirts of the village.
8. We shall be supplied with all that is needful and necessary.
9. The reason is plain and evident why the paper should be given up.
10. No wonder that he trembled and quaked when he did not know the cause of the explosion.
11. The Italian tried and experimented in every way to explain and represent to us what he wanted.
12. He has been a joy and delight to us and has brought to our home a new and larger happiness and felicity.
13. What sad and doleful music that organist plays!
14. The young man was enticed and decoyed to the place of his death and murder.
15. By pushing and pressing and urging we made our way through the crowd.
16. He delays, pauses, and dwells too long on each minute subdivision to be interesting.
17. The poor animal since the accident has been dwindling and wasting away.
18. No more impudent and shameless conduct has been seen here this season.
19. I was sorry to blame and censure him.
20. A brave, bold and resolute boy, he has made a noble man.

21. This is all that we can do with our limited and finite powers.
22. She is ill from care, anxiety, and solicitude.
23. Then our little plans will all be extinguished and annihilated.
24. Why not be sanguine and hopeful until you know the result?
25. I fear anything so infectious and pestilential.

EXAMPLES FOR CORRECTION OR CRITICISM IN VERBOSENESS.

26. The reason why she came home was on account of her illness.
27. The best explanation of his conduct is to be attributed to his early associations.
28. I shall go from thence to Boston.
29. From whence did it come?
30. You can do it equally as well.
31. She is a widow woman with several children.
32. It has ragged extremities at both ends.
33. From hence where will you go?
34. They both came to see me to-day.
35. It is owing to an old hatred which has actuated him to seize the property.
36. You and I both agree in this instance.
37. In the universal patriotism of all our people is the nation's bulwark.
38. You have my grateful thanks and sincere gratitude for this favor.
39. All my friends without exception are invited.
40. For two men to have precisely the same name is a great inconvenience to both of them.
41. Our own littleness and insignificance seem never so evident as when in a great crowd of many other persons who know nothing of us and who care nothing for us.
42. This is an original recipe of his own.
43. He bears this with great equanimity of mind.
44. We ought to respect an old veteran who has fought for us.
45. This has been thought to be a universal panacea for every political evil.
46. The wrong was too intolerable to be borne.
47. He has returned again to us.

48. They all unanimously consented to the change.

49. A gale of wind took off the unfinished roof of his prison house.

50. There is a fortune in a new discovery.

51. "Network is anything reticulated or decussated at equal distances with interstices between the intersections."

52. The different branches of study in this course mutually reflect light on each other.

53. He has been heard to reiterate again and again the story in which he gives an account of the impediments and hinderances that obstructed his way to the final success in which he at last won his wealth and reward.

54. The wealth of this man in its rich accumulations has hidden and obscured from the public gaze the unscrupulous and unworthy means by which it was gathered and acquired.

55. In his habitual silence on this subject which comes from his taciturn disposition, he simply reveals a characteristic unwillingness to lay open his mind to others.

56. Our state of mind at any one time is but the result of the different circumstances which just then determine our mental condition.

EXAMPLES FOR CORRECTION OR CRITICISM IN CIRCUMLOCUTION.

57. After having dinner at a small edition of a once large hotel which had been burned the year before, near Ausable Chasm, and finding that the boat would not leave Port Kent for several hours, and that the railway train was not much more convenient, probably for the same reason that the boat arrives so late because of the few local passengers, I decided it would be more pleasant to be travelling in some way than to remain idle at this uninteresting hotel, and so was taken by horse and carriage in a beautiful ride along Lake Champlain, to Plattsburg.

58. When many duties crowd upon you which you feel have a claim upon your best efforts, and you are, therefore, in doubt which first to attempt, then choose always that which is not most remote in its interests and associations, but the one which touches most closely your immediate surroundings and your nearest obligations.

59. He came to me as if something was troubling him about which he wished to speak, and when, seeing his perplexity, and desiring to relieve him from it, I said, "I see that things are not going right with you," he answered in perhaps not these words, but in what meant the same, that while on the train he had taken out his pocket-book to examine a paper which was in it, and in some way he had probably dropped the pocket-book on the floor when he thought he had put it in his pocket, and so would like to borrow from me ten dollars to get home.

60. An admirable piece of advice to follow is to abstain from interesting yourself in the affairs of others when there is not any request or indication that your services are desired; but to give your earnest attention to what immediately concerns yourself.

EXAMPLES OF CONCISENESS TO BE APPROVED OR TO BE CRITICISED.

61. "Christianity a failure! Then man is a failure. Then the race is a failure. Then the government of God is a failure. The man whose face is seamed and ridged all over with the fruits of vice says virtue is a failure. The bloated, besotted, drivelling inebriate says temperance is a failure. The highwayman and the murderer say law is a failure. The reckless violators of the laws of health say the science of medicine is a failure. The owl says light is a failure. Is it any wonder that men may be heard to say that Christianity is a failure? It's an old cry. Every single century since Christ it has sounded out. But somehow this thing we call Christianity does not fail."—*Herrick Johnson*.

62. "All hail, public opinion! To be sure, it is a dangerous thing under which to live. It rules to-day in the desire to obey all kinds of laws, and takes your life. It rules again in the love of liberty, and rescues Shadrach from Boston Court-House. It rules to-morrow in the manhood of him who loads the musket to shoot down—God be praised!—the man-hunter, Gorsuch. It rules in Syracuse, and the slave escapes to Canada. It is our interest to educate this people in humanity, and in deep reverence for the rights of the lowest and humblest individual that makes up our numbers. Each man here, in fact, holds his property and his life dependent on the constant presence of an agitation like this of anti-slavery. Eternal vigilance is

the price of liberty; power is ever stealing from the many to the few. The manna of popular liberty is gathered each day, or it is rotten. The living sap of to-day outgrows the dead rind of yesterday. . . . All clouds, it is said, have sunshine behind them, and all evils have some good result; so slavery, by the necessity of its abolition, has saved the freedom of the white race from being melted in luxury or buried beneath the gold of its own success. Never look, therefore, for an age when the people can be quiet and safe. At such times despotism, like a shrouding mist, steals over the mirror of Freedom." — *Wendell Phillips*.

63. "Thousands have reflected on a Diarist's power to cancel our Burial Service. Not alone the cleric's good work is upset by him but the sexton's as well. He howks the graves and transforms the quiet worms, busy on a single poor peaceable body, into winged serpents that disorder sky and earth with a deadly flight of zigzags, like military rockets, among the living. And if these are given to cry too much, to have their tender sentiments considered, it cannot be said that history requires the flaying of them."—*George Meredith*.

64. "We are all disgusted by gossip; yet it is of importance to keep the angels to their proprieties. The smallest insect will draw blood, and gossip is a weapon impossible to exclude from the privatest, highest, selectest. Nature created a police of many ranks. God has delegated himself to a million deputies. From these low external penalties, the scale ascends. Next come the resentments, the fears, which injustice calls out; then, the false relations in which the offender is put to other men; and the reaction of his fault on himself in the solitude and devastation of his own mind."—*Emerson*.

65. "To read the reports of the Poor-Law Commissioners, if one has faith enough, would be a pleasure to the friend of humanity. One sole recipe seems to have been needful for the woes of England — 'refusal of out-door relief.' England lay in sick discontent, writhing powerless on its fever-bed, dark, nigh desperate, in the wastefulness, want, improvidence, and eating care, till, like Hyperion down the eastern steeps, the Poor-Law Commissioners arose, and said, let there be workhouses, and bread of affliction and water of affliction there! It was a simple invention; as all truly great inventions are. And see, in any quarter, instantly as the walls of the workhouse arise, misery and necessity fly away, out of sight, out of being, as is fondly hoped, dissolve into the inane: industry, frugality,

rise of wages, peace on earth and good-will towards men, do—in the Poor-Law Commissioners' reports—infallibly, rapidly or not so rapidly, to the joy of all parties, supervene."—*Carlyle.*

66. "A disbanding army is a thaw. The whole bends, cracks, rolls, crashes, plunges. Mysterious disintegration; Napoleon gallops along the fugitives, harangues them, urges, threatens, entreats. The mouths which in the morning were crying 'Vive l'Empereur!' are now agape. He is barely recognized; the Prussian cavalry just come up, spring forward, fling themselves upon the enemy. Teams rush off; the guns are left to take care of themselves; the soldiers of the train take the horses to escape. Wagons upset with their four wheels in the air, block up the road. They crash, they crowd, they trample upon the living and the dead. Arms are broken. A multitude fills roads, bridges, valleys, woods, choked up by the flight of forty thousand men. No more comrades; no more officers; no more generals. Inexpressible dismay."—*Victor Hugo.*

EXAMPLES FOR CRITICISM OR CORRECTION.

Clauses and important words of the sentence so placed as to lose their force.

1. He delights in presenting subjects which he can be most heretical in.
2. Though he was able and even brilliant yet he was far from being one of the leaders of the club, with all his gifts.
3. He held this office in the church for more than thirty years as if with a divine right to it.
4. Success in life is in what we are, and not in what we have, as some seem to think.
5. Why of all matters pertaining to the welfare of the institution should he say of the most important so little?
6. This is the most valuable experience which the nation thus far has passed through.
7. His conduct during all his public career showed him to be not only a politician but a statesman.
8. He will accomplish the great work which he has been assigned to.

9. But keep this thought in mind and you will ultimately succeed whatever may be the difficulties.

10. Petty deception is an evil which most persons are sometimes guilty of.

11. In their prosperity my friends shall never hear of me, but always in their adversity.

12. At this critical moment he showed great errors of judgment, to say no worse.

13. What a triumph it was to know that this achievement he had planned and brought about.

14. Several novels and two or three popular magazines were on the table, and an open writing desk.

15. It can be done by this man and by only this man.

16. There is nothing more foolish than envy of the good fortune of others.

17. It is what you do and not what you say that convinces men of your sincerity.

18. There have been no suffering and privation here.

19. And this is the man who once was the idol of his party.

20. It must be indeed wrong for an organization to prevent a boy from learning a trade or a man from working at it because the man and the boy are not members of the organization.

21. This statement is not so much dependent on as it is involved in what has been said before.

22. I have often touched on themes kindred to but not immediately connected with my present subject.

EXAMPLES FOR CORRECTION OR CRITICISMS IN THE WRONG USE OR THE OMITTED USE OF CONNECTIVES.

1. Our military school at West Point has a picturesque situation on the Hudson River, and gives a training which proved its value in the Civil War; and is a place much visited by foreigners and who always seem surprised at the precision and finish of the drill which the cadets display.

2. I knocked down the man in my haste to escape. I did not wish to do him serious injury. I should not have done so, had I not known that my only chance of life was in freeing myself from him. Others

were in pursuit. They, I knew, would not hesitate in their rage to strike the fatal blow.

3. Hazing is a custom that in its old form has nearly passed out of our larger colleges; and if it appears now, it is most often in the initiations into the secret organizations, and which the student is not compelled to enter, so that one now usually suffers from hazing by choice and not by force.

4. We came to the river. It was too high for fording. We had then to travel northward several miles. Here was a bridge. It was a bridge with a toll house. The keeper seemed to be one of the Seven Sleepers. At last he was aroused. We then went on our wearisome way. We arrived at our destination at early daybreak.

5. It was a delightful walk which we took one day in the Adirondacks, and what we especially enjoyed was that although we were walking several hours, we never wholly lost sight of the beautiful group of lakes that makes the particular spot where our cottage is so pleasant; and thus we have come to be very much attached to them, and so like to keep them always in view, and which because we often caught unexpected glimpses of them that day made our walk unusually enjoyable.

Change the following sentences to the Periodic Structure.

1. What a number of men is in this degrading business who ought to be able to do something worthy of human beings.

2. These young men had been trained at home to promptness, diligence, and honesty; and so when thrown upon their own resources in this new country they soon showed in their rise to wealth and influence the value of early discipline.

3. There are many things taught in these days which we may fail to know without suffering from our ignorance.

4. He spoke eloquently, and so won over the jury to his side.

5. Rigorous discipline is essential not only to success but to safety in the Army and the Navy.

6. She has a sweet, sympathetic voice, and therefore gives pleasure to all her hearers who are not critical.

7. It is impossible for a new man, if at all indolent, to have any success here, because of the scarcity of openings, the close competition, and the energy of the native inhabitants.

8. The fire swept on, and with its advance gained force and range, and left in ashes the town, and in terrible desolation the surrounding country for miles in every direction.

9. He came now to the crisis of his life, struggled, fell back, got courage again, made another vigorous effort, stood firm and strong against the heavy odds, and finally conquered.

10. He walks rapidly so as to get the benefit of the exercise.

11. The general was now compelled to take the defensive, having been surprised by the arrival of the fresh troops on the opposite side.

12. I should urge you to come out of your sick room, get the strength of this invigorating air, enjoy this constant sunshine, and know again what it is to live, if you were here.

13. He came upon me suddenly so that I had no time to avoid him or to prepare for him.

14. We have no opportunity to make money or to spend money.

15. Why should he disgrace himself and his friends by getting money in this way, when he could have whatever he needed by asking for it?

16. You must act promptly, taking the risk of mistake, or else you must perhaps let slip the only opportunity that you will have to gain your object.

17. There are to be accommodations for a larger attendance at the next football game than ever before, I hear.

18. The number of subjects to be taught multiplies, and so must the means of instruction be increased.

19. The enemies of the public school are in favor of this measure; the friends of the school are opposed to it.

20. He had the years of youth, yet he had the wisdom of age.

Rearrange the parts of the following sentences, when necessary, in the gradation of a Climax.

1. It is a hopeless, wearisome, painful undertaking.

2. Andrew Jackson announced, Washington feared and Jefferson foreshadowed the danger of sectional divisions.

3. All these institutions have been subverted, radically changed and rudely shaken.

4. He had administered government and war; he had patronized

learning; he had preserved and extended an empire; he had founded a polity; he had repurchased the old lands and rebuilt the old dwelling.

5. By whose strong grip has the corpse of a Republic once fallen ever been raised? Where, in what age and in what clime have the ruins of constitutional freedom renewed their youth and regained their lost estate?

6. Intemperance has produced more misery, crime, want, distress, and idleness, than all other causes put together.

7. He acted out his plans in a suffering, loyal, earnest life.

8. So great and unsullied a consecration, so signal an illustration of the moral sublime, explains the profound feeling that attended the death of a man of no official position, of no literary, or scientific, or social distinction, and publicly known only as an orator from whose opinions there was often general and strong dissent.

9. A man whose donations were crowns; who raised himself from obscurity to a crown; who broke down the awful barrier of the Alps; whose will was feared as destiny; who changed the face of the world; who was the greatest leader of armies that modern history has known, is a man who has taken out of our hands the question whether he shall be called great.

10. They entreated; they expostulated; they requested.

11. The next reckoning day for this world will be set by the Nihilist —not by the Puritan who put his foot on the necks of prostrate kings in the name of the Lord of Hosts, enfranchising conscience and making an end of star-chambers, who feared God, loved liberty, and hated oppression.

12. A man learns that on the whole it is safer in the world not to shirk and hesitate and dodge.

13. Where else shall we find memorials of patriotism like the corner where the farmers of Middlesex fell with withering fire upon the Britons retreating from that bridge; the field in which the minute-men gathered; the farm on which the Revolutionary stores were hidden; the site of the first church and of the first school.

14. "The days will grow to weeks, the weeks to months, the months will add themselves and make the years, the years will roll into centuries, and mine will ever be a name of scorn."

15. In our early struggles, John Jay was the conscience, Jefferson was the heart, and Hamilton was the head.

16. Victory returned his sword, necessity stained, liberty unsheathed it.

Change the following sentences, when necessary, to the Antithetic Structure.

1. If you regulate your desires according to the standard of nature, you will never be poor; if according to what men think of you, you will never become a possessor of wealth.

2. Homer was the greater genius; Virgil a poet of more artistic merit; in the one we must admire the man; in the other what the man did. Homer hurries us with a commanding impetuosity; Virgil with his attractive majesty is more of a leader. Homer scatters with a generous profusion; Virgil bestows with magnificence and yet with care.

3. "The Puritans hated bearbaiting, not because it gave pain to the bear but because it gave pleasure to the spectator."

4. I love the country, but for the town I have even hatred.

5. The individual is nothing; the state represents every interest and relation.

6. We measure genius by quality, not by the amount of it.

7. Your general never saw an army till he was forty; my general never saw the smallest part of an army till he was ten years older.

8. They aimed at the rule, not at the power to destroy their country.

9. Success evokes applause, but it is silenced by defeat.

10. Faith inspiring to effort, and doubt which paralyzes action, contend for the mastery.

11. Man wishes to be happy, and has a constant fear of being miserable.

12. A writer who had the art of being minute without tediousness, and a general without permitting himself to become confused.

13. A dramatist who seldom pierces the breast, but he always gives delight to the ear, and often adds improvement to the understanding.

14. . . . . "My way of life
Is fall'n into the sear, the yellow leaf,
And that which should accompany old age,
As honor, love, obedience, troops of friends,

> I must not look to have ; but, in their stead,
> Curses, not loud but deep, mouth-honor, breath,
> Which the poor heart would fain deny, and dare not."

15. "Let your search and criticism always have for its purpose that you may find that which you may believe, not that you may find what you need not believe."

16. The external part of the church has a charm which the inward has not.

17. "Who is the man who has dared to call into civilized alliance the wild and inhuman inhabitant of the woods?—to delegate to the merciless Indian the defence of disputed rights, and to wage the horrors of his barbarous war against our brethren?"

Change the structure of the following sentences from the *declarative* form to the *interrogative*, and from the *interrogative* to the *declarative*.

1. You would wish to ruin yourself in public opinion to gratify your resentment.

2. They shall bend their neck to the cruel yoke, for the want of your help.

3. With undoubted right on my side, I am to be thus despoiled.

4. We should suspend our resistance, we should submit to an authority like this.

5. You believe that the pure system of Christian faith which appeared eighteen hundred years ago, in one of the obscurest regions of the Roman empire, at the moment of the highest mental cultivation, and of the lowest moral degeneracy, originated in the unaided reflection of twelve Jewish fishermen on the Sea of Galilee.

6. Has tyranny thus triumphed; have the hopes with which we greeted the French Revolution been crushed; has a usurper plucked up the last roots of the tree of liberty and planted despotism in its place?

7. Must I wound his ear with the news of your revolt; must he hear from me that neither the soldiers raised by himself, nor the veterans who fought under him, are willing to own his authority?

8. You are Christians; and, by upholding duelists, you will deluge the land with blood, and fill it with widows and orphans.

9. You will give your suffrage to this man, when you know that by withholding it, you may arrest this deadly end.

10. Does he suppose me less capable of gratitude for his patriotism, or sympathy for his sufferings, than if his eyes had first opened upon the light of Massachusetts, instead of South Carolina?

11. All the wealth of universal commerce, all the achievements of successful heroism, all the establishments of this world's wisdom, cannot secure to the empire the permanency of its possessions.

12. A title deed like this ought to become the acquisition of the nation.

13. Was it the winter's storm beating upon the houseless heads of women and children, was it disease, was it the tomahawk, was it the deep malady of a blighted hope, a ruined enterprise and a broken heart aching in its last moments at the recollection of the loved and left beyond the sea, was it some, or all of these united, that hurried this forsaken company to their melancholy fate?

14. You are a scholar, and the land of the Muses shall ask your help in vain.

15. You are a mother, rejoicing in all the charities of domestic life; you are a daughter rich and safe in conscious innocence and parental love, and thousands among the purest and loveliest of your sex shall glut the markets of the Orient, and be doomed to a fate inconceivably worse than death.

16. This is then the genuine fruit of the pious care of our ancestors for the security and propagation of religion and good manners to the latest posterity.

17. The miseries of man are in contemplation.

18. The farmer in cultivating his lands, the mariner navigating his vessel on the ocean, professional men in their various pursuits, contribute as really as the statesman in his cabinet to the prosperity of the country.

INDEX

Abbreviations, 210
"Ability" and "capacity," 265
Abruptness, obscurity from, 107
Abstract words used for concrete, 103; and concrete words, exercises, 283
Accuracy, philosophical, 66
"Adherence" and "adhesion," 265
Adjectives and adverbs, arrangement of, 111; errors in use of, examples, 283
"Admire," 229
Adverbs and adjectives, arrangement of, 111; errors in use of, examples, 283
Affectation of unnaturalness, 197
Affectations, literary, 167
Aim of discourse, necessity of interest in, 200
Alison, A., faulty construction, 108, 111, 120; testimony to English language, 43
"Alone" and "only," 265
"Alonely," 19
Alternative, hypothetically expressed, 118
"Alternative," 230
Ambiguous words, dangers from, 102
American and English usage, 217
Americanisms, 35; exercises on, 214
Americans should use pure English, 45
"Among" and "between," 265
Anacoluthon, 120
Analogies, 73; variety of, desirable, 188
"Ancient" and "antiquated," 265
"And" beginning sentences, 150

"Anon," 230
"Antiquated" and "ancient," 265
Antithesis, 157; exercises in, 305
Apathetic style unnatural, 195
Aphoristic style obscure, 146
Apologetic style unnatural, 195
Apostrophe an aid to energy, 162
"Apparent" and "obvious," 266
"Apprehend" and "comprehend," 266
"Apprehensive," 266
Archaisms, to be used, when, 20
Arnold, Dr., on popular condensed style, 142
"As," 230
Audience in mind when writing, 129
"Averse from" *vs.* "averse to," 266
"Awful," 230

Barbarism of style, 10, 23
"Base," 230
"Bayonets think," 139
Beautiful in nature and in character, 167
Beauty an ultimate conception, 164
Beauty, excessive, not elegant, 169
"Belittle," 230
"Beside" and "besides," 266
"Betrayal," *vs.* "betrayment," 266
"Between" and "among," 265
Bible, purity of style, 38; heaven and hell presented specifically in, 137
Blundering constructions, 65, 254
Boyle, Roche, blunders of, 94
Brimley, G., obscurity of, 90
Bryant, W. C., 30

Burke, E., diatribe against metaphysicians, 100; effective diffusiveness in description, 146; his style made easy things difficult, 92; idea of beauty, 165; too elaborately precise, 66

"Calculate" for "think," 231
California, Spanish words in, 47
"Can but" vs. "cannot but," 231
Cant and slang, exercises in, 222
"Capacity" and "ability," 265
Carlyle, degrading effect of German studies on his style, 52; recklessness as to style, 28
"Caucus," 35
Chalmers, T., faulty construction, 108
"Chastity" and "chasteness," 267
China, concise description of, 142
Chinook dialect, 46
Choate, R., command of etymological meaning of word, 63; command of language, 71; sources of his fine diction, 75
"Christen" for "baptize," 267
"Christianization," 231
"Christless," 231
Cicero, failure to improve language, 29
Circumlocution, examples of, for correction, 297; of thought, 143; obscurity from, 107
Climax, 157; exercises in use of, 303
Cobbett, W., on use of "it," 56
"Coeval" and "contemporaneous," 267
Coleridge, S. T., neologisms, 27, 29, 30; on capacity of language, 91; on connectives, 58; on empty thought, 68
Colloquialisms, 49; exercises in, 219
Colonization and commerce, English, the language of, 43
Combinations of words, many possible, 113
Command of language, 70, 71; an acquisition, 76

"Common" and "mutual," 272
Commonplace in imagery, 175
"Community," 231
Comparison, errors in, 248
"Compassionate," "pitiful," and "piteous," 272
Composition, scholarly care in, 52
Compound words, 231; barbarous, 25
"Comprehend" and "apprehend," 266
"Concept," 21; and "conception," 267
Conciseness, affected, 145; an element of force, 139; excessive, 64, 104; examples of, 298
Concrete and abstract words, exercises, 283
Concreteness essential to oral discourse, 197
"Conditioned," 231
"Conduct," 231
"Conform with" vs. "conform to," 267
Conjunctive beginnings, care in, 150
Connectives, errors in use of, 57, 251; exercises in use of, 301
Construction, blunders in, 254; clearness of, 107; extreme care in, 122; loose, destroys precision, 67; of sentence and energy, 148
Constructions, inelegant, 173
"Contemporaneous" and "coeval," 267
"Continual" and "continuous," 267
Contractions, 23, 210
Contrast, usefulness of, 158
Conversation and public speaking, different styles in, 135; freedom of style in, 49
Cowper, H. Miller's criticism of, 70
Creation of new words, 23
Critical study of language, 72
Cushing, Caleb, command of English, 75
"Custom," "habit," "usage," 270

"Decided" vs. "decisive," 268
"Declension," 233
"Deed," 233
"Deicide," 28
"Deity," 233
Delicacy an element of elegance, 164; and vividness, 181
"Delicious" vs. "delightful," 268
Delight in writing a source of ease, 203
Delivery, period effective in, 153; variety of, 188; and style, reciprocal effect of, 188
"Delusion" vs. "illusion," 268
Demosthenes and Cicero contrasted, 147
Dependent clauses, bungling construction of, 173
"Depravity" and "depravation," 268
"Deputize," 233
DeQuincey, T., early "penury of words," 76; on grammatical faults of most writers, 56; style injured by archaisms, 22; intemperate style of, 132; use of slang, 51
Description, concise, 142
Descriptive writing sometimes marred by conciseness, 146
"Desk" for "pulpit," 233
Dialects, 46
"Diction" and "style," 268
Dictionaries, discreet use of, 52
"Differ with" vs. "differ from," 268
Diffuseness, excessive, 103; sometimes required, 145
Digression, 119
"Disbelief" and "unbelief," 268
Discrimination in thinking, 68
Distention causes obscurity, 104
Distinctness of thought, 181
Diversities in style, natural, 166
Dogmatic style, 194
"Donate," 233
"Don't," 233
Douglas, S. A., on classical education, 45

"Doxologize," 234
Drama, Greek love of, 185
Dramatic quality of oral discourse, 198
"Drouth," 234
"Drive" and "ride," 273

"Effectuate," 234
Effeminacy not elegance, 166; of taste a token of decay, 178
Elegance of style, 7, 164; and energy, 176; promoted by precision, 82
Ellipsis, excessive or careless, 117; examples of erroneous, 249, 290
Emerson, R. W., obscure conciseness of, 146; over-conciseness of, 64
Emphatic clauses, wrong arrangement in, 116
Emphatic sentence, growth of, 69
Emphatic words, location of, 149
"Endow" and "endue," 269
"Energize," 234
Energy of style, 7, 124; means of, 134; exercises in, 292
"England" for "Britain," 234
English language, excellence of, 41; rapid spread, 42; three kinds of, 16
English poetry, 39
English temperament, 166
Enthusiasm requisite for forcible writing, 127; unbalanced, 131; vs. "fanaticism," 269
Epitaphs, blundering, 116
"Epoch," and "era," 269
Erasmus, wedded to Latin, 11
Errors in use of prepositions, 223; miscellaneous, exercises on, 224; in comparison, exercises on, 248; in the use of verbs, from ellipsis, 249; in use of tenses, 249; in use of moods, 250; in use of the subjunctive, 250; in use of connectives, 251; in use of synonyms, 251; in use of pronouns, 283; of adjectives and adverbs, 284; of qualifying clauses, 287; in order of

thought, 288; in use of ellipsis, 290; in introduction of irrelevant matter, 291
"Eternal" and "everlasting," 269
Etymology, misleading, 33; neglect of, 63
"Evangelization," 234
"Eventuate," 234
Everett, E., never employed contractions, 23; style in conversation, 50
"Everlasting" and "eternal," 269
"Except" and "unless," 270
Exclamation an aid to energy, 101
"Exhumate," 234
Expansions of words, 24; exercises, 211
"Expect" for "think," 234
Expression, excessive care for, 69
Extemporaneous and written discourse, 135
Extemporaneous speech, period in, 153
"Extreme," 234
Eye, appeal to, in oratory, 99

Facetiously coined words, 24
"Fall" for "autumn," 234
"Falsehood" for "falseness," 270
"Fancy" and "imagination," 270
"Fellowship," 234
Feminine qualities of thought, 165
Figurative language and energy, 156; exercises, 275
Figurative uses, 73
Figurative and literal use of same word, 60
Figure, excessive use of, 60
Figures of speech, right use of, 162
Finical imagery, 175
"Firstly" for "first," 235
Fitness of expression to subject, 193
"Fix," 235
"Fixity" for "fixedness," 235
Fontenelle's rule "to understand myself," 89
Force, purity of style imparts, 39

Forcible composition and thought, 125; conditions of, 128
Foreign words, importation of, 32
Foster, J., method of, 93; quotation from, 81
Fox, C. J., speaking in Parliament, 189
Froude, obscurity of style, 118

General words used for specific, 103
Generic and specific words, exercises, 280
"Genius" vs. "talents," 270
German writers, corrupting effect on English, 51
German construction, 119, 154
Gibbon, misplacement of "only," 112
"Gift" as a verb, 235
God, name of, as apostrophe, 162
"Gospel" as an adjective, 235
Gough, J. B., power in pantomime, 105
Gray's Elegy, possible transpositions of words, 113
Grimm, Jacob, on English language, 41
Grote, neologisms, 27
"Guess," inelegance of, 172
Guizot, F., testimony to English language, 42

"Habit," "custom," "usage," 270
Hall, R., subjection to Johnsonian dialect, 70
Hallam, on misplaced inflections, 57
"Happify," 235
"Hardy" and "rugged," 273
"Haste" and "hurry," 270
Heart-beats, power of, if combined, 129
"Heavenly-mindedness," 235
"Healthy" and "healthful," 62, 270
Hearers, fitness of expression to, 194
"Heaven" as synonym of "God," 235
Henry, Patrick, and colloquial dialect, 17

"Hope" for "hope for," 235
"How?" 235
"Humbug," 14
"Humility," 20
"Hurry" and "haste," 270
Hyperbole an aid to energy, 161; may assist precision, 82

"Idiot," 19
Illiterate, influence of, on speech, 45
"Illusion" vs. "delusion," 268
Illustration, variety in, 187
"Illy" for "ill," 236
Imagery, 96, 97; and figure not identical, 156; commonplace in, 175; easy command of, 183; inelegance of, 174
"Imagination" and "fancy," 270
Imitation, servile, 69
Immigrants to U. S., effects on language, 46
"Imperative" and "imperious," 271
"Implicit," 236
Impressiveness and energy, 124
Impropriety of style, 10
"In spite of," 271
"Inaugurate," 236
"Incident" for "liable," 237
Indefinite thought, energy not adapted to, 126
Indiscriminate thinking, 68
Individuality of style, 7
Inelegance, Macaulay's effective, 174
Inelegant constructions, 173
Inelegant language, 171
Inflections, misplaced, 57
Intemperance of style, 131, 132
"Intend" for "mean," 237
Intensity may be diffuse, 147
Interest in aim of discourse, 200
Interrogation an aid to energy, 158
Inversion, misplaced or excessive, 173
Inverted sentence, 117
Involuted style, 58
Irony, 161
"Irreligionist," 237

Irrelevant matter, introduction of, 121; examples, 291
Irving, W., style in conversation, 50
"It," errors in use of, 56, 248
"Ize," words in, 24

"Jeopardize," 237
Johnson, Dr., Latinized style, 32; on The Rehearsal, 138; style, criticised by Hazlitt, 187; two styles of, 135
Journalists, new words by, 29

Kant, long sentence by, 119

Language, love of, 39
"Lay" and "lie," 237
"Learn" for "teach," 271
"Lengthy," 237
"Lethal weapons," 101
"Lieve" for "lief," 237
"Like" and "love," 271
Lincoln, A., method of, in debate, 93
Literatures, national, decline of, 178
Long and short words, exercises in use of, 292
"Long" as a noun, 237
Loose style, causes of, 68
Lord's Prayer, purity of style, 40
Loring, C. G., faulty construction, 109
"Love" and "like," 271
Lowell, J. R., neologisms, 30; on archaisms, 20
Luther, "Reformation of," 102

Macaulay, T. B., effective use of detailed description, 147; omission of words, 55
Mason, Jeremiah, method with juries, 159
Mastering subjects of discourse, habit of, 199
Mastery of words, 72
Maurice, F. D., on hidden meanings in words, 72

"Mean" for "means," 237
"Memories" for "reminiscences," 271
"Methinks," 237
Michael Angelo, picture of Virgin Mary, 194
"Mighty" for "very," 238
"Militate with," 238
Milton, J., angels not described by, 127; neologisms, 29, 32; prose style, 58; use of antithesis in Paradise Lost, 158; vocabulary limited, 78
"Missionate," 238
"Moment" and "minute," 271
Mongrel imagery, 176
Monotony of construction, 107, 186
Moods and tenses of verbs, 56; errors in use of, 250
Moore, Thomas, getting his *word*, 74
"Moot," 238
"Mutual" and "common," 272

Napoleon, intensity of his thinking, 89
National usage, 15
Naturalness of style, 7, 192
Negligence in construction, 123
Neologisms, dictionaries of, 14
"Nervous," 102
New words, exercises with, 212; principles governing, 27
New York State, Dutch and Welsh in, 46, 47
"News," 238
Newspaper, condensed style demanded for, 142
Niagara Falls, beauty and sublimity of, 177
"Nice," 238
"No," "whether or," 238
Noah entering the ark, 101
Northwestern U. S., foreign languages in, 47
"Notify," 238
Number of words, energy dependent on, 139

Object in view required for forcible style, 129
"Obligate," 238
Obscurity from absence of thought, 87; from vague thought, 88; from affectation, 90; from profoundness, 92; from rapidity of thought, 94; how removed, 101
"Observation" and "observance," 272
Obsolescent words, 20; and moral decay, 21
Obsolete words, 19
Omission of words, 55
"One, the, and the other," 118
"Only" and "alone," 265; misplacement of, 112
Onomatopoetic style, 138; examples, 294
"Onto," 239
"Open up," 239
Oral delivery, excessive precision in, 66
Order, excessive, 173
Order of thought, wrong, 116; examples, 288
Ornament, elegance not simply, 160
Orthography, similar, dangers from, 62
"Ought," 239

"Painful," 20
Parenthesis, abuse of, 119
Park, Professor, on barbarisms, 23
Passionate style, 131
"Paternal" and "fatherly," 272
Paul, St., antithetical passage from, 158
Periodic structures, 152; abuse of, 153; exercises in, 302
Perspicuity, 7, 17; purity of style, an aid to, 38; distinguished from precision, 54; as affected by imagery, 96; affected by words of discourse, 100; affected by construction, 107; energy not same as, 124; exercises in, 275

Philosophy, study of, affects language, 91
Pierrepont, Judge, in trial of Surratt, 99
" Pitiful," " piteous," and " compassionate," 272
" Pity " and " sympathy," 273
" Plead " as preterite, 239
" Plenty " for " plentiful," 239
" Plowman homeward plods," etc., 18 ways of reading, 113
Poetry, obsolete words in, 21
Political parties' watchwords, 85
Population of the world, vastness illustrated, 127
Portrait, unconsciousness essential to, 8
Position of words, relative, 113, 114
Practice in composition, 202
Prayer, Book of Common, tautological phrases in, 140
Prayer, obsolete words in, 22
Precision of style, 7; defined, 54; violations of, 55, 60; foundation of, in thought, 68; inducements to, 79; not pedantic, 80; promotes clearness and energy, 81; promotes elegance, 82; approved for its own sake, 84; a popular style, 84; exercises in, 248
" Predicate " for " found," 239
" Prejudices," 20
Prepositions ending sentence, 149; errors in use of, 223
" Prevent," 33
" Pride " and " vanity," 272
Prior, M., faulty construction, 108
" Profanity " and " profaneness," 240
" Professor " for " communicant," 240
" Progress " as a verb, 240
Prolific writers natural writers, 202
Pronouns and antecedents, 108; repetition with different antecedents, 108; errors in use, examples of, 283

Propriety distinguished from precision, 54
Provincialisms, 35; English, 38; in America, 46
Prussian dictionary, Government, 13
Public speakers use limited vocabulary, 77; successful, 92
Public speaking, pure English adapted to, 40
Pure words an aid to energy, 134
Purism, 11
Purity of style, 7; defined, 10; standard of, 11; violations of, 19; reasons for cultivating, 37; an essential of culture, 48; how acquired, 49; exercises in, 209

Qualifying clauses, arrangement of, 114; examples of errors in use of, 287
Qualifying words, excess of, 141
Quincy, Josiah, fine-spun oratory, 200
Quintilian on precision, 79
" Quite " for " very," 240
" Quiz," origin of, 12

" Raise," 240
Randolph, J., hyperbole of, 82
Rapidity of speech, dangers from, 94
" Rather," " had," or " would " preceding, 240
" Rational " for " reasonable," 273
Reading, classic English to be preferred, 51
Redundancy, excessive, 65
Refinement of perception, 169
Reinhard, on use of pronouns, 110
" Reluct," " reluctate," 240
" Remorse," 240
" Remove, an infinite," 241
Republican institutions favor debasement of language, 45
" Resentment," 19
" Retrospect " as a verb, 241
Richter, J. P., variety of illustrations, 188

"Ride" and "drive," 273
"Rugged" and "hardy," 273

"Sang," 241
"Save" for "except," 241
Saxon and Norman synonyms, 140
Saxon element in English, 40
Saxon style, 100; strength of, 134
Saxon words, 52; when not to be used, 136; substituted for Latin or Greek derivatives, exercises, 279
Scott, Walter, use of colloquialism new to him, 74
"Scripturality," 241
"Security" and "safety," 273
Self-forgetfulness in composing, 200
"Self-love" and "selfishness," 273
Self-possession essential to eloquence, 130; consistent with heat of style, 148
"Selfsame," 241
Sensitiveness of feeling, 182
"Sensual" and "sensuous," 273
Sentence, ending of, 149
Shakespeare, vocabulary limited, 78; fertility of his mind, 203
"Shall" and "will," 241
"Shew" for "shewed," 242
Short words an aid to energy, 137; abuse of, 138; and long words, exercises in use of, 292
"Shortcomings," 242
Shylock, example of interrogative style, 160
"Sidehill," 242
Simplicity of language essential to vividness, 183; in construction of sentences, 198
Slang, 36, 50; popular, 84; examples, 222
Smallness not essential to beauty, 165
Solecism of style, 10
"Solemnize," 242
Soliloquy, oral discourse in, 130
"Some" for "somewhat," 242
"Soul" compounds with, 242

Southey, R., and "deicide," 28; rules of composition, 80
"Spake," 241
Spanish language, prevalence of, 42
Specific words an aid to energy, 136; and generic words, exercises, 280
Spencer, H., theory of style, 104, 122
Spenser, E., Faerie Queene, archaic style of, 22; compared with Bible, 38
"Spiritual-mindedness," 242
"Sprang," 241
Standards of English usage, 17
"Station" vs. "depot," 242
Stormont, Lord, style of, in Parliament, 189
"Stricken" for "struck," 242
Strutting in discourse, 195
Studied beauty, 178
Style, defined, 3; popular conceptions of, 4; is thought, 6; qualities of, 6, 7; and delivery, reciprocal effect of, 188; and "diction," 268
Subjects of discourse, fitness of expression to, 193
Subjunctive, use of, 56; examples of wrong use, 250
Sumner, C., classical allusions in speeches, 97
"Sundown," 243
"Sympathy," 63; and "pity," 273
Synonyms, confounding of, 60; knowledge of, necessary, 73; errors in use of, 251; lists of, 255, 260
"Systemize," 243

"Talent" vs. "talents," 243; vs. "genius," 270
Tautology and conciseness, 140; examples of, for correction, 295
Taylor, Jeremy, learned style of, 97
"Telegram," 30
"Temper" for "anger," 243
Tenses and moods, 56; errors in use of, 249

"Thalagram," 30
"Thanks!" 243
"That" for "thus," 244
"The," omission of, 273
"Then" used adjectively, 244
"This" for "thus," 244
Thought, quickness of, 142
Tonic effect of qualifying word, 143
"Transpire," 244

"Ugly" for "ill-natured," 244
"Un-" 244
"Unbeknown," 244
"Unbelief" and "disbelief," 268
Uncouth words, 171
"Undertaker," 62
Unfinished imagery, 175
Unimportant thought, energy not adapted to, 126
"Unless" and "except," 270
"Unreason," 244
"Unwisdom," 244
Usage *vs.* learning, 11; the ultimate standard, 12; national, 15; as influenced by laws of a language, 15; must be reputable, 16; standards of, 17; "habit," "custom," 270

Vagueness, remedy for, 89
"Vanity" and "pride," 272
"Variate," 245
Variety essential to beauty, 184; in method of discussion, 185; in construction, 186; in illustration, 187

Verboseness and conciseness, 141; scholastic, 142; as to certain parts of speech, 143; examples of, 295
Versatility of thought, 185
Vision, figure of, an aid to energy, 161
Vivacity and energy, 124
Vividness an element of elegance, 180
Vocabulary, extensive, not command of language, 70; retentive control of, necessary, 74; not necessarily large, 77; of children, 77; of public speakers, 77
Vulgarisms, 35

"Was" for "were" with "you," 245
Webster, D., use of colloquialisms, 49; command of language, 71; questionable use of relative pronoun, 110; self-possession, 132
Wellington, Duke of, style affected by fame, 8
"Were" for "was," 245
Whately on vacuity of style, 88
Whitefield and the sailor, 198
"Whole" for "all," 245
Wise, H. A., mixed imagery of, 96
Words condemned by critics, 217; confounded, list of, 263
Wordsworth, W., on obscurity of style, 93; poetry of, elegance in, 168; inelegancies used by, 172

Zest in writing, 203

ENGLISH LANGUAGE AND LITERATURE

Messrs. CHARLES SCRIBNER'S SONS wish to call your attention to the following list of books. Many of them have become widely known and are generally recognized as the leading authorities. Several have recently been issued and an acquaintance with these will be found particularly desirable.

No pains have been spared in securing the ablest authors, as well as the ones best fitted by experience in teaching, to understand the needs which are constantly being felt.

These books can be examined by teachers without expense, and the terms enabling this will always be cheerfully quoted upon request.

EARLY ENGLISH REPRINTS

Edited with Introduction and Notes by EDWARD ARBER. Stiff paper covers, 16mo.

> ADDISON'S CRITICISMS OF PARADISE LOST. 50 cents *net*.
> BACON'S HARMONY OF THE ESSAYES. $2.50 *net*.
> MORE'S EUTOPIA. 50 cents *net*.
> MILTON'S AREOPAGITICA. 25 cents *net*.
> SIDNEY'S APOLOGIE FOR POETRIE. 25 cents *net*.

A complete list of these and the twenty-five additional volumes will be sent on application.

ENGLISH COMPOSITION

Eight Lectures delivered at the Lowell Institute. By BARRETT WENDELL, Professor of English in Harvard College. 12mo, $1.50.

CONTENTS: I. Introduction to the Elements and Qualities of Style in General—II. Words—III. Sentences—IV. Paragraphs—V. Whole Compositions—VI. Clearness—VII. Force—VIII. Elegance.

Professor Wendell has now given to the public the means of obtaining results in teaching English, similar to those which have characterized his remarkably successful work in Harvard College. Accuracy, ease, and grace in writing are the natural results of this author's method. A large amount of practice is required in accordance with the simple and practical suggestions of the book.

> "I have used this work with success, and shall continue to use it."
> —Prof. F. H. STODDARD, University of the City of New York.

> "The best thing of its kind I have ever seen."—Principal ALBERT HALE, Boston.

> " Admirable . . . I shall recommend it to my students in oratory."
> —Prof. T. C. TRUEBLOOD, University of Michigan.

OUTLINES OF ENGLISH LITERATURE

By WILLIAM RENTON, Lecturer to the Scottish Universities. 12mo, with diagrams, $1.00 net.

CONTENTS: First Period [600-1600], pages 9-112: I. The Old English Metric and Chronicle [600-1350], a. Anglo-Saxon: b. Anglo-Norman—II. The Renascence [1350-1500]—III. The Reformation [1550-1600]—IV. The Romantic Drama [1550-1650]. Second Period [1600-1900], pages 132-232—V. The Serious Age [1600-1700]—VI. The Age of Gaiety [1650-1750]—VII. The Sententious Age [1700-1800]—VIII. The Sympathetic Age [1800-1900]—Appendix: Literature of America [1600-1900]—Index: Conspectus of British and American Poetry.

The general arrangement of the book and valuable diagrams showing the division of literature according to ages and characteristics combine to make this manual especially fitted to use in the class-room.
Criticism is supplemented by exposition, with extracts to exhibit the fashion of a period, or the style of a master. The number of authors indicates the importance of a period, and intrinsic power the importance of an author. American literature is considered as a part of the whole, but a brief summary of its history and general characteristics is also given.

THE ENGLISH NOVEL

Being a Short Sketch of its History from the Earliest Times to the Appearance of Waverley. By WALTER RALEIGH, Professor of Modern Literature at University College, Liverpool. 12mo, $1.25 net.

CONTENTS: I. The Romance and the Novel—II. The Elizabethan Age: Euphues—III. The Elizabethan Age: Sidney and Nash—IV. The Romance of the Seventeenth Century—V. The Beginnings of the Modern Novel—VI. Richardson and Fielding—VII. The Novels of the Eighteenth Century—VIII. The Revival of Romance—IX. The Novel of Domestic Satire: Miss Burney, Miss Austin, Miss Edgeworth—X. Sir Walter Scott.

This book furnishes critical studies of the work of the chief English novelists before Scott, connected by certain general lines of reasoning and speculation on the nature and development of the novel. Most of the material has been given by the author in the form of lectures to his classes, and possesses the merit of being specially prepared for use in the class-room.

THE JACOBEAN POETS

By EDMUND GOSSE, Hon. M.A., Trinity College, Cambridge. 12mo, $1.00 net.

This little volume is an attempt to direct critical attention to all that was notable in English poetry from 1603-1625. It is the first book to concentrate attention on the poetry produced during the reign of James I. Many writers appear here for the first time in a book of this nature. The aim has been to find unfamiliar beauties rather than to reprint for the thousandth time what is already familiar.

THE POETRY OF TENNYSON

By HENRY VAN DYKE, D.D. Fourth Edition. Revised and enlarged with Poetry. 12mo, $2.00.

As a critical study of the great poet-laureate, this book cannot be surpassed. For preparatory work in connection with English requirements for admission to colleges, it will be found serviceable. Its use, wherever the life and writings of Tennyson are being considered, will be found to afford special advantages.

"No truer or more sympathetic presentment and analysis has been made of the works of our greatest living poet."—Mr. E. C. STEDMAN.

HEROES AND HERO WORSHIP. By Thomas Carlyle. People's Edition. 12mo, 40 cents.

SARTOR RESARTUS. By Thomas Carlyle. People's Edition. 12mo, 40 cents.

CHAUCER FOR SCHOOLS. Edited by Mrs. H. R. Haweis. 8vo, $1.00.

WILLIAM SHAKESPERE

A Study in Elizabethan Literature. By BARRETT WENDELL, Assistant Professor of English at Harvard College. 8vo, 439 pages, $1.75.

The purpose of this study is to present a coherent view of the generally accepted facts concerning the life and work of Shakespere. To accomplish this the first endeavor is to glance at the known facts of Shakespere's life; then follows a consideration of the condition of English literature at the time when his literary activity began; then critical attention is paid, in chronological order, and with all the details possible, to all of the works commonly assigned to him. Finally the resulting impression of his individuality is defined as fully and clearly as is possible.

CONTENTS: I. Introduction—II. The Facts of Shakespere's Life—III. Literature and the Theatre in England until 1587—IV. The Works of Shakespere—V. Venus and Adonis, and The Rape of Lucrece—VI. The Plays of Shakespere from Titus Andronicus to The Two Gentlemen of Verona—VII. The Plays of Shakespere from A Midsummer-night's Dream to Twelfth Night—VIII. Shakespere's Sonnets—IX. The Plays of Shakespere from Julius Cæsar to Coriolanus—X. Timon of Athens, and Pericles, Prince of Tyre—XI. The Plays of Shakespere from Cymbeline to Henry VIII.—XII. William Shakespere. Authorities, etc.

THE ART OF EXTEMPORE SPEAKING

Hints for the Pulpit, the Senate, and the Bar. By M. BAUTAIN, Vicar-General and Professor at the Sorbonne. Edited by a member of the New York Bar. With addition, rules of debate, etc. 12mo, $1.50.

"This work has no counterpart or rival in the English language. Other works teach how to write; this contains suggestions on the art of speaking—easily, agreeably, forcibly."—*The Christian Observer*.

THE SCIENCE OF ENGLISH VERSE

By SIDNEY LANIER, late of Johns Hopkins University. 12mo, $2.00.

Mr. Lanier does not content himself with merely combating vigorously the false methods which have become traditional in English prosody, but presents most interesting and valuable suggestions for a truer method; treating verse almost entirely as analogous with music—and this not figuratively, but as really governed by the same laws, little modified. His forcible and skillful use of the most modern investigations in acoustics in supporting this position makes the book not only a contribution to literature, but, in the best sense, to physical science.

SELECT POEMS OF SIDNEY LANIER

Edited, with an Introduction and Notes, by MORGAN CALLAWAY, Jr., Ph.D., Associate Professor of English Philology in the University of Texas, formerly Fellow of the Johns Hopkins University; author of "The Absolute Participle in Anglo-Saxon." 12mo, $1.00 net.

"This edition of the 'Select Poems of Sidney Lanier' is issued in the hope of making his poetry known to wider circles than hitherto, especially among the students of our High Schools and Colleges. To these, as to older people, the poems will, it is believed, prove an inspiration from the standpoint both of literature and of life."
—FROM THE PREFACE.

ESTIMATES OF LANIER'S POETRY.

"As a master of melodious meter only Tennyson, and he not often, has equaled Lanier. . . . Enough has been said to hint to those personally unacquainted with Lanier's works, that, from an æsthetic view, his career is one of the most remarkable, if not the most remarkable, yet lived by an American."—WILLIAM R. THAYER, editor of "Best Elizabethan Plays," etc., in *The Independent*, N.Y.

"His poems, which have been gathered in a volume, constitute the most characteristic specimens of American verse to be found in any similar collection. They are thoroughly and completely American. Thoughtless critics have pronounced them obscure, but other generations will undoubtedly appreciate the splendid exaltation, the subtle suggestions, the glowing thoughts, the wonderful harmonies of an imagination not inferior to Emerson's."—JOEL CHANDLER HARRIS, author of "Uncle Remus," etc.

ELOCUTION

The Sources and Elements of its Power. A Text-book for Schools and Colleges, and a book for every Public Speaker and Student of the English Language. By Rev. J. H. MCILVAINE, D.D. 12mo, $16.75.

This is an original and thoroughly practical manual, arranged with special reference to class-room use and convenience of students. Nearly half the work consists in the exhibition of the intellectual, moral, æsthetical, and physical sources of power in delivery; the other part contains several chapters on phonology and treats in detail the articulation, accent, and pronunciation, the relation of the vocal organs to vocal culture, the qualities and powers of the voice, etc.

Descriptive Catalogue of Educational Publications sent free. Privileges of Examination, Introductory Prices, Regular Rates to Instructors, to Libraries, and to the Trade, will be cheerfully furnished upon application.

CHARLES SCRIBNER'S SONS

153-157 FIFTH AVENUE, - - NEW YORK CITY

www.ingramcontent.com/pod-product-compliance
Lightning Source LLC
Chambersburg PA
CBHW031856220426
43663CB00006B/651